US FOREIGN POLICY IN THE MIDDLE EAST

Over the last 60 years, Washington has been a major player in the politics of the Middle East. From Iran in the 1950s, to the Gulf War of 1991, to the devastation of contemporary Iraq, US policy has had a profound impact on the domestic affairs of the region. Anti-Americanism is a pervasive feature of modern Middle East public opinion. But, far from being intrinsic to 'Muslim political culture', scepticism of the US agenda is directly linked to the regional policies pursued by Washington.

By exploring critical points of regional crisis, Kylie Baxter and Shahram Akbarzadeh elaborate on the links between US policy and popular distrust of the United States. The book also examines the interconnected nature of events in this geo-strategically vital region. Accessible and easy to follow, this book is designed to provide a clear and concise overview of complex historical and political material. Key features include:

- maps illustrating key events and areas of discontent;
- text boxes on topics of interest related to the Arab–Israeli wars, Iranian politics, foreign interventions in Afghanistan and Iraq, the wars of the Persian Gulf, September 11 and the rise of Islamist movements; and
- further reading lists and a selection of suggested study questions at the end of each chapter.

US Foreign Policy in the Middle East: The roots of anti-Americanism provides students and researchers insight into the popular discontent generated by decades of US policy in the Middle East.

Dr **Kylie Baxter** is a researcher at the National Centre of Excellence for Islamic Studies, the University of Melbourne, Australia. Her research focuses on Islamic politics and conflict in the Middle East. She is also the author of *British Muslims and the Call to Global Jihad* (Melbourne: Monash Asia Institute Press, 2007).

Associate Professor **Shahram Akbarzadeh** is Deputy Director of the National Centre of Excellence for Islamic Studies, the University of Melbourne, Australia. His research focuses on Australian Muslims, international relations and Islamic politics. He is also the author of *Uzbekistan and the United States: Islamism, Authoritarianism and Washington's Security Agenda* (London: Zed Books, 2005).

US FOREIGN POLICY IN THE MIDDLE EAST

The roots of anti-Americanism

Kylie Baxter and Shahram Akbarzadeh

Routledge
Taylor & Francis Group

LONDON AND NEW YORK

First published 2008
by Routledge
2 Park Square, Milton Park, Abingdon, Oxon, OX14 4RN

Simultaneously published in the USA and Canada
by Routledge
270 Madison Avenue, New York, NY 10016

Transferred to Digital Printing 2008

Routledge is an imprint of the Taylor & Francis Group, an informa business

Typeset in Garamond by Prepress Projects Ltd, Perth, UK
Printed and bound in Great Britain by TJI Digital, Padstow, Cornwall

British Library Cataloguing in Publication Data
A catalogue record for this book is available from the British Library

Library of Congress Cataloging in Publication Data
Baxter, Kylie.
US foreign policy in the Middle East : the roots of anti-americanism / Kylie Baxter and Shahram Akbarzadeh.
    p. cm.
Includes bibliographical references and index.
    ISBN-13: 978-0-415-41048-9 (hardback)
    ISBN-10: 0-415-41048-7 (hardback)
    ISBN-13: 978-0-415-41049-6 (pbk.)
    ISBN-10: 0-415-41049-5 (pbk.)
    [etc.]
1. United States—Foreign relations—Middle East. 2. Middle East—Foreign relations—United
States. 3. United States—Foreign public opinion, Middle Eastern. 4. Middle East—Public opinion.
I. Akbarzadeh, Shahram. II. Title. III. Title: United States foreign policy in the Middle East.
DS63.2.U5B37 2008
327.73056--dc22
                    2007042998

ISBN 10: 0-415-41048-7 (hbk)
ISBN 10: 0-415-41049-5 (pbk)
ISBN 10: 0-203-92830-X (ebk)

ISBN 13: 978-0-415-41048-9 (hbk)
ISBN 13: 978-0-415-41049-6 (pbk)
ISBN 13: 978-0-203-92830-1 (ebk)

CONTENTS

List of maps   viii
Acknowledgements   ix

Introduction   1

1 The Middle East in the Colonial Period   8

Introduction   8
The fall of the Ottomans and the Hashemite Dynasty   10
The Sykes–Picot Agreement of 1916 and the balfour declaration of 1917   13
The post-war era: the King–Crane commission and the Mandates   17

2 Great Power Influences, Zionism and the Middle East   25

Introduction   25
Zionism: the road to statehood   26
Zionism during the war   33
Al-Nakba/the Israeli War of Independence   37
Conclusion   42

3 Israel and the Arabs at War: Superpower Dimensions and the Israeli–US Alliance   46

Introduction   46
1956: the Suez War   47
1967: the Six-Day War   49
1973: the Yom Kippur/Ramadan War   56
1982: the Lebanon War   60
2006: the July War   63
Conclusion   65

4 Islamism and the Iranian Revolution   **70**

    Introduction   69
    Historical background   71
    The Iranian Revolution   76
    The Shia dimension   85
    Conclusion   85

5 Proxy War: the Superpowers in Afghanistan   **89**

    Introduction   89
    Historical context   90
    Reasons for the Soviet decision   93
    Regional reactions   96
    The role of the United States   97
    Case study: the Stinger controversy   98
    Resolution of the Afghan conflict   101
    Conclusion   104

6 Wars in the Persian Gulf   **109**

    Introduction   109
    Historical background   110
    Iran–Iraq tension   114
    The superpowers' involvement   118
    After the Iran–Iraq War   123
    Regional tensions: water and oil   124
    Operation Desert Storm   128
    Outcomes of Desert Storm   131
    Conclusion   132

**7 Israel and Palestine: the Failure to Find Peace and the Role
   of the United States**   **136**

    Introduction   136
    The first uprising: Intifada 1987   140
    The emergence of HAMAS   141
    The Oslo Accords (September 1993)   142
    Oslo's failure and the al-Aqsa Intifada   144
    Israel's security wall   151
    The Gaza withdrawal   152
    Conclusion   155

8 The Iraq 'Adventure' and Arab Perceptions of the Unites States   **160**

Iraq: the road to war   161
Arab discontent   170
Conclusion   172

Conclusion   **177**

The United States and Israel   179
The United States and the Palestinians   180
The United States and Iraq   183
The United States and the Middle East: where to from here?   185

Index   187

MAPS

0.1 The Middle East   x
3.1 Post-1967 borders   50
4.1 Iran   78
6.1 Iraq   112
7.1 Israel   137

ACKNOWLEDGEMENTS

The authors would like to thank the School of Political and Social Inquiry at Monash University for its support during the development of *US Foreign Policy in the Middle East: The roots of anti-Americanism*. Thanks also to Rebecca Barlow and Abhijit Mitra of the Centre for Muslim Minorities and Islam Policy Studies staff for their invaluable research assistance. Finally, we would like to express our appreciation to the students of Monash University for their lively debate and sustained enthusiasm for Middle Eastern studies, which helped us develop and refine this book.

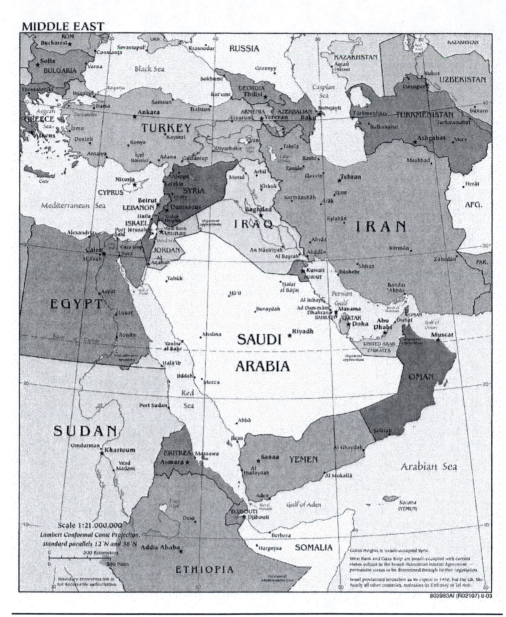

Map 0.1 The Middle East. Reproduced with permission from the UN Cartographic Section.

Introduction

The United States of America occupies a central place in global politics. As the sole superpower, the United States is able to exert an unrivalled influence in the international system. Indeed, some social commentators believe that 'America affects, directly and indirectly, the lives of every individual, community and nation on the planet' (Sardar and Davies 2002: 58). As is the case with all great powers, this pervasive presence has triggered a range of responses, and states and leaders throughout the international system in part define themselves on the basis of their relationship to Washington. History demonstrates that a unipolar system often engenders concerns about the great power's use of its influence. Thus, Washington's rise as the global power-broker has led to a concurrent rise in anti-Americanism.

Anti-Americanism is a complex social and political mindset that permeates the political discourse of many parts of the global community. In recent decades, anti-Americanism has become most closely associated with the Muslim Middle East. The extensive research carried out by the Pew Research Center confirms that, whereas public perceptions of the US have been largely negative for decades, 'in recent years that broad dislike has taken on an aspect of outright fear' (Pew Research Center 2005). In the aftermath of the terrorist attacks of September 11, 2001, it appeared to many Westerners that Middle Eastern anti-Americanism had entered a new and violent chapter. As social pundits rushed to ask 'why do they hate us?', more nuanced voices attempted to contextualize this violent explosion of anti-American sentiment within a long and complex history of US foreign policy and intervention in the Middle East. In a political climate marked by fear and uncertainty this was not an easy task.

The United States has been a major force in Middle Eastern politics since the 1950s. Following the close of the Cold War, Washington emerged as the region's major power-broker, often as influential in local decision-making processes as the regional states themselves. In addition to its political influence, the United States displayed an increasing willingness to apply more traditional 'hard power' tools to further its regional agenda. US foreign policy is conceived and implemented in order to advance the national interest of the state. This is true of the foreign policy of every state in the international system. The difference lies in the special position the United States currently occupies in international relations. In the post-Cold War world, the United States is a hyperpower, essentially a state capable and prepared to exert its political or military will in a unilateral manner (Litwak 2002). In the unipolar world that emerged in the late twentieth century, Washington displayed a marked tendency to direct its power and influence toward the Middle East. This is a result of the region's geo-strategic importance, its energy reserves and its often unstable political climate. The constant presence of the United States – as a military force, political power and a controversial cultural icon – has engendered a range of regional responses. Anti-Americanism is one such response.

Anti-Americanism is often dismissed as envy, cultural disparity or, at worst, implacable hatred. Such essentialist interpretations deny the basic principles of cause and effect. The underpinnings of Middle Eastern anti-Americanism require exploration, contextualization and debate. In this respect, the months that followed September 11, 2001, are revealing. It was in late 2001 that Washington prepared to launch its 'war on terror', initially a military invasion of Afghanistan to oust the Taliban and eradicate the al-Qaeda organization. Despite the Bush administration's public assurances that the new military campaign was not a 'war against Islam' (Bush 2006), it quickly became clear that the battlefields would be exclusively in the Muslim Middle East. By 2003, the Middle Eastern focus of this conflict was acknowledged even within the American political discourse:

> . . . the "war on terrorism," which is, in truth, not a global war on all terrorist organizations – so far, the FARC in Colombia and the Irish Republican Army seemed to have escaped much attention from the Bush administration – but principally upon "Islamism," that violent political movement antipathetic to modernity and to the West, and especially to their expression through American power. The motivating core of this movement appears to be more "Arab" than "pan-Islamic," and often stems from the Saudi-funded spread of Wahhabism.
> (Donnelly 2003)

As is the case in all wars, it was the civilians of Afghanistan and Iraq who suffered as the 'war on terror' gained pace. The high civilian death toll associated with the prosecution of the military campaigns was seemingly dismissed by the administration and the US military establishment as 'collateral damage'. The repressive nature of the Taliban's rule in Afghanistan and the reality of Saddam Hussein's dictatorial rule in Iraq led many to question why civilians, oppressed under both leaderships, should be paying the price of the 'war on terror'. Since the events of 2001, international public opinion has swung dramatically against the Afghanistan military campaign, which was ostensibly started to capture the Saudi Arabian dissident Osama bin Laden. This public rejection peaked as the highly problematic nature of extending the war against transnational terrorism to the state of Iraq became ever more evident.

The underpinning logic of the Bush administration appeared to pivot on certain assumptions, the most damaging of which was an apparent determination to minimize the role of cause and effect in the ways in which the United States was viewed in the Middle East. In the first years of the twenty-first century, powerful voices in Washington and in the US media appeared to subscribe to the belief that Arab anti-American sentiment was driven by, or at least fed by, a fundamental dislike of America, its culture and its people. As David Khairallah, a member of the American-Arab Anti-Discrimination Board, pointed out in 2004, 'from reading and hearing the US media, you would think Arab anger towards the US is almost genetic' (quoted in Al-Arian 2004: 71) This essentialist mindset was already evident in the days following September 11, 2001, when President George W. Bush declared to the world at large that the time had come to make a choice: 'either you are with us or you are with the terrorists' (Bush 2001). This binary understanding of the world did not take into account the complex perspectives that many in the Middle East hold towards the United States, responses that are a result of historical experience and political realities. A rejection of the terrorism perpetrated on September 11 was evident throughout the region, demonstrated in spontaneous public displays such as candlelight vigils in Tehran (Garthwaite 2004: 279). However, despite a rejection of the tactics employed, in the Middle East the events of September 11 were placed within a broader historical and political context. This contextualization was not matched in the United States. As the Bush administration positioned the United States as the champion of 'freedom' in a battle between good and evil, an interpretation that glossed over decades of US oppression and intervention, critical voices began to emerge. These voices were empowered only as the chain of events triggered by the attacks on September 11 began to extract a much, much greater human cost in the Middle East.

As the global community has gained a sense of distance and perspective on the attacks of September 2001, and perhaps been somewhat immunized against the initial horror through the blood-letting of Bali, Madrid, London, Afghanistan and Iraq, political space has emerged for new, more nuanced perspectives. External interventions and domestic realities both feed anti-American sentiment in the Middle East. Such perspectives have evolved as part of a broader response to the role of the United States as an external player and to the local conditions of political repression and intolerance of dissent. It is vital to note that even these internal or domestic structures are often linked to the historic role of the United States.

Throughout the second half of the twentieth century, Washington played a key role in maintaining the position of 'friendly' undemocratic regimes. Despite the rhetoric of generations of US leaders, democracy promotion in the Middle East is a dangerous undertaking for US interests. In the Cold War years socialism was a powerful force in the region, and in the unipolar world Islamic alternatives have proven popular. This willingness of many in the Middle East to express their preference for such alternatives through the ballot box has greatly complicated Washington's position. In the Cold War, Washington could not afford to risk its access to oil, its strategic hold on the Middle East or its position vis-à-vis the Soviet Union by endorsing democratic experiments. Consequently, Washington backed authoritarian leaders who were willing to commit to the US sphere of influence. This is a tradition that dates back to the stark example of Iran in the 1950s. As a result of this gap between Washington's rhetoric and the reality of its regional policy, dissent against local despots often developed an international angle, with popular opinion targeting Washington for its role in propping up existing regimes. This interplay of local factors and international trends provides the backdrop to modern anti-Americanism.

As this book demonstrates, the relationship between the United States and the Middle East has been one of dynamic change in the past century. Indeed, popular assumptions regarding the US role, and the Arab response,

BOX 0.1

The **Cold War** refers to the period between the end of the Second World War and the early 1990s, during which the United States and the Soviet Union engaged in a battle for regional and global influence. This conflict was marked by economic, ideological and military competition, brinkmanship and proxy wars. Cold War considerations influenced many conflicts during this period including the Korean War, the Vietnam War and the conflict in Afghanistan in the 1980s. It also contributed to numerous other tensions in the Middle East as the two superpowers armed and supported states within their sphere of influence. The Cold War drew to a close in the late 1980s and formally ended with the demise of the Soviet Union in 1991.

are challenged by even the briefest historical survey. Ussama Makdissi points out that the growth and prosperity of the United States in the nineteenth century and America's own revolutionary history encouraged many activists in the early twentieth-century Middle East to view the emergent world power as a natural ally and friend to the region's many nationalist movements.

> The influence of an idea of a benevolent America reached its apex among Arabs during and immediately after World War I. President Woodrow Wilson's proclamations on self-determination reinforced a notion among nationalist elites in the Arab world that the United States was different from the European powers.
>
> (Makdissi 2002: 544)

The hope that Washington would act as a champion for universal human rights and self-determination has echoed through the twentieth century. But this hope has rarely been fulfilled. The US support for self-determination has been belied by its involvement in Iran and its response to the political processes in Lebanon and the Occupied Territories. As this book explores, when contextualized in the history of the region, cultural or essentialist readings of the relationship between the United States and the Middle East are revealed as having scant relevance. The rise of Middle Eastern anti-Americanism may be more constructively understood as a defensive rejection of the hypocrisy in US rhetoric and action, and the ways in which America uses its unrivalled power to influence and intervene in other states.

This book places the current relationship between the Middle East and the United States within the historical context of the last century. In the early twentieth century the United States was not a major player in Middle Eastern politics, as an isolationist tendency was dominant in US foreign policy thinking. Yet it was within this colonial period that the state system that characterizes the modern Middle East was formed. Moreover, the early decades of the twentieth century offer an important insight into the ways in which Middle Easterners viewed and understood the 'West' and thus, by extension, came to see the United States. The mistaken belief that Washington would assist anti-colonial movements and champion Arab self-determination provided the genesis of the sense of betrayal that marked the mid-twentieth century. In this period, the inherently self-interested nature of US foreign policy began to collide with the altruistic political statements of the US leadership. It is this process that is the underlying focus of Chapter 1.

Chapter 2 explores the impact of the Zionist movement on the political geography of the Middle East. Not only did the establishment of Israel transform the region's map, it forever altered the political discourse of the Arab world. The United States did not play a central role in the establishment of Israel. It was the dynamics of the international system and the efforts of the Zionist movement that produced the only state in the Middle East without a Muslim majority. Chapter 3 explains how the Cold War placed new pressures on the Middle East. As Israel became repeatedly embroiled in regional conflicts (in 1956, 1967, 1973, 1982 and 2006), Washington was drawn progressively closer to Tel Aviv. By the last Arab–Israeli war, in July 2006, Washington's regional role had degenerated into acting as little more than a cheerleader for Israeli policy. Washington's shift from potential champion of Arab self-determination to its position in July 2006 was dramatic. Chapters 2 and 3 outline how such a significant reorientation of the US role occurred.

Chapter 4 provides an introduction to Islamic politics. The major concepts of political Islam, or Islamism, are investigated in order to provide a context for the pivotal events of the 1979 Islamic Revolution in Iran. The Iranian Revolution was a vital turning point in the political history of the Middle East. It sparked a new, more assertive period of regional political organization, of which anti-Americanism became an intrinsic aspect. This focus on the Islamic Revolution in Iran in early 1979 is followed by the exploration in Chapter 5 of the Soviet invasion of Afghanistan, which occurred later that year. Events in Afghanistan have played a central role in Islamic politics as a result of the murky relationship between the United States and the 'Arab-Afghan' movement. This was a movement of volunteers from the Middle East and beyond who entered Afghanistan to participate in militant resistance against Soviet occupation. The establishment of al-Qaeda and the 'globalizing' of a mindset of anti-Western confrontation were the key outcomes of this conflict.

Chapter 6 focuses on the geographic heartlands of the Middle East, the regions surrounding the Persian Gulf. The Iran–Iraq War of 1980–88 and the international conflict of 1991 are explored here. This eight-year conflict between two major Middle Eastern states saw the issues of national identity, religious sectarianism and international involvement assume new heights of importance. The United States emerged from the 1980s as the world's sole remaining superpower and the 1991 Gulf War is a reflection of this 'new world order'. The regional role of the United States in the post-Cold War world dominates Chapters 7 and 8. Chapter 7 tracks the relationship between Israel and the Palestinians, beginning with the hopes of the Oslo Accords and the period of US diplomacy in the 1990s. These hopes were submerged by the Palestinian Intifadas, increased acts of terrorism and the splintering of the Palestinian leadership in 2007. Chapter 8 explores US strategy in the 'war on terror', and the virtual destruction of the state of Iraq.

This book provides a contextualized insight into anti-Americanism in the Middle East by offering a chronological account of major flashpoints in the region's history. Understanding the history of Washington's role in the Middle East enables a clear insight into why anti-Americanism was able to take hold in the Middle East.

REFERENCES

Al-Arian, Laila (2004) 'Perceptions of the US in the Arab World', *The Washington Report on Middle Eastern Affairs,* Vol. 23, No. 7, pp. 66–75.

Bush, George W. (2001) 'Address to a Joint Session of Congress and the American People', 20 September, available at www.whitehouse.gov/news/releases/2001/09/20010920-8.html.

Bush, George W. (2006) 'Address to the UN General Assembly', 19 September, available at www.whitehouse.gov/news/releases/2006/09/20060919-4.html.

Donnelly, Thomas (2003) 'The Underpinnings of the Bush Doctrine', *AEI Online,* 31 January, available at www.aei.org/publications/pubID.15845/pub_detail.asp.

Garthwaite, Gene (2004) *The Persians* (London: Blackwell).

Litwak, Robert (2002) 'The Imperial Republic after 9/11', *The Wilson Quarterly* (Summer), pp. 76–82.

Makdissi, Ussama (2002) 'Anti-Americanism in the Arab World: An Interpretation of a Brief History', *Journal of American History*, Vol. 89, No. 2, pp. 538–58.

Pew Research Center (2005) 'Global Opinion: The Spread of Anti-Americanism', in *Trends 2005*, available at http://pewresearch.org/assets/files/trends2005-global.pdf.

Sardar, Ziauddin and Davies, Merryl Wyn (2002) *Why Do People Hate America?* (New York: Disinformation Press).

CHAPTER 1

The Middle East in the Colonial Period

INTRODUCTION

The early twentieth century was a time of unparalleled change in the Middle East. The fall of the Ottoman Empire and the establishment of a system of distinct nation-states signalled a new phase in regional history. Over the first half of the twentieth century, the emergent state-based nationalisms interacted with pre-existing loyalties based along sectarian, ethnic and tribal lines. The Western imposition of territorial boundaries irrevocably changed the Middle East. It provided a stable system of states that were plagued by endemic political instabilities. This new political configuration simultaneously provided the opportunity for the consolidation of regional alliances and, often ineffectually, submerged ethnic and sectarian tensions. The political machinations of the colonial powers of France and, particularly, Britain and the emergent role of the United States are the topic of many excellent historical texts. As a brief introduction to the colonial period and its impact on the politics of the Middle East, this chapter will explore three major documents: the Husayn–McMahon Correspondence, the Sykes–Picot Agreement and the Balfour Declaration. These three seemingly contradictory British foreign policy initiatives were designed to consolidate the United Kingdom's regional alliances and influence in the region. From the perspective of the Arab world, they set the scene for a history of Western influence and intervention that spanned the twentieth century.

The contemporary geo-political landscape of the Middle East is the product of direct colonial administration, client protectorate systems of governance and the Mandate system set up by the League of Nations. With the notable exception of Saudi Arabia, the fledgling states of the Middle East all experienced various degrees of colonial administration, with the most intense periods of control during the First and Second World Wars. Colonial administration was a significant impediment to the region's political development within the international system. The preference for direct administration by colonial powers created a situation in which the local leaderships were limited in their exposure to the international stage. Moreover, long after the period of formal colonial rule had ended, Britain and France continued to manipulate key aspects of state sovereignty, such as trade and security issues.

This is the vital historical background against which contemporary Western involvement in this region must be analysed. In Western discourse, the colonial period has been largely relegated to history. In the Middle East, however, the situation is different. The colonial period fundamentally shaped the political system of the region, and many of the regional delineations created in this period continue to cause instability. Consequently, history and the West's role within it are given much greater prominence in contemporary debates within Middle Eastern circles. The role of the colonial powers had significant influence on the ways in which Middle Easterners came to understand and respond to external political involvement. The United States, a predominantly isolationist power in the early twentieth century, was not a major player in the colonial divisions and machinations of the era. Indeed, during the colonial period the role of the United States in the Middle East was premised on Wilsonian idealism favouring self-determination of colonized peoples. Over time, however, this idealistic approach was increasingly tempered by Cold War pragmatism and self-interest and, finally, supplanted by policies of direct intervention.

BOX 1.1

The **Ottoman Empire** spanned six centuries and was centred in Anatolia, in modern Turkey. At its peak in the 1500s the Ottoman Empire controlled swaths of land throughout the Middle East and Europe. The Empire's decline began in the late sixteenth century and its territory steadily decreased until the nineteenth century. Geopolitics forced Constantinople to ally itself with Germany in the First World War (1914–18), and post-war treaties divided up the Ottoman lands. The last vestiges of Ottoman rule were abolished in the early 1920s, when Mustafa Kemal Ataturk established the Republic of Turkey.

THE FALL OF THE OTTOMANS AND THE HASHEMITE DYNASTY

Ottoman rulers, buoyed by the merging of temporal and Islamic authority in the structure of the Caliphate, had maintained centralized control of the entire Middle East for hundreds of years. However, in the first two decades of the twentieth century, the Ottoman Empire became increasingly vulnerable to internal tensions and external pressures. In October 1914 the Ottoman Empire concluded a treaty with Germany that led to its entering the First World War against Russia and, by extension, the United Kingdom. Traditional Ottoman fear of imperial Russia's regional agenda clearly influenced this fateful decision. Indeed, had the Ottomans elected to remain neutral in this conflict, regional history might have taken a very different course. However, geo-political considerations at the time pushed the Ottomans into action, and the commitment to the German alliance set in motion a chain of events that led to the eventual downfall of their system of centralized governance and the disintegration of the Ottoman Empire into a series of distinct nation-states.

London was well aware of the geographical and historical importance of the Middle East, and the German–Ottoman alliance only solidified a determined and sustained British interest in the region. As the war developed, British military and political leaders sought opportunities to weaken and destabilize Germany's Ottoman ally. In small pockets of the Arab world, this new alignment of forces was also seen as an opportunity. For some regional leaders, Ottoman rule, although imbued with Islamic legitimacy, was increasingly perceived as domination by non-Arab forces. Encouraged by this predisposition towards anti-Ottoman rebellion, Britain began to look for allies within the Arab world. It was in this climate that a handful of Arab tribal leaders began to view their own interests and

BOX 1.2

The **Caliphate** was the political-religious entity that emerged after the death of the Prophet Muhammad in AD 632. The role of the Caliph (successor) was ostensibly endowed with full political and religious authority, but throughout history the position of Caliph often functioned as the titular or symbolic head of the Muslim community. Tensions over the process of succession to the Prophet Muhammad led to the entrenchment of the Sunni–Shia division within Islam. The most powerful of the Caliphs, the Abbasid dynasty (750–1258), fell to Mongol forces in 1258. The position was revived sporadically and then institutionalized in Constantinople in 1517 as part of the legitimization of the Ottoman Empire. The position was consigned to history with the abolition of the Ottoman Empire and the establishment of modern Turkey in 1924.

those of the British state as aligned. The Hashemite family emerged as the major player in this delicate and complex political scene. Descended from the Prophet Muhammad, this central Arabian tribal family had both historical legitimacy and political ambitions. The family was headed by Husayn ibn Ali, who had been appointed by the Ottomans as the Sharif of Mecca in 1908. Emboldened by the war, the Hashemite clan, in league with the British, made its play for regional influence and prestige, advancing its aims with the language of Arab nationalism and self-determination. In the first decades of the twentieth century, the Hashemite dynasty became a major political player in the Middle East. The Hashemites occupied key positions in the politics of Syria until 1920, Saudi Arabia until 1924 and Iraq until the 1950s, and they remain the royal family of Jordan.

The first major international involvement of the Hashemites occurred in the context of Ottoman entry into the First World War. The Husayn–McMahon Correspondence was a series of letters exchanged between Sharif Husayn of Mecca and the United Kingdom's High Commissioner in Egypt, Henry McMahon. Aware of Britain's interest in destabilizing the Ottoman Empire from the east, Husayn approached the British authorities with an outline of the conditions under which he would lead an Arab revolt against Ottoman rule in the Hijaz. In return, Husayn aimed to secure land for Arab, or more correctly *Hashemite*, self-rule.

In many ways, the Hashemite proposal reflected the broader international system of the time. Recourse to Great Power patronage became a key theme of international relations in this period as nationalist movements sought to better their positions within a fluid international environment. Seen in the context of local political realities, the Hashemite determination to secure British support becomes even more understandable. The balance of power on the Arabian Peninsula was unsettled, and the Hashemites were competing for authority against other tribal groups. Husayn viewed a relationship with the United Kingdom as a way to buttress his leadership claim in the face of both Ottoman opposition and

BOX 1.3

The **League of Nations** was an international body that emerged at the close of the First World War. It was officially formed at the Paris Peace Conference of 1919–20 and essentially represented the political will of the Allied victors of the war. The governing principle of the organization was to negotiate the peaceful settlement of international tensions. The League of Nations did not have its own military force and was dependent upon the Great Powers to enforce its decisions. The League dissolved as a result of the outbreak of the Second World War and was replaced by the United Nations.

competition from other Arabs. However, his negotiations with the British were far from clear-cut, and the exact tract of land slated for Arab self-rule in the Husayn–McMahon Correspondence has long been the subject of academic and political conjecture. At the centre of this debate is the future of the land known as Palestine. As will be discussed, the disposition of Palestine in the Husayn–McMahon deliberations became an issue of increasing importance to all actors, particularly as Zionist settlement in the region intensified. Despite the ambiguity of his arrangement with the British, Husayn initiated a rebellion in the Hijaz, and the British aided it significantly. This became known as the Arab Revolt of 1916.

As Matthew Hughes points out, it was a 'great coup for the British to have the Hashemites, descendants of the Prophet Muhammad and guardians of Mecca and Medina, on their side', yet Husayn's revolt was heavily dependent on British supplies to sustain it (Hughes 1999: 74). The combination of British support and an implicit lack of popular legitimacy was to plague the Hashemites in the post-war period. This aside, as a result of the uprising against Ottoman rule and the concurrent British endorsement of the Hashemite claim, as the First World War came to a close many in the Arab world expected that a new era in Arab history, marked by some form of political self-determination, was at hand.

The Arab nationalist movement has sparked much controversy among modern academics. The role played by political beliefs in academic inquiry is evident in an analysis of the various positions taken regarding the nature of the Hashemite movement. Among others, the Israeli historians Ephraim and Inari Karsh assert that Husayn 'was not an Arab nationalist but an aspiring imperialist bent on empire-building' (Karsh and Karsh 1999: 232). The tribal and dynastic intentions of the Hashemite family are indeed evident. However, in the all-important popular historiography of the region, the Hashemite movement is often presented as an Arab nationalist uprising against Ottoman rule. Mary C. Wilson argues that Arab nationalism 'was spawned in the cities of the Fertile Crescent among a class of provincial notables that had lost power because of changes in Istanbul between 1908 and 1914' (1991: 189). The most constructive interpretation may well be that the Arab Revolt of 1916 was caused by a blend of political opportunism, nationalist inclinations, financial incentive (which was provided by the British) and dynastic ambition. The degree to which the broader Arab world embraced nationalist self-determination became a matter of lively political and academic debate largely because of the significant implications the question has had in the Arab–Israeli battle for historical legitimacy.

Considering the political ramifications of this period, it could be argued that the nationalist versus dynastic credentials of the Arab Revolt are not as important as the generic British endorsement of Arab self-determination.

It is important to remember that at this point the entire region was still under Ottoman rule; therefore, McMahon's letters constitute nothing more than a vague statement of future British intent. The British framers of the correspondence allowed themselves significant room to manoeuvre. Nevertheless, the letters also constitute – and more importantly were perceived by future observers to have constituted – a promise, made explicit in the text: 'Great Britain is prepared to recognize and uphold the independence of the Arabs' ('McMahon–Hussein Correspondence'). Yet the wording of the documents is careful not to specify precisely what regions along the Mediterranean coastal plain were considered 'not purely Arab' and thus excluded from support for Arab self-rule. The Syrian coastal plain was an area long coveted by the French because of the presence of their regional allies the Maronite Christians. Seen in this light, the wording of the McMahon letters appears to relate less to the ethnic composition of the region than it does to the British desire to keep their wartime allies on their side. Such motives were typical of the colonial powers' decisions regarding the Middle East. In any case, in the post-war period the lack of a clearly defined fate for Palestine became one of the central points of contention arising from the correspondence, as from 1920 the British held that Palestine was excluded from the area intended for Arab independence. This position was hotly, if, as some argue, retrospectively, contested. Various interpretations of the British 'promise' circulated the Middle East, and the United Kingdom became increasingly viewed as perfidious.

The various interpretations of the Husayn–McMahon Correspondence tend to hinge on the wording of the correspondence itself. At its core, the correspondence can be seen as deliberately ambiguous and designed to allow the British room to manoeuvre as the fortunes of war changed. As the fall of the Ottoman Empire loomed, regional and international interest in the fate of Palestine began to assume ever greater proportions.

THE SYKES–PICOT AGREEMENT OF 1916 AND THE BALFOUR DECLARATION OF 1917

The Husayn–McMahon Correspondence was not the only negotiation conducted by Britain during this period. Concurrent plans were afoot among the wartime allies. The Sykes–Picot Agreement of February 1916 effectively subdivided the defunct Ottoman Empire. The plan received Russian endorsement in late 1916, and became public when it was revealed by the anti-imperialist Bolsheviks after the 1917 Revolution. The agreement carved up the Middle East on the basis of the economic and geo-strategic interests of France and the United Kingdom. The two colonial powers sought to assure their maritime access to and political domination of the areas of the Middle East already under their influence. The Sykes–Picot

Agreement is usually understood by pro-Arab historians as a contradiction of the spirit, if not the letter, of the Husayn–McMahon Correspondence, which at a minimum provided a generalized endorsement of Arab self-determination.

The Sykes–Picot Agreement restricted the area reserved for absolute Arab sovereignty to the Arabian Peninsula. Ephraim and Inari Karsh remind us that the Husayn–McMahon Correspondence never led to 'an official and legally binding agreement' (Karsh and Karsh 1999: 235). They also argue that the two documents are not contradictory, as both agreements allow for a tract of land for Arab self-rule. In this view, regional politics of this period were simply a long process of manipulation and double-dealing in which all actors attempted to maximize their post-war positions. This appears a valid point, particularly when one acknowledges the dynastic ambitions of the Hashemite family. However, it is clear that the objective informing the Hashemites' dealings with the British in 1915 was to attain a more extensive outcome than Arab self-rule in the Arabian Peninsula. Moreover, with regard to McMahon's letters, it is evident that the British too were referring to a greater swath of the Middle East.

The 1915 correspondence did not figure in the construction of the Sykes–Picot Agreement. Indeed, the Middle East envisaged in this agreement was a markedly different geo-political entity and was premised on the solidification of external influence. The rationale for Russia's endorsement is evident: imperial Russian interests were served by the acquisition of land in Anatolia. French and British regions were clearly delineated. In contrast to, or perhaps because of, the ambiguous treatment of Palestine in the Husayn–McMahon Correspondence, this area was clearly marked for joint administration by the allies. This demonstrates an increasing awareness of the region's controversial status and an acknowledgement of the Russian Orthodox Church's interest in the cities of the Holy Land. Once Britain had secured its own interests and appeased its wartime allies, the amount of land left with which to honour the Husayn–McMahon Correspondence was severely curtailed and basically limited to the Arabian Peninsula.

Both the Husayn–McMahon and Sykes–Picot negotiations were conducted by a handful of local and international power-brokers. This reality supports the depiction of the Arab nationalist movement as a limited elitist movement rather than a grassroots expression of popular will. However, the existence of the agreements reflects a broad-based awareness that the geo-political future of the region was an open question at this juncture. It is instructive to view the agreements as demonstrating two trends: the notional desire for autonomy within the Middle East and the determination of external powers to maintain their interests. Yet these trends were not the sole factors influencing the political processes of the Middle East at this time. In addition to the Arabs and the colonial powers, the Zionist movement also had significant interest in the future of the

Ottoman lands. Explored in detail in the following chapter, the political Zionist movement was a Jewish nationalist movement that had originated in Europe in the late nineteenth century. Zionism sought to effect the national reconstitution of the Jewish people in the biblical land of Israel, a land known at that time as Palestine.

The confusion generated by the Husayn–McMahon Correspondence and the interventionist mindset evident in the Sykes–Picot Agreement were further intensified on 2 November 1917. On this day the Balfour Declaration passed the British Cabinet, turning the fate of Palestine into a major international issue. A public letter to the Zionist patron Lord Rothschild, this document was a major turning point in the history of the Middle East. Given the vital importance of this declaration, it is worth quoting in full:

Dear Lord Rothschild,

I have much pleasure in conveying to you, on behalf of His Majesty's Government, the following declaration of sympathy with Jewish Zionist aspirations which has been submitted to, and approved by, the Cabinet.

'His Majesty's Government view with favour the establishment in Palestine of a national home for the Jewish people, and will use their best endeavours to facilitate the achievement of this object, it being clearly understood that nothing shall be done which may prejudice the civil and religious rights of existing non-Jewish communities in Palestine, or the rights and political status enjoyed by Jews in any other country.'

I should be grateful if you would bring this declaration to the knowledge of the Zionist Federation.

Yours sincerely,

Arthur James Balfour

(Foreign Office 1917)

The declaration was the culmination of an intense Zionist lobbying effort that had spanned several decades. Whereas the Sykes–Picot plan for allied administration of the Holy Land and for the broader fragmentation of the region had confounded the Zionists' nationalist intentions for Palestine (Sachar 2005: 353), the Balfour Declaration constituted a major step forward for the Zionist project.

From the beginning there was an inherent contradiction. As Avi Shlaim points out, at the time of the document's release, Palestine was home to around 690,000 Arabs and 85,000 Jews (1995: 24). The United States was emerging into the international spotlight, and the ideal of self-determination of peoples, as expressed in the proclamation of President Woodrow Wilson's Fourteen Points, was becoming a feature of Western political discourse. Considering the low ratio of Jews to Arabs in

Palestine, the Balfour Declaration can be seen to not sit easily with the self-determination principle. In fact the Balfour Declaration marks the beginning of a political and academic struggle for Israeli versus Palestinian legitimacy that spans the twentieth century. For example, Alan Dershowitz utilizes the same figures as Shlaim to argue against the opposing view that Jewish self-determination, in the area inhabited by Jews, was in line with the Wilsonian idea of self-determination. Reflecting traditional Zionist discourse, Dershowitz also makes the point that 'a Jewish homeland would not be carved out of a pre-existing Palestinian state . . . after all there had never been a Palestinian state in this area' (2003: 32). Yet as this chapter has shown, a *pre-existing state system* was simply not present in the Middle East at all in this period. These modern political debates pivot on the concept of national legitimacy, an issue that remains at the heart of the Israeli–Palestinian conflict.

The demographic 'facts on the ground' go some way to explaining the furore the document sparked in Arab political circles at the time. Sahar Huneidi contends that the depth of Arab anger towards the Balfour Declaration was well understood by the British authorities, who delayed the formal release of the text in Palestine for several years (2001: 28). For Britain, the declaration functioned as a public endorsement of the Zionist movement, but more importantly it solidified in the eyes of the global community London's post-war dominance over Palestine (Sachar 2005: 357). By assuming the role of regional power-broker, London was staking its claim in the post-war Middle East.

In a clear acknowledgement of the increasing role of the United States, the declaration was floated in Washington and received the support of the Wilson administration on 16 October 1917. The passage of this brief yet historically explosive document was aided at different times by factors as diverse as individual sentiment, geo-strategic considerations and alliance-building. In addition to the issues surrounding the reality of demographic imbalance, the problematic term 'national home' was unknown in the parlance of international relations at this time. The term had first been employed by the Zionists in lieu of the more explicit terminology of statehood at the 1897 World Zionist Conference (Sachar 2005: 360), in order to allay Ottoman concerns about the Zionist enterprise in Palestine. Yet with the passing of the Balfour Declaration it entered the international system. Dershowitz argues that the debates generated by the controversial declaration effectively helped incorporate the notion of 'national home' into international law (Dershowitz 2003: 32). The actual intentions of Britain, beyond yet another broad-brush statement of support for a people, are difficult to ascertain. Like other foreign policy statements before it, the declaration was careful not to bind the British government to exact outcomes. The Balfour Declaration did not compel the British government to endorse a specific, territorially defined Jewish 'national home'. Rather, it functioned as a statement of support for the existence of a 'national home' *somewhere* in the already hotly contested land of Palestine.

As the period 1915–17 drew to a close, self-interest emerged as the predominant characteristic of politics in the Middle East. From Husayn's self-interested launching of the Arab Revolt to secure the prosperity of his lineage, to the British manoeuvrings to better their position against their wartime enemies, the Middle East was manipulated for the benefit of political elites. In this way, the early twentieth-century experience of the Middle East mirrors that of most developing regions. In the period after the First World War, local resentment of colonial powers and the enforced status quo took on strong anti-Western overtones, and culminated in calls for national self-determination.

These trends were aided by changes in the international system that resulted from the actions of a new player on the international scene, the United States. As a result of its entry into the First World War, the United States entered the politics of the Middle East. President Woodrow Wilson's Fourteen Points, proclaimed in 1918, signalled a new phase in international relations, with the American endorsement of self-determination made explicit. Many contemporaries believed that the new era would be defined by a sense of transparency in international relations and self-determination for the ex-Ottoman regions. Throughout the Middle East, Arabs were keen to wrest the future from external forces. They were not to succeed.

THE POST-WAR ERA: THE KING–CRANE COMMISSION AND THE MANDATES

In the post-war period, the spirit of the imperial carve-up evident in the Sykes–Picot Agreement was ascendant, albeit with concessions to the idealism of the Wilsonian worldview dominant in Washington. This blending of worldviews is evident in the proclamation of Article 22 of the League of Nations Covenant, confirmed on 28 June 1919.

> To those colonies and territories which as a consequence of the late war have ceased to be under the sovereignty of the States which formerly governed them and which are inhabited by peoples not yet able to stand by themselves under the strenuous conditions of the modern world, there should be applied the principle that the well-being and development of such peoples form a sacred trust of civilization. The best method of giving practical effect to this principle is that the tutelage of such peoples should be entrusted to advanced nations who by reason of their resources, their experience or their geographical position can best undertake this responsibility, and who are willing to accept it, and that

this tutelage should be exercised by them as Mandatories on behalf of the League.

(League of Nations 1919)

It was on this basis that the Mandate system was conceived and applied to the Middle East. The role of the proposed Mandatory powers was confirmed at the San Remo Conference of April 1920, which divided the remains of the Ottoman Empire among the allied victors. In line with the intentions of the wartime negotiators, France retained its influence in Syria and the United Kingdom was assured of its continuing presence in Mesopotamia and Palestine.

The United States played an often overlooked role in the immediate post-war period. As tensions flared between the Arabs and the colonial powers, the United States suggested a fact-finding commission to investigate the popular will of the region's people. Initially envisaged as a tripartite initiative, the tour of the King–Crane Commission to the Middle East in 1919 was completed only by two US delegates, because of increasing tensions between the French and the British. The Commission tendered its report on 28 August 1919; it was the intention of Washington that the report would play a role at the San Remo Conference in deciding the region's fate. During this period the United States publicly renounced territorial ambitions in the region. The report's preamble stated this clearly:

> The American people – having no political ambitions in Europe or the Near East; preferring, if that were possible, to keep clear of all European, Asian, or African entanglements but nevertheless sincerely desiring that the most permanent peace and the largest results for humanity shall come out of this war – recognize that they cannot altogether avoid responsibility for just settlements among the nations following the war, and under the League of Nations.
>
> (King–Crane Commission 1919)

However, the body of the report clearly suggests that the United States could act as a major player in the region, taking on a role that would eclipse that of the colonial powers. By the time it reaches its conclusion, the report appears to be little more than a call for an American Mandate in Syria. This controversial document, leaked to the public several years after its submission, was predominantly concerned with the French role in Syria and the local response there to the looming implementation of the Mandate system. Retrospectively, however, the report has gained attention for its clear indication of the opposition of Palestinian Arabs to the implementation of the Balfour Declaration and the establishment of the envisaged 'national home' in Palestine for the Jewish people.

No British officer, consulted by the Commissioners, believed that the Zionist program could be carried out except by force of arms. The officers generally thought that a force of not less than 50,000 soldiers would be required even to initiate the program. That of itself is evidence of a strong sense of the injustice of the Zionist program, on the part of the non-Jewish populations of Palestine and Syria. Decisions, requiring armies to carry out, are sometimes necessary, but they are surely not gratuitously to be taken in the interests of a serious injustice. For the initial claim, often submitted by Zionist representatives, that they have a "right" to Palestine, based on an occupation of 2,000 years ago, can hardly be seriously considered.

(King–Crane Commission 1919)

Overall, the King–Crane Commission found that the region's people rejected the application of Article 22 of the League of Nations Covenant, which endorsed Mandate rule, and that they instead desired independent Arab rule and an immediate end to Zionist settlement. By 1919, it was clear that the French intended to cleave off the coastal plain of Syria in order to protect the political power of their regional allies there, the Maronite Christians. The King–Crane Report advocated against any division of sovereignty between Lebanon and Syria and endorsed the position of the Hashemites, notably the kingship of Husayn's son Faisal. In specific relation to Zionism, the report found that, in order to preserve the Wilsonian vision of self-determination, a positive stance on Zionism should be reconsidered. The report stated that, 'if the wishes of Palestine's population are to be decisive as to what is to be done with Palestine, then it is to be remembered that the non-Jewish population of Palestine – nearly nine tenths of the whole – are emphatically against the entire Zionist program'. The report acknowledged the Balfour Declaration, but stressed the caveat in it that 'nothing shall be done which may prejudice the civil and religious rights of existing non-Jewish communities' (Foreign Office 1917). The King–Crane Commission found that the establishment of a Jewish home in Arab Palestine against the wishes of the overwhelming majority of the inhabitants was clearly prejudicial to their civil rights.

In conclusion, the report recommended that 'only a greatly reduced Zionist program be attempted by the Peace Conference, and even that, only very gradually initiated . . . Jewish immigration should be definitely limited, and . . . the project for making Palestine distinctly a Jewish commonwealth should be given up' (King–Crane Commission 1919).

The submission of the report caused uproar among America's allies, France and the United Kingdom, both of which were close to securing their interests through the the post-war negotiations. The leading role of these two allies in the negotiations was evident, and the recommendations of the King–Crane report eventually played no part in the formulation of international or US policy. This outcome prompted denouncements against the US administration for falsely raising hopes among the Arab participants in the fact-finding study regarding their ability to avoid the imposition of Mandate rule (Helmreich 1974: 139).

At the San Remo Conference in 1920, the Mandates for the Middle East were officially conferred. After discussions with the United States, the Mandates were confirmed by the United Nations in 1922 and came into effect in September of the following year. The French received the Mandate for Syria, and subsequently blessed the creation of Lebanon as a distinct entity. This decision was taken in order to assure the political dominance of the new state's Christian majority. The decision had historical precedent as, under Ottoman rule, the Maronite Christians had attained some degree of autonomy in 1861 in the region of Mount Lebanon. In the rapidly changing post-war climate, the Maronites pushed their claim under the French for a greater tract of land, which was to house a Christian majority and be independent from the predominantly Muslim area of Greater Syria. The State of Greater Lebanon was therefore created on 1 September 1920, with Beirut as its capital. The affiliated Christian communities held a thin majority, so a political system was created in order to preserve the status quo. The seeds of Lebanon's future instability were sown in this period as a system of governance based on proportional sectarian representation, or confessionalism, emerged.

This system was confirmed in the so-called National Pact that accompanied Lebanon's formal independence in 1943. This unwritten agreement served to institutionalize the power relationships that had been the aim of the state's founding. The Christian-to-Muslim proportion of representation in the parliament was set at six to five. It was decided that the president was always to be a Maronite Christian, the prime minster a Sunni Muslim, and the speaker of the Assembly (a largely ceremonial role)

BOX 1.4

Confessionalism is a system of governance that aims to provide integrated leadership in societies marked by the presence of multiple sectarian or religious groups. Most closely associated with Lebanon, confessionalism institutionalizes power-sharing arrangements based on representation by religious affiliation. In this system, different positions in the government are reserved for members of a particular community. Although it was intended to foster national cohesion in a multi-faith state, this system has proven vulnerable to challenge as communities cling to institutionalized political power even as demographic changes mean that the national balance of power has shifted.

a Shia Muslim. The increasing politicization of the Lebanese Shia in the late twentieth century was, in part, a response to this institutionalized under-representation and marginalization. This power-sharing system crumbled in 1975 with the onset of the Lebanese civil war and was problematically renegotiated in the Taif Accords of 1990, which reset the parliamentary representation balance at five to five – a proportion that is, as many Muslims argue, still unrepresentative of the demographic make-up of Lebanon. The seeds of dissent sown in the Mandate period can therefore be seen as having continued to have a profound effect on Lebanon's history. The same is true of the neighbouring Mandate for Palestine.

Post-war negotiations assured the British of their dominant position in Palestine, and the Balfour Declaration was incorporated into the wording of the British Mandate there. In an acknowledgement of the increasing influence of the United States and its self-determination ideal, the League of Nations conferred the Mandates in accordance with the Type A allocation system, which required the Mandatory powers to provide tutelage for independent statehood and not simply continue under the model of colonial exploitation. In order to provide some overarching governance, the newly established League of Nations was given the power to oversee the administration of the Mandates, and the Mandatory powers were required to report to the international body. In reality, as Leon Carl Brown points out, the League of Nations did little to constrain the actions of the Mandatory powers, which, since the international body was drawn from European powers with their own imperialist traditions, is not surprising (Brown 1984: 250).

Tension between France and the United Kingdom over the spoils of war was a major factor in the post-war period. The United Kingdom, duty bound to honour at least some portion of its wartime promises, attempted to appease the Hashemites. Although London was not in a position to offer the independence discussed in the deliberations with Husayn during the early years of the war, the Hashemite sons, Abdullah and Faisal, were rewarded with positions of power in the new British Mandates. Despite these concessions, Husayn entered the post-war period an embittered and still divisive figure in regional politics. He remained in the Hijaz, where he had declared his kingship in 1916. However, Husayn was not the only British ally in the region. Abdul-Aziz ibn Saud, the Wahhabi Emir of Riyadh, had also nurtured his links with the British. Ibn Saud was a leading figure in the al-Saud tribal family, which also had political ambitions in the Arabian Peninsula (Kostiner 1995: 47). As the period of Saudi ascendency commenced in the early 1920s, the British did nothing to halt the Hashemite fall, and al-Saud rule of the Arabian Peninsula was recognized in 1929. Kamal Salibi suggests that, compared to Husayn, the Hashemite sons and the al-Saud family were more 'practical men who were willing to give and take, and settle for what was ultimately achievable in given circumstances' (Salibi 1993: 24).

21

In Palestine, the League of Nations had charged the British authorities with the creation of 'self-governing institutions'. As mentioned, the Balfour Declaration was incorporated into this Mandate, thus securing a place for the notion of a Jewish 'national home' among the international legal norms that related to this region. However, the Arab communities of Palestine were also to be protected under the guidelines established by the Balfour Declaration and, more explicitly, under the terms of the Mandate. In 1921 the United Kingdom designated a section of Mandatory Palestine as a protectorate under Husayn's son Abdullah. Again, the influence of Ottoman norms is evident, as this region had experienced some degree of autonomy under Constantinople's rule. The installation of Abdullah was a British tactic aimed at convincing the Hashemite family not to oppose the French decision to remove Faisal from the short-lived Syrian kingdom (Rogan 1999: 241). Abdullah agreed, and this region, the Kingdom of Transjordan, was immediately closed to Zionist settlement, an act that some Zionists pointed to as a contradiction of the Balfour Declaration. The state of Jordan did not become a member of the United Nations until December 1955.

The map of the Middle East changed rapidly in the first few decades of the twentieth century. The fall of the Ottoman Empire, widely seen as a moment of opportunity for self-determination in the Arab world, led instead to the imposition of external, Western rule. Although the agency of local leaders and the intentions of the Zionist movement played a part in this result, the region was shaped primarily by the external power-brokers of the time, and all actors were beholden to the will of distant European powers. This is evident in the creation of states such as Jordan and Lebanon, both the result of the colonial desire to appease and endorse local constituencies. The colonial masters continued through the Mandate system to act for the new Arab states on the international stage, retaining control over foreign relations and security. The formal objectives of the Mandates explicitly included the notion of a transition to sovereignty, but

BOX 1.5

Wahhabism is an Islamic movement formed by the Islamic preacher Muhammad ibn 'Abd al-Wahhab (1703–92). This puritanical movement focuses on absolute monotheism and advocates a return to the Islamic texts. Wahhabism also rejects all cultural accretions to the faith, including Sufi traditions such as saint veneration. The movement came to prominence after it was adopted by the al-Saud family in 1744. Following their rise to power in the Arabian Peninsula in the twentieth century, Wahhabi doctrines formed the political basis of the modern state of Saudi Arabia.

the implementation of the Mandate system clearly limited exposure to statecraft and diplomacy in the Arab world. This was to become strikingly evident as the new Arab states struggled to deal with the ascendency of Zionism in the region.

REFERENCES

Brown, Leon Carl (1984) *International Politics and the Middle East: Old Rules, Dangerous Game* (London: IB Tauris).

Dershowitz, Alan (2003) *The Case for Israel* (New York: John Wiley and Sons).

Foreign Office (1917) 'The Balfour Declaration', 2 November, available at www.mideast.web.

Helmreich, Paul C. (1974) *From Paris to Sevres: The Partition of the Ottoman Empire at the Peace Conference of 1919–1920* (Athens, OH: Ohio State University Press).

Hughes, Matthew (1999) *Allenby and the British Strategy in the Middle East 1917–1919* (London: Frank Cass).

Huneidi, Sahar (2001) *A Broken Trust: Herbert Samuel, Zionism and the Palestinians* (London: IB Tauris).

Karsh, Ephraim and Karsh, Inari (1999) *Empires of the Sand: The Struggle for Mastery in the Middle East 1789–1923* (Cambridge, MA: Harvard University Press).

King–Crane Commission (1919) 'The King–Crane Commission Report 1919', available at www.mideastweb.org. (Reproduced from 'First publication of King–Crane report on the Near East, a suppressed official document of the United States government' (1922)).

Kostiner, Joseph (1995) 'Prologue of the Hashemite Downfall and Saudi Ascendency: A New Look at the Khurma Dispute 1917–1919', in Asher Susser and Aryeh Shmuelevitz (eds), *The Hashemites in the Modern Arab World* (London: Frank Cass).

League of Nations (1919) 'Covenant of the League of Nations 1919', available at www.mideastweb.org/leaguemand.htm.

'McMahon–Hussein Correspondence, 1915–1916' (1915–16), available at www.mideastweb.org/mcmahon.htm.

Rogan, Eugene L (1999) *Frontiers of the State in the Late Ottoman Empire* (Cambridge: Cambridge University Press).

Sachar, Howard (2005) *A History of the Jews in the Modern World* (New York: Vintage Books).

Salibi, Kamal (1993) *A House of Many Mansions: The History of Lebanon Reconsidered* (London: IB Tauris).

Shlaim, Avi (1995) *War and Peace in the Middle East* (London: Penguin).

Wilson, Mary C. (1991) 'The Hashemites, the Arab Revolt and Arab Nationalism', in Rashid Khalidi (ed.), *The Origins of Arab Nationalism* (New York: Columbia University Press).

SUGGESTED FURTHER READING

Firro, Kais (2003) *Inventing Lebanon: Nationalism and the State under the Mandate* (London: IB Taurus).

Shepherd, Naomi (2000) *Ploughing Sand: British Rule in Palestine, 1917–1948* (New Brunswick, NJ: Rutgers University Press).

Sluglett, Peter (1976) *Britain in Iraq, 1914–1932* (London: Ithaca Press for the Middle East Centre, St Antony's College, Oxford).

Suraiya, Faroqhi (2004) *The Ottoman Empire and the World around It* (London: IB Taurus).

Tripp, Charles (2007) *A History of Iraq*, third edition (Cambridge: Cambridge University Press).

Winslow, Charles (1996) *Lebanon: War and Politics in a Fragmented Society* (London; New York: Routledge).

Zamir, Meir (1985) *The Formation of Modern Lebanon* (London: Croom Helm).

SUGGESTED STUDY QUESTIONS

1   Compare patterns of imperial intervention in the Middle East after the First World War with contemporary patterns of external involvement in the region. Are contemporary patterns of intervention reflective of imperial intervention in the Middle East?

2   What were the specific factors giving rise to the ideology of nationalism in the Middle East?

3   What role has nationalism played in the politics of the Middle East?

4   How would you define pan-Arab nationalism?

5   What factors led to the demise of pan-Arab nationalism?

CHAPTER 2

Great Power Influences, Zionism and the Middle East

INTRODUCTION

The colonial period in the Middle East was marked by the intervention of external powers in the political development of the region. The establishment of the modern system of nation-states was the key outcome of this period. This state system remains the organizing political principle of the region, yet the instabilities inherent in these states still linger. The division of the Ottoman lands into Arab states is one aspect of the Middle East's twentieth-century history. The establishment of the state of Israel is another pivotal moment in the political development of the region. This chapter explores the Zionist movement and the establishment, through a mixture of international politics and conflict, of a Jewish state in the Middle East.

The conflict engendered by the establishment of Israel remains a fierce influence in Middle Eastern politics. The plight of the Palestinian people, which spanned the twentieth century and continues to the current day, remains a central factor in Middle Eastern perceptions of the international system, a system that is often understood as weighted against the interests of the Arab world. The intertwining of Israel and the United States is a feature of the Middle Eastern political landscape, and the correlation between anti-Israeli sentiment and anti-Americanism is significant. The United States was not the major force behind the establishment of Israel, but as the twentieth century progressed and regional politics drew Washington and Tel Aviv ever closer, it is this relationship that became central to Arab dissatisfaction with the United States. In order to provide a clear analysis of this relationship, this chapter will explore the Zionist movement and the establishment of Israel in 1948.

ZIONISM: THE ROAD TO STATEHOOD

Israel has its origins in the Eastern European nationalist movement known as Zionism. Crystallizing around the Hungarian-born Viennese Jew Theodor Herzl, political Zionism sought to reconstitute Jewish life on a national basis. Although often understood as the father of modern Zionism, Herzl was part of a pre-existing tradition of Jewish thought. In formulating his position, Herzl drew on previous work such as that of the Russian Jew Leo Pinsker, who had argued the importance of a national territory for the Jewish people. The Zionist movement spanned the European continent and the movement's early thinkers were motivated by differing concerns, dependent on their national and socio-political situations. In Eastern Europe, Zionist thinkers emphasized the security to be gained by communal reconstitution, as violent anti-Semitism manifested itself in the form of pogroms and massacres that threatened the physical existence of the Jewish people there. In Western Europe, the situation was more complex, with both institutionalized anti-Semitism and increasing assimilation obstructing progression while also threatening the spiritual and cultural uniqueness of the community.

An assimilated Jew, Herzl, whose 1896 publication *The Jewish State* is one of modern Zionism's foundational texts, reacted strongly against the increasing anti-Semitism that characterized the European Jewish experience. The emergence of a Jewish nationalist movement in Europe

BOX 2.1

Theodor Herzl (1860–1904) was the founder of political Zionism. A journalist, playwright and lawyer in Vienna, Herzl was the prototype of a successful, assimilated European Jew. He extended the thought of Leo Pinsker and others after his own faith in assimilation was tested during the Dreyfus affair of 1894. His seminal publication was *The Jewish State* (1896), which launched the modern Zionist movement. Herzl also founded the World Zionist Organization (WZO), which began the long process of lobbying the international community for a Jewish homeland. In the early years of the twentieth century the WZO considered various locations, including Uganda, for the establishment of a 'national home' before focusing its attention on the region of Palestine – the ancestral, biblical homeland of the Jewish people.

at this time is unsurprising, for nationalism was both a curse and an opportunity for the Jewish people. As European nationalisms intensified, Jews were increasingly marginalized, although simultaneously Jewish thinkers assimilated nationalist doctrines into their own worldviews. The term 'Zionism' (Zion is a biblical name for Jerusalem) was coined in 1885 to describe a movement that was first and foremost nationalist and, although fleeting consideration was given to nationalist reconstitution in places such as Western Australia and Africa, it generally focused on the right of the Jewish people to reclaim a national existence in the biblical land of Israel, which for 2000 years had been known as Palestine.

The Zionist claim to the land of Palestine is based on several key points, each given varying degrees of emphasis depending on the orientation of individual proponents. First, there is a biblical connection between the Jewish people and the land. According to Jewish tradition, God promised a geographically defined tract of land to the Jewish patriarch Abraham and his descendants. During the biblical era, there were periods of Jewish sovereignty over the land, symbolized historically by the construction of the First and Second Temples in Jerusalem, the holiest location in the Jewish tradition. With the destruction of the Second Temple in 70 CE the period of Jewish sovereignty ended and the majority of Jews were scattered throughout Europe, the Middle East and Asia in what became known as the Jewish Diaspora. The region known as Palestine passed under the rule of Arabs, Crusaders and, finally, the Ottomans. However, the historical and religious memory of the land, and particularly of the city of Jerusalem, became ritualized within the Jewish tradition and remained a focal point of Jewish identity. Although the vast majority of Jews resided in the Diaspora, a small contingent remained in the region of Palestine, many located in or around Jerusalem. This figure fluctuated dramatically throughout history, ranging from a few thousand to nearly a quarter of a million, and was affected by upheavals such as the Crusades (Sachar 2005: 260–3).

BOX 2.2

Leo Pinsker (1821–91) was a Russian-Polish doctor. Pinsker's faith in the assimilationist policies of the time was shaken by pogroms in Odessa in 1871 and 1881. In response to official ambivalence towards, and even endorsement of, anti-Semitic violence in Russia, he became an ardent Jewish nationalist. In 1882 Pinsker authored an anonymous pamphlet titled *Auto-Emancipation* in which he argued that a Jewish homeland was the only solution for the Jewish people. The publication sparked controversy within the European Jewish communities, and made Pinsker the intellectual forerunner to the Zionist movement.

BOX 2.3

The **Crusades** were a series of Christian military expeditions that began in the late eleventh century to counter the territorial expansion of the Islamic Empire. The campaigns continued sporadically for several centuries. The Crusades were endowed by the Latin Church's hierarchy with religious significance, and participation was often seen as a religious act. At different times, Crusades were called in order to conquer Muslim land, contain Islamic expansion and to retake the Holy Land. Crusades were also called to confront 'heresy' within the Christian community, most notably in the Albigensian crusade (1209–29). The excesses and brutality of the Crusades are well documented.

Driven by the central belief that Jews could not prosper without a state, Zionism was in many ways as much a nationalist as a religious movement.[1] Its leaders called for a revival of Hebrew as the national language of the Jewish people, rejecting the more commonly spoken Yiddish as the language of the ghettos of Europe. This focus on linguistics as a communal unifying force had clear nationalist overtones. Indeed some Zionists, heavily influenced by socialism, paid little attention to the religious connotations of their movement. From the late 1880s, the Zionist movement began sending Jews to Palestine to rebuild a communal presence. Zionism was only one aspect of a diverse and dynamic Jewish political scene in Europe. Various organizations, such as the Bund, initially opposed the Zionist programme of national reconstitution in Palestine, advocating alternative strategies to enhance the standing of Europe's Jews. Often the Jews most attracted to emigration, whether because of religious belief or political conviction, were young, single people. This led to a dynamic and youthful mindset in the early Zionist community. Socialism was a powerful political ideology in early twentieth-century Europe, and its influence can be identified in the central Zionist focus on working or reclaiming the land itself in Palestine. As the Zionist movement grew in popularity, it became more complex, and came to encompass secular, socialist and religious streams.

Buoyed by the Balfour Declaration in 1917, Zionist leaders began a serious international campaign to build and legitimize a viable community in Palestine. The Western origins and mindset of the movement's founders were reflected in the political methodology adopted by the movement, and a fundamental characteristic of Zionism became the determination to ally itself with a powerful external actor. The movement's leaders worked in the international arena to achieve this aim. Considering the realities of the international system of the time, British support was particularly valuable to Zionist ambitions.

BOX 2.4

The Jewish Labor Federation of Lithuania and Poland, known as the **Bund**, was a Russian-Jewish socialist organization formed in 1897. The Bund had a complex relationship with Zionism, especially in relation to the Zionist focus on migration to Palestine, which the Bund ideologically rejected. Although the Bund shared Zionist concerns about the desirability, or feasibility, of assimilation, its members shared an internationalist, socialist perspective that sought to improve the socio-political standing of Jews as a recognized national minority within their states of residence. Linked to its desire to operate within the European context, the Bund also tended to endorse Yiddish as the 'national' language of the Jewish people, in opposition to the Zionist advocacy of Hebrew. As the twentieth century progressed, and anti-Jewish agitation in Russia increased, many Bundists did migrate to Palestine, where they formed the backbone of socialist organizations in the pre-state and early state periods.

As discussed, in the aftermath of the First World War the League of Nations had conferred upon the United Kingdom a Mandate for Palestine. This was a Type A Mandate, meaning the region was to receive interim tutelage in preparation for independent statehood. Reflecting the political mindset of the United Kingdom, a pivotal state in the League of Nations, the Balfour Declaration, with its support for a 'national home' for the Jewish people, had been incorporated into the Mandate. This had given the Zionist movement, and its objective of securing a national community for Jews in the region, international legitimacy. However, since the historical scattering of Jews in the Diaspora, the land of Israel had been populated by Arabs, a reality creating a serious obstacle to the Zionist dream of Jewish sovereignty in the region. Under the terms of the Mandate, the United Kingdom was theoretically required to assist the areas under its influence to develop the capacity for self-governance. Moreover, the Balfour Declaration itself had stipulated that the civil and religious rights of the non-Jewish communities were to be protected. Arguably, the British had set themselves up for failure, as the task of preparing a region for self-rule while endorsing the existence of two competing nationalisms was fraught with difficulties. As a result, the Mandate authorities found themselves increasingly engaged in attempts to manage the disintegrating relationship between the two growing communities.

Global politics significantly influenced the United Kingdom's administration of the Mandate for Palestine. After the close of the First World War, the European powers hoped to avoid further bloodshed.

However, in the 1920s and 1930s further conflict appeared increasingly inevitable, and managing the Nazi threat became a growing preoccupation of the British political elite. At the same time the United Kingdom, fettered by its contradictory promises to both Arabs and Jews, found its authority seriously challenged in Palestine. Both communities intensified their commitment to their competing claims to the land and to national self-determination. As immigration swelled the ranks of both communities, the situation became ever more tense.

Despite the inclusion of the Balfour Declaration in the Mandate, the British were soon placed in a position in which they sought to reassess their alliances in this pivotal region. The first of many British policy backflips occurred in 1922 with the publication of a government document known as a White Paper, which by imposing an economic criterion for immigration to Palestine was aimed at stemming the flow of young Jews from Europe. Perceived by Zionists as a repudiation of the promise made by Balfour in 1917, the 'Churchill' White Paper moved away from the implicit promise of support for statehood that many Zionists had perceived as the eventual outcome of the ambiguous notion of a national home.

> [T]he status of all citizens of Palestine in the eyes of the law shall be Palestinian, and it has never been intended that they, or any section of them, should possess any other juridical status.
>
> ('The British White Paper of 1922')

This document can be understood as a public acknowledgement by the British government that a communal conflict was brewing in Palestine. Members of the Zionist movement, although bitterly disappointed, remained largely committed to a diplomatic resolution through the auspices of its relationship with the United Kingdom. This policy of political adaptation was a vital component of the early Zionist movement. The European roots of the movement helped immeasurably as the Zionist leadership, familiar with Western applications of international relations, sought to develop their case for Palestine through the Western corridors of power.

Intellectually, early Zionism displayed an often naive belief that the dual claim to the land would resolve itself over time. Overall, the Arab question was minimized by many early Zionists. The Arab understanding of Zionism, and indeed Zionism's understanding of itself, was as a predominantly nationalist movement of Western origins. For the Arab population in Palestine, then, the Zionists were foreign settlers. Consequently, it was difficult for many Arabs not to see Zionism as just another form of colonization of Arab lands.

Palestinian political identity is one of the more complex dimensions of this political history. Issues of Western-centric and Orientalist thought

BOX 2.5

Orientalism traditionally refers to the study of Eastern cultures, languages and peoples. Since the late 1970s, however, the term has been associated with the late Professor Edward Said. In his 1978 text *Orientalism*, Said critiqued Western studies of the East, arguing that most scholarship had been informed by stereotypes and false assumptions formed in the eighteenth and nineteenth centuries. Said's thesis has in turn been critiqued by post-colonialist theorists who suggest it works to disenfranchise the cultures of the Middle East.

need to be addressed in any exploration of Palestinian nationalism in the inter-war period. Arabs, both Muslim and Christian, had resided as a majority in the land of Palestine since the Jewish expulsion in 70 CE. Some tribes, such as the Bedouin, were nomadic, some had settled in villages and pursued an agrarian lifestyle, and others had become traders and merchants. The concept of nationalism, as espoused in the Zionist movement, was an inherently Western one, spawned and nurtured in late nineteenth-century Europe and expressed in the language of European political thought. By contrast, the identity of the Arabs of Palestine can be understood as organic, premised on the relationship between the land, the tribe and the community. This explanation highlights the complexities of a collision between different forms of political identity.

The religious dimensions of Palestine, more specifically Jerusalem, made the contrasting claims of its communities even harder to resolve. Jerusalem is a holy site in the Islamic faith, surpassed in importance only by Mecca and Medina. As mentioned earlier, it is also the most sacred location in the Jewish tradition. That the veneration of Jerusalem is also central to the Christian tradition further complicated the fate of this contested city.

Overall, it is reasonable to view Jewish and Palestinian identities as having a symbiotic relationship throughout the pre-state period, with each reinforcing and intensifying the other. As Zionist immigration increased, Arabs began to organize politically to counter the perceived threat. This in turn caused a hardening of Zionist claims to Palestine.

This reality was acknowledged by some within the Zionist movement. Some, often those influenced by a more socialist leaning, called for a federation-style approach – a uniting of the Arab and Jewish workers – to construct a new state. Others, such as Ze'ev Jabotinsky (1880–1940), who led a splinter faction called Revisionist Zionism, advocated a more hardline response. This group broke from the broader Zionist movement over the mainstream's acceptance of the terms of the 1922 White Paper. Revisionist Zionism advocated a territorial understanding of a future Jewish state that corresponded with the biblical promise (that is, both banks of the River

Jordan) and called for an immediate declaration of Jewish sovereignty over the land. Although understanding the need for Great Power patronage, this faction was dissatisfied with the diplomatic manoeuvrings of the Zionist Executive and demanded immediate action to achieve the dream of a Jewish state in Palestine. The precursor to the modern Israeli right wing, Revisionist Zionism focused on the need for a strong military capability to ensure the borders of a future state. Although Jabotinsky's line was rejected as too extreme by many within the Zionist movement, he did, unlike many of his fellow Zionists, acknowledge the reality of Palestinian identity and foresaw the inevitability of conflict between these two nationalisms.

> Every indigenous people will go on resisting alien settlers as long as they see the hope of ridding themselves of the danger of foreign settlement. This is how the Arabs will behave and go on behaving so long as they possess a gleam of hope of preventing 'Palestine' from becoming the Land of Israel.
>
> (Jabotinsky 1923)

As Jabotinsky predicted, the situation in Mandate Palestine grew progressively worse. The Arab Revolt of 1936–39 demonstrated the intractable determination of Palestinians and their increasing willingness to resist Zionist intentions. The British government, sliding towards another European conflict, struggled to resolve the situation. The 1937 Peel Commission is the most well known of a range of British fact-finding missions that attempted to extricate the United Kingdom from the tangle of the competing claims in Palestine. The Peel Commission recommended partition, accompanied by transfer of land and populations, as the only feasible solution. Publication of the Commission's report sparked controversy within the Zionist camp and outright condemnation from the Arab states. For most Zionist leaders partition offered the pinnacle of the Zionist dream: the legitimacy of statehood in place of the ambiguous

BOX 2.6

The **Arab Revolt of 1936–39** was a period of intense violence and civil conflict in Mandate Palestine. It was led by the Arab Higher Committee and targeted both Jewish and British interests. Initially, protestors declared a general strike and boycott and lobbied the Mandate authorities to end Jewish immigration to Palestine and to cease the sale or transfer of land to the Zionist movement. The situation rapidly spiralled away from civil protest, however, and a period of communal violence between Zionists, Arabs and the British authorities ensued.

status of a 'national home'. Despite internal differences regarding the land allocated, the Zionist mainstream eventually accepted this plan. The Arab position was, however, unequivocal. Representing both the Palestinian Arab and wider Arab perspectives, seen in this period as indivisible, the Arab states declared the partition of Palestine unacceptable and decried the proposal as illegitimate, an example of an imperial power promising to a Western minority land that was not theirs to give. That the British proposed partition, a project fraught with uncertainty and logistical challenges, revealed their awareness that nationalism on both sides was intense and growing.

ZIONISM DURING THE WAR

As another European war loomed, the United Kingdom identified Arab support against Germany as more important than maintaining its commitment to the small transnational Jewish minority. Thus, in a new White Paper in 1939 London reversed the partition plan. Crushing the hopes of the Zionists, this document was clearly an attempt to secure Arab support on the eve of the Second World War. It asserted that Jews were to remain a minority without the security of statehood in the land of Palestine.

> It has been urged that the expression 'a national home for the Jewish people' offered a prospect that Palestine might in due course become a Jewish State or Commonwealth . . . His Majesty's Government therefore now declare unequivocally that it is not part of their policy that Palestine should become a Jewish State. [It is] contrary to their obligations to the Arabs under the Mandate, as well as to the assurances which have been given to the Arab people in the past, that the Arab population of Palestine should be made the subjects of a Jewish State against their will.
>
> ('The British White Paper of 1939')

Despite this devastating setback, most Zionist organizations called a truce against the Mandate authorities and assisted the United Kingdom and its allies in the confrontation with Hitler's Germany. Many Jews from Palestine fought in Britain's Jewish Battalions, gaining vital military experience throughout the course of the war. This strengthened an already well-developed Zionist military capability. Military organization and experience were key components of the Zionist experience in the pre-state period. For example, the Haganah had been established in 1920 as a clandestine force for the defence of Jewish settlements. Various splinter groups also existed, such as the fiercely nationalist Irgun, the armed wing

BOX 2.7

Pre-state Zionist military organizations included the **Haganah**, the **Irgun Zvai Leumi** and the **Stern Gang**. The Haganah was formed in 1920 to defend Jewish settlements in Palestine. It represented a mainstream Jewish political position, and a series of more radical groups splintered from it as the political dynamics of the Mandate period became more intense. The Irgun militia was one such group; it emerged in 1931 and by 1936 was closely associated with the Revisionist movement. The Irgun employed violence against both the British authorities and the Arabs, and was responsible for a 1946 attack on the British authorities' headquarters in Jerusalem's King David Hotel. The Stern Gang (also called Lehi) emerged from the Irgun in 1940. It was the most radical and marginal Zionist militia and was condemned by the mainstream Zionist movement. The Stern Gang was involved in political assassinations and attacks against British personnel and infrastructure.

of Revisionist Zionism, which had been established in 1931 and advocated a policy of armed reprisal against both Arab and British targets. The Irgun elected to hold to the wartime truce, however, and consequently a further splinter group emerged: Lehi, also known as the Stern Gang, was established in 1940 and exhorted its followers to refuse to serve in the Jewish Battalions against the Axis powers (Heller 1995: 70–6).

By the close of the Second World War, many in the Zionist community had gained significant combat experience and military training and were already organized into various efficient fighting structures. With the Allied victory came awareness of the full scale of the devastation of the Holocaust, and Zionist belief in the immediate need to establish a Jewish state became ever more absolute. Outrage and desperation among international Jewry had grown steadily throughout the final years of the war, as information about the systematic destruction of Europe's Jewish communities seeped out. This can be seen in initiatives such as the Zionist Biltmore Program of 1942, developed in the United States. Given the contradictions and confusion evident in the position of the United Kingdom, it was not surprising that the Zionist community agitated against British rule as the war ended. The Haganah undertook acts of sabotage and maintained its defence of Jewish settlements against Arab attacks, while marginal groups such as the Irgun adopted a more violent programme, including acts of terrorism that culminated in a bomb attack against the British authorities in their headquarters at Jerusalem's King David Hotel in 1946.

By 1947 Palestine was in a state of chaos. Zionist factions were waging a war of rebellion while Palestinian militias launched raids on Jewish settlements and British military installations. The violence had assumed the form of a cyclical, communal war of attrition, with civilians dying on either side. The United Kingdom, recovering from its own war of survival and realizing that the sun was setting on the British Empire, referred the matter of Palestine to the United Nations. After deliberation, the United Nations passed Resolution 181, on 29 November 1947, in favour of the partition of Palestine into two states. A redevelopment of the Peel Commission recommendation, the UN resolution was plagued by the same challenges and shortcomings.

The partition would have been a geographic and demographic disaster, with the security of neither community assured. The planned Jewish state included a population of approximately 500,000 Jews and just below 400,000

BOX 2.8

The **Holocaust** was a campaign of systematic mass killing of Jews, Gypsies and others by Nazi Germany during the Second World War. Anti-Semitism, which had ebbed and flowed throughout European history, was institutionalized under the Nazi regime. As Nazi Germany strengthened its hold on Europe, the targeted extermination of Jews, Gypsies, intellectuals, homosexuals and the disabled increased. Europe's Jews were first forced into ghettos and concentration camps. At the Wannsee Conference of 1942, the Nazi hierarchy endorsed the 'Final Solution', a plan for the physical annihilation of European Jewry. By 1945, the Holocaust had claimed the lives of an estimated 6 million Jews, and the European Jewish communities had been largely decimated.

BOX 2.9

The **Biltmore Program** refers to the outcomes of an international Zionism conference held at the Biltmore Hotel in New York City on 9–11 May 1942. The conference was attended by nearly 600 local and international delegates, including leading Zionist figures such as Chaim Weizmann and David Ben Gurion. The conference adopted eight key resolutions that were then ratified by the Zionist General Council in Palestine. These included a call for the immediate implementation of the 'original purpose' of the Balfour Declaration, a complete rejection of the British White Paper of 1939, and increased and unlimited Jewish immigration to Palestine. Despite some internal dissent, often based on support for a binational resolution with the Palestinian Arabs, the Biltmore Program quickly gained acceptance as the platform of the Zionist movement.

Arabs, so in reality it would have been binational, with Jerusalem placed under UN-administered trusteeship (Galnoor 1995: 285). Furthermore, at the time of the resolution the Zionist community owned only some of the land allotted to Jews. The structural weaknesses of the partition plan may have been deliberate, with the United Nations attempting to ensure that neither the Zionists nor the Palestinians were in a position to exercise absolute dominance over the other. Resolution 181, like the Peel Commission before it, caused some dissent within Zionist ranks, but since it offered the international recognition of statehood, the Zionists eventually accepted it. Flapan suggests that Ben Gurion and many others in the Zionist leadership viewed acceptance as a logical and pragmatic move, citing Ben Gurion's statement that 'in the wake of the establishment of the state, we will abolish partition and expand to the whole of Palestine' (quoted in Flapan 1987: 22). This indicates that the Zionist leadership's support for partition was premised on the expectation that the territory allotted would be expanded in the coming conflict that they had viewed as inevitable since the mid-1940s.

The Palestinians, represented by the Arab Higher Committee (which had been formed by the Arab League to address the question of Palestine), rejected Resolution 181 completely. The Arab League declared the partition plan illegal and threatened force if it was implemented. The role played by non-Palestinian regional Arab actors in this period is extremely problematic, and set a precedent for the misrepresentation and exploitation of the Palestinian political perspective. The Arab states, reacting with hyperbole and propaganda that exaggerated their ability to defeat the Zionist community in conflict, were hasty to take the mantle of representation from the Palestinian people. The decision to reject Resolution 181 had disastrous consequences, with the resulting conflict establishing only one of the two states envisaged by the international body.

BOX 2.10

David Ben Gurion (1886–1973) was born in Poland to a family of Zionist activists of socialist persuasion. He migrated to Palestine and matured into a Zionist leader deeply involved in the military and political planning for the establishment of the state of Israel. Upon its foundation, he became the state's first prime minister and is often referred to as the 'father of the nation'. Ben Gurion remained active in Israeli politics for decades, serving again as prime minister from 1955 to 1963.

AL-NAKBA/THE ISRAELI WAR OF INDEPENDENCE

The Zionist leadership, drawing on the legitimacy offered by the UN partition plan, declared independent statehood on 14 May 1948. The decision to declare statehood was a brave one, cautioned against by Washington and London. The level of international trepidation about the potential for conflict was so high that on the eve of Israel's independence the United States called for a ten-year cooling-off period on Resolution 181. American representatives suggested that during this period Palestine should be placed under a trusteeship administered by the United Nations or the United States (Tal 2004: 83). The possibility of coming so close to statehood only to see it delayed in the international arena may have spurred the Zionist leadership into action. The Israeli declaration, although citing the new state's desire for peace, did not stipulate borders, an omission that has been seen as a clear indication of the leadership's awareness of the inevitability of regional conflict.

The Israeli declaration prompted a chain of events that revealed the importance of Palestine in the global order at this time. The emergent post-war superpowers, the United States and the Soviet Union, both immediately recognized the new state. When added to the UN mandate established by Resolution 181, the dual superpower endorsement effectively established the international legitimacy of the new state of Israel. The dynamics of the early Cold War period may well have prompted recognition by the superpowers. Some sources indicate that President Truman, viewed by some historians as the 'midwife' at Israel's birth, struggled with the decision to endorse Israel immediately, but domestic pressures, splits within the administration itself, and intelligence indicating that the Soviet Union would do so, may have forced his hand (Ganin 1979). Concerns regarding the new state's possible Soviet leanings were intensified by the traditional socialist underpinnings of the Zionist movement. In the context of a rapidly developing Cold War, Washington was worried about the possibility of a pro-Soviet state in the region.

The day after Israel's declaration of independence a combined Arab force invaded the new state, starting the first major Arab–Israeli war. The Arab invasion of 15 May 1948 was the culmination of the low-intensity conflict that had already been embroiling Mandate Palestine. In effect it signalled a new phase in the pre-existing conflict between Arabs and Zionism as it expanded the conflict into a regional inter-state war. With varying degrees of intensity, these two communities had been locked in a struggle over the land and its future political status since the turn of the century. More immediately, the Zionist and Arab communities in Palestine had been conducting a low-intensity war since the announcement of Resolution 181 on 29 November 1947. This period of conflict between Zionist and Arab militias can be understood as a guerrilla war, with significant loss of civilian life. Palestinian fighters, ill-equipped and unable to mount a regular army, engaged in commando raids and incursions against Zionist settlements. Initially, the Zionist forces limited themselves to containment operations, but in April 1948, only a month before the declaration of independence, the inevitability of a broader regional conflict triggered a significant tactical change.

Plan Dalet, also known as Plan D, was a highly contested Zionist military operation in the pre-state period. To the Zionists, Plan D was an aggressive defence measure aimed at securing the areas allocated to the Jews under Resolution 181 from hostile or *potentially* hostile Arab factions, a designation that often included Arab civilians. Arabs identified Plan D as a Zionist attempt to expropriate their land. The objectives of Plan D included the capture of Arab villages, a tactic that the Haganah had not previously attempted. As David Tal points out, Palestinian civilians were already fleeing the region, and the goal of Plan D to 'seize territory and impose Jewish authority' only reinforced this trend (2004: 100). The roots of the Palestinian refugee crisis can be traced back to this period, pre-dating the May 1948 war.

Palestinian civilians were most affected by this conflict. In addition to the possibility of Zionist military action, many traditional community leaders, including landowners and the leaders of the Arab Higher Committee, fled Palestine in this period (Flapan 1979). Such losses only added to the sense of panic as the Palestinian community found itself lacking stable leadership in a time of crisis. In April 1948, a Zionist militia operation resulted in the deaths of civilians in the Arab village of Deir Yassin, a community that had signed a non-aggression pact with its Jewish neighbours. News of the killings spread quickly. Although the Zionist Executive issued a formal apology, fears of further massacres at the hands of Zionist forces clearly contributed to the exodus of Palestinians from the region and may even have precipitated the entry of the Arab states into the conflict (Hogan 2001: 332). It is important to note that violence against civilians was perpetrated by both sides. For example, Palestinian factions responded to the massacre at Deir Yassin by killing medical staff at Hadassah Hospital on Mount Scopus.

In addition to the climate of fear and violence, traditionally some Zionist accounts have also suggested that regional Arab leaders, influenced by miscalculations of their own military strength, encouraged Palestinians to leave and return after the Arab armies had defeated the Zionists, although this view is strongly contested.[2] The varied arguments and interpretations demonstrate the complexity characterizing the highly politicized history of the Palestinian exodus and consequent refugee problem. For the Palestinian fighting forces, the impact of the population's instability was significant. By the close of April 1948, the irregular military capabilities of the Palestinian fighters had been seriously degraded, if not destroyed (Elam 2002: 52). As Rashid Khalidi comments, by the Israeli declaration on 15 May 1948, the Palestinian people were in a state of chaos. Khalidi states that 'weak political institutions, factionalism and a lack of leadership', compounded by international ambivalence and Arab self-interest, combined to render the community unable to maintain a military position against the better organized Zionists (2001: 12–14). The collapse of local resistance to partition triggered, or perhaps forced, an Arab tactical switch from supporting the Palestinian irregular fighters into committing regular national army deployments. Thus, the Arab states, bound by pan-Arab solidarity and their own propaganda regarding their ability to defeat an emergent Jewish state, declared war on Israel. Egypt, Transjordan, Syria, Lebanon and Iraq committed troops and regional conflict began in earnest.

The perspectives of the superpowers would have been a serious consideration for the invading Arab states. It bears remembering that the United States and the Soviet Union had both recognized Israel's declaration of independence, thus affirming their support for the existence of the state. The potential willingness of one, or both, of the superpowers to intervene to protect the new state was unknown and could not have been discounted by the Arab war planners. Although the 1948 war has been understood in Israeli historiography as a struggle for survival, some modern Israeli historians suggest that, considering the position of the superpowers, the Arab military campaign may have been waged with more limited objectives. Different understandings of aim and objective, as well as contradictory interpretations of events, are significant features in any study of the Arab–Israeli wars. This is especially the case in the 1948 war, which is at the heart of myth-making and the creation of national identity for both communities.

Traditionally, the 1948 war has been understood by Israelis as a 'David and Goliath' conflict. Israeli research of the Revisionist school, however, suggests that this image, like much about the traditional discourse surrounding the conflict of 1948–49, is questionable. Although political geography does lend itself to such an interpretation, it has been suggested that 'the Arab Goliath was suffering from extreme poverty, domestic discord and internal rivalries' (Thomas 1999: 81). The Revisionist school, spearheaded by historians such as Avi Shlaim and Simha Flapan, asserts that the 'David and Goliath' paradigm was not reflected in the combat strength of the two sides in the actual fighting. Despite its much smaller size, Israel was able to match and then increase its numerical strength vis-à-vis the Arab armies. Poor leadership and coordination affected the Arab armies, with individual states – especially Transjordan and Egypt – seeking to better their own position. In the field, an Arab tendency to initially underestimate, and then to overestimate, the combat strength and capabilities of the Israelis had a devastating effect on troop morale.

BOX 2.11

The **Gaza Strip** is a strip of coastal land that borders both Israel and Egypt. Its major city is Gaza City. The Gaza Strip is 41 kilometres long and between 6 and 12 kilometres wide; its total area is approximately 360 square kilometres. Between 1949 and 1967, Gaza was administered as an occupied territory by Egypt. Its population swelled significantly as a result of the 1948–49 conflict and has continued to increase exponentially since that time. Gaza was under Israeli military occupation from 1967 until 2005, during which time Israeli settlers established a series of communities there. Factional infighting between Fatah and HAMAS followed the Israeli withdrawal, and eventually led to HAMAS rule in June 2007. Today Gaza is home to approximately 1.5 million people. Gaza is one of the world's most densely populated tracts of land and has chronic problems of housing and unemployment.

This morale differential in the field, the contrasts in degree of political will and military training, the impact of the apparent and public superpower support for the state of Israel, and the need for the new Arab states to hold back some of their forces to protect the status quo at home are some of the factors that explain the Arab defeat. In addition, Western arms embargoes on the conflict limited the ability of all parties to rearm their forces, and although all states involved received smuggled weapons from various quarters, the Israeli forces clearly benefited from a major arms lift from Czechoslovakia (Elam 2002: 57). This arms deal, originating in the Soviet Union, suggested a Cold War dimension to the conflict that would become inherent in future Arab–Israeli wars.

By the close of the inter-state conflict in January 1949, the state of Israel had emerged victorious. Moreover, it had gained control of a significantly greater territorial mass, and attained a greater strategic depth, than that which was stipulated in the 1947 partition plan. Israel proudly recalls this war as the 'war of independence'. As the baptism of fire for the new state, it occupies a central place in the national history of Israel. The Arabs, however, have a very different view. The 1948 war is seen as the catastrophe – al-Nakba – of the Palestinian people. A mirror image of the Israeli perspective, al-Nakba is at the heart of the Palestinian account of history, recounting dispersion and exodus. By 1949, between 600,000 and 700,000 Palestinians were refugees (Flapan 1987: 83). Whereas traditional Zionist discourse focuses on interpretations that privilege theories such as the idea that Arab leaders encouraged Palestinians to leave their homes, Revisionist historians and Arab sources place greater weight on factors such as the implementation of Plan D and the dynamics of the conflict. The central cause of the Palestinian exodus aside, the reality remains that

BOX 2.12

The **West Bank** is an area of land between Jordan and Israel. It is predominantly inhabited by Palestinians. As a result of the war of 1948–49, Jordan took control of the West Bank, including Jerusalem's Old City in East Jerusalem. Jordan governed the West Bank until it fell under Israeli control in the 1967 war. Israel then formally annexed East Jerusalem, leaving the remainder of the West Bank as occupied or disputed territory. After the 1967 war, and more intensively after 1977, Israeli settlers established both state-sanctioned and non-state-sanctioned communities in many parts of the West Bank. Today the West Bank is home to approximately 2.5 million Palestinians, 260,000 Israeli settlers and a further 185,000 Israeli Jews living in East Jerusalem. Similar to the Gaza Strip, the West Bank is not formally recognized as part of any state.

hundreds of thousands of people were displaced and herded into refugee camps along Israel's borders with Arab states. The desire to return became the foundational component of Palestinian political identity. The close of the war saw the remaining Palestinian territory of Gaza, with between 200,000 and 300,000 Palestinians, come under the administration of Egypt; the West Bank, with its population of between 400,000 and 450,000, was controlled by Transjordan. Neither state had a vested interest in encouraging Palestinian independence. Thus, the refugees emerged as 'double victims', displaced from their land as a result of the Zionist dream of a Jewish state in Palestine and then failed by the Arab world.

Despite the clear military victory, this was a costly war for Israel, with 1 per cent of its population, around 6,000 people, dying in the conflict (Shalim 2000: 34). Moreover, there was no comprehensive peace: the key 1949 issues of borders and refugees remained unresolved, as they do even today. Israel insisted that its responsibility was first and foremost to the resettlement of Jewish refugees from the Holocaust and the Second World War. Hundreds of thousands of Jews who had lived throughout the Arab world poured into Israel as a result of increased persecution in the aftermath of the establishment of the Jewish state. In terms of nation-building, Israel's ability to create a cohesive national identity from the disparate mix of local Jewish people, refugees and Holocaust survivors was nothing short of remarkable. The role of repeated state-to-state conflicts in forging this identity should not be underestimated. Meanwhile, in the aftermath of the 1948–49 war, the Arab states called for resettlement of the Palestinians displaced during the conflict. The Arab League, still representing the Palestinian people, forced the pan-Arab position on the refugees: return or compensation, and the acknowledgement of Israeli liability. Israel, for its part, pointed to the Arab role as the aggressor in the conflict. This oppositional dynamic, which did nothing to alleviate political uncertainty for the refugees, soon developed an internal logic, and the situation remained unchanged for decades.

CONCLUSION

For the United States, the establishment of a Jewish state was a mixed blessing. North American Jews had been settling in Palestine since the turn of the century. Sachar reports that by 1900, nearly 1,000 North Americans had relocated to Palestine; this figure grew significantly over the coming decades (2005: 704). This opened channels of familial interest and influence between the American Jewish community and the new state. The United States had provided a weak voice of caution in the international arena through the ill-fated King–Crane Commission of 1919. However, similar to the rest of the international community, by the eve of the Second World War the United States was relegated to being little more than a bystander in a process of conflicting nationalisms in Mandate Palestine. The scale of devastation wrought by the Holocaust was keenly felt in the United States and led to strong levels of support for the establishment of a Jewish state. However, as has been explored in this chapter, the United States was not a major player in the establishment of the state of Israel. Yet Washington quickly came to see Israel as a regional ally in the decades following its independence, a topic to be examined in Chapter 3.

The 1948 Arab–Israeli war is perhaps one of the most controversial wars in modern history. The centrality of this conflict in the formulation of a cohesive national identity for both Israelis and Palestinians is undeniable. In both symbolic and literal terms, the refugee crisis sparked by this conflict remains at the crux of the Arab–Israeli dispute. As Flapan asserts, resolution of this key point, historically speaking, has been further complicated by the fact that the two national narratives are 'diametrically opposed and equally inadequate' (1979: 301). The traditional Israeli discourse has asserted a lack of Israeli culpability and focused on the supposed role of the Arab leaderships, whereas the Arab historiography glosses over the concept of self-flight and the internal dissolution of political structures and focuses instead on forced expulsion. Unfortunately these interpretations, which leave little room for reconciliation, still remain influential in the political and public mind and have been further entrenched by nearly six decades of conflict. For the Palestinians, caught up in a conflict and then a political game of blame attribution, the events of this period were an unmitigated disaster, with even the unsatisfactory promise of partition lost. For Israel, its establishment was assured with this victory, but the peace that its founders called for in the declaration of statehood proved elusive.

NOTES

1 For a full exploration of Zionism see Vital (1982, 1987).
2 See Flapan (1987). Flapan contends that it is nonsensical to suggest that the Arab leadership, knowing their armies would rely on the local population for food and shelter, would encourage their departure from the battle zone.

REFERENCES

'The British White Paper of 1922', available at www.mideastweb.org/1922wp.htm.

'The British White Paper of 1939', available at www.mideastweb.org/1939.htm.

Elam, Yigal (2002) 'On the Myth of the Few against the Many', *Palestine–Israel Journal of Politics, Economics and Culture*, Vol. 9, No. 4, 50–7.

Flapan, Simha (1979) *Zionism and the Palestinians* (London: Croom Helm).

Flapan, Simha (1987) *The Birth of Israel: Myths and Realities* (New York: Pantheon Books).

Galnoor, Itzhak (1995) *The Partition of Palestine: Decision Crossroads in the Zionist Movement* (Albany, NY: State University of New York Press).

Ganin, Zvi (1979) *Truman, American Jewry and Israel 1945–1948* (New York: Holmes & Meier).

Heller, Joseph (1995) *The Stern Gang: Ideology, Politics and Terror 1940–1949* (London: Frank Cass).

Hogan, Matthew (2001) 'The 1948 Massacre at Deir Yassin Revisited', in *Historian*, Vol. 63, No. 2 (Winter), pp. 309–33.

Jabotinsky, Ze'ev (1923) 'The Iron Wall' (in Russian), available in English at www.mideastweb.org/ironwall.htm.

Khalidi, Rashid (2001) 'The Palestinians and 1948: The Underlying Causes of Failure', in Eugene Rogan and Avi Shlaim (eds), *The War for Palestine: Rewriting the History of 1948* (Cambridge: Cambridge University Press).

Sachar, Howard (2005) *A History of the Jews in the Modern World* (New York: Vintage).

Shlaim, Avi (2000) *The Iron Wall: Israel and the Arab World* (London: Penguin Books).

Tal, David (2004) *War in Palestine 1948: Strategy and Diplomacy* (London: Routledge).

Thomas, Baylis (1999) *How Israel Was Won: A Concise History of the Arab–Israeli Conflict* (Lanham, MD: Lexington Books).

Vital, David (1982) *Zionism: The Formative Years* (Oxford: Clarendon Press).

Vital, David (1987) *Zionism: The Crucial Phase* (Oxford: Clarendon Press).

SUGGESTED FURTHER READING

Bar-Siman-Tov, Yaaov (1987) *Israel, the Superpowers and the War in the Middle East* (London: Praeger).

Black, Ian and Morris, Benny (1996) *Israel's Secret Wars: A History of Israel's Intelligence Services* (Cambridge: Cambridge University Press).

Bregman, Ahron (2000) *Israel's Wars 1947–1993* (London: Routledge).

Bregman, Ahron (2003) *A History of Israel* (London: Palgrave Macmillan).

Cohen, Israel (1950) *Contemporary Jewry: A Survey of Social, Cultural, Economic and Political Conditions* (London: Methuen).

Cohen, Michael Joseph (1978) *Palestine, Retreat from the Mandate: The Making of British Policy* (London: Paul Elek).

Daphne, Trevor (1980) *Under the White Paper: Some Aspects of British Administration in Palestine from 1939 to 1947* (Munich: Kraus International).

El Badri, Hassan, El Magdoub, Taha and Dia El Din Zohdy, Mohammed (1978) *The Ramadan War, 1973* (New York: Dupuy Associates).

El-Eini, Roza (2006) *Mandated Landscape: British Imperial Rule in Palestine, 1929–1948* (London: Routledge).

Heller, Joseph (2000) *The Birth of Israel, 1945–1949: Ben Gurion and His Critics* (Gainesville: University Press of Florida).

Herzl, Theodore (1960) *The Completed Diaries of Theodore Herzl*, ed. by Raphael Patai, trans. by Harry Zohn (New York: Herzl Press and Thomas Yoseloff).

Herzl, Theodore (1988) *The Jewish State* (New York: Dover).

Hirst, David (2003) *The Gun and the Olive Branch: The Roots of Violence in the Middle East* (London: Faber).

Karsh, Efraim (2000) *Israel: The First Hundred Years* (London: Frank Cass).

Kurz, Anat (2005) *Fatah and the Politics of Violence: The Institutionalization of a Popular Struggle* (Brighton: Sussex Academic Press).

Lockman, Zachery (2004) *Contending Visions of the Middle East: The History and Politics of Orientalism* (New York: Cambridge University Press).

Macfie, A.L. (2002) *Orientalism* (London: Longman).

Massad, Joseph Andoni (2006) *The Persistence of the Palestinian Question: Essays on Zionism and the Palestinians* (New York: Routledge).

Meyer, Michael (1990) *Jewish Identity in the Modern World* (Seattle: University of Washington Press).

Nasser, Jamal R. (1991) *The Palestine Liberation Organization – From Armed Struggle to the Declaration of Independence* (New York: Praeger).

Peleg, Yaron (2005) *Orientalism and the Hebrew Imagination* (Ithaca, NY: Cornell University Press).

Peres, Shimon, in collaboration with Patrick Girard (1999) *The Imaginary Voyage* (New York: Arcade).

Qassem, Naim (2005) *Hizbullah: The Story from Within*, trans. by Dalia Khalil (London: Saqi).

Rogan, Eugene and Shlaim, Avi, eds (2001) *The War for Palestine: Rewriting the History of 1948* (Cambridge: Cambridge University Press).

Roth, Stephen, ed. (1988) *The Impact of the Six Day War: A Twenty Year Assessment* (London: Macmillan).

Rubenstein, Amnon (1984) *The Zionist Dream Revisited: From Herzl to Gush Emunim and Back* (New York: Schocken Books).

Sahliyeh, Emile F. (1986) *The PLO After the Lebanon War* (Boulder, CO: Westview Press).

Said, Edward (1995) *Orientalism* (London: Penguin).

Said, Edward (2001) *The Edward Said Reader*, ed. by Moustafa Bayoumi and Andrew Rubin (London: Granta).

Said, Edward, with David Barsamian (2003) *Culture and Resistance: Conversations with Edward Said* (Cambridge, MA: South End Press).

Said, Edward, with Amritjit Singh and Bruce G. Johnson (2004) *Interviews with Edward Said* (Jackson, MS: University Press of Mississippi).

Said, Edward, with by Gauri Viswanathan (2004) *Power, Politics and Culture: Interviews with Edward W. Said*, (London: Bloomsbury).

Smith, Charles D. (2004) *Palestine and the Arab–Israeli Conflict* (Boston: Bedford/St Martins).

Sprinzak, Ehud (1999) *The Ascendance of Israel's Radical Right* (New York: Oxford University Press).

Sprinzak, Ehud (1999) *Brother against Brother: Violence and Extremism in Israeli Politics from Altalena to the Rabin Assassination* (New York: Free Press).

SUGGESTED STUDY QUESTIONS

1   What is 'Zionism', and what role do religion and the ideology of nationalism play in the Zionist paradigm?

2   To what extent do current foreign policies of Western powers towards the Middle East appear to be informed by an Orientalist mindset?

3   What has been the historical impact of the Balfour Declaration on the psychology of Palestinian leadership?

4   What role does religion play in the dispute between Palestine and Israel?

5   How can the outbreak of conflict between Israel and the Lebanese militia Hezbollah in 2006 be contextualized within the long history of Arab–Israeli violence?

CHAPTER 3

Israel and the Arabs at War

Superpower Dimensions and the Israeli–US Alliance

INTRODUCTION

The Arab states of the Middle East were created through a mixture of local alliances, imperial interest and the processes triggered by the fall of the Ottoman Empire. The state of Israel was voted into existence at the United Nations and consecrated through a costly regional war. The creation of Israel, although a fulfilment of the Zionist dream, had a dramatic and divisive impact on the region and its international relations. Few states in history have engendered the passionate responses that Israel has evoked in its short history. As explored in the previous chapter, the fractious final years of the Mandate notwithstanding, the major patron of the Zionist movement was the United Kingdom. However, in the late 1940s the United Kingdom's power was waning, the devastation of the Second World War and the turbulent end of the colonial period sapping the strength of this one-time regional power-broker.

For the United States, the establishment of Israel was to have a profound and lasting influence on the formulation of foreign policy. The limited role of the United States in the pre-state period reflects the balance of power in international relations in the first decades of the twentieth century. As the influence of the colonial powers of France and the United Kingdom diminished, the Cold War superpowers – the United States and the Soviet Union – gained increasing prominence in the Middle East. From 1948 onwards, and particularly in the pivotal war of 1967, the Israeli–US relationship gained strength. By the close of the Arab–Israeli war of 1973, Washington had gained a position unrivalled by other Western powers.

The creation of a Jewish state in the heart of the Arab Middle East was both the culmination and commencement of a struggle between two peoples in one land. In the contemporary period, this conflict, which has ebbed and flowed for nearly one hundred years, is one of the greatest factors in the formulation of US policy in the region and a major contributing force to the dynamics of Arab anti-Americanism. This chapter will explore the conflicts that have characterized the Arab–Israeli relationship and the impact of Cold War bipolarity.

1956: THE SUEZ WAR

The establishment of Israel and the subsequent war signalled the end of lasting peace in the region. The all-pervasive Cold War greatly affected the Middle East, with superpower interest in the region steadily increasing as the international tension between Washington and Moscow gained pace. In 1956, a war broke out that signalled the finality of the 'changing of the guard' in relation to external power-brokers and their influence in the Middle East. This war involved Egypt and the tripartite allies of Israel, France and the United Kingdom. Known as the Suez War, the lead-up to this conflict is characterized by economic and post-colonial considerations.

Egypt's charismatic president, Gamal Abdul Nasser, came to power in 1953. In line with the post-colonial initiatives of the time, Nasser sought to industrialize the state, and his major project was the construction of the Aswan Dam. Nasser approached the United Kingdom and the United States for funding and received assurances of a US$250 million loan. Yet in mid-July 1956 this offer was rescinded, mostly because of Nasser's increasing overtures to the Soviet Union. Washington formally withdrew its offer of funding for the project on 19 July 1956, and the World Bank rescinded its offer of credit four days later (Ricker 2001: 67). Nasser, lacking revenue to complete his project, took the controversial step of nationalizing the Suez Canal. The Suez Canal is a lifeline in the largely landlocked Middle East. The waterway, built by Egyptian labour in the late 1880s, had historically been under the control of a French and English consortium, the Suez Canal Company. Nasser's decision to nationalize the canal had two consequences: it deprived France and the United Kingdom of profits, and Israel of waterway access. This infuriated the colonial powers, leading to the formation of an alliance of convenience. A secret tripartite operation, code-named Operation Musketeer, was agreed upon by Israel, France and the United Kingdom, and the canal was taken by a combined military force on 29 October 1956.

Although the assault was a military success, it was a political disaster for the allied forces. The widespread protests in the Arab world were expected but the emergent powers of the Soviet Union and the United States uniting in their condemnation of the tripartite aggression was not (Choueiri 2000: 185–6). The depth of Washington's anger was evident in its decision to call for 'collective military, economic and financial sanctions' against Israel unless it withdrew (Bar-Siman-Tov 1987: 54). This call was blocked in the United Nations Security Council by the dual veto of Israel's allies in the conflict, France and the United Kingdom. Underscoring the dynamics of the international system, Washington was forced to quickly abandon this tactic, as sanctions against Israel would also suggest the need for sanctions against Britain and France. In a Cold War context, Washington could not penalize its own closest allies.

The tension triggered by this conflict was ratcheted up as the Soviets threatened retaliatory attacks on London and Paris, and Washington brought significant political and economic pressure to bear on the United Kingdom, including a threat to withhold vital support for the British currency (McNamara 2003: 59). Eventually, the allies were forced to withdraw in a débacle that contributed to the resignation of the British Prime Minister Anthony Eden. By its conclusion in March 1957, the conflict had killed between 2,500 and 3,500 people, mainly Egyptians. Yet in the aftermath of the Suez War, Nasser emerged a hero, for he had forced a dual superpower endorsement of an Arab position. The short-lived United Arab Republic (1958–61) was, in part, a political outcome of this conflict and the prestige it afforded Nasser. Moreover, as a consequence of this war, the United States was widely perceived in the Arab world as having endorsed an Arab post-colonial stand against the colonial powers of the United Kingdom and France. This led to a belief that the United States, emerging onto the international stage, would act as a force for Arab self-determination. This favourable perspective would, however, not prove lasting. For Israel the outcomes of this conflict were problematic, the willingness to align itself with the former colonial masters only lending credence to regional accusations of neo-colonialism.

BOX 3.1

The **United Arab Republic** (UAR) was established between Egypt and Syria in 1958. The establishment of the Republic was seen as the first step in the creation of a broader Arab entity. However, the pan-Arab agenda was frustrated by the power and self-interest of nation-state leaders, notably Nasser. The Syrians became increasingly discontented with the arrogance of the Egyptian military in the supposedly equal relationship. The UAR collapsed in 1961 after a coup in Syria brought a secessionist group to power and the dominance of state-based considerations was assured.

In the post-war period Nasser, frustrated by the lack of American support, turned to the Soviet Union and received significant funding and military hardware. With this step, Cairo embarked on a pathway that would see Egypt, despite the rhetoric of non-alignment, become a virtual Soviet 'client state'. Nasser's increasing disillusionment as a result of this US policy orientation is clearly expressed in speeches throughout the late 1950s.

> America refuses to see the reality of the situation in the Middle East and forgets also its own history and its own revolution and its own logic and the principles invoked by Wilson. They fought colonialism as we fight colonialism. . . . How do they deny us our right to improve our condition just as they did theirs? I don't understand, brothers, why they do not respect the will of the peoples of the Arab East? . . . We all call for positive neutrality. All the peoples of the Arab Middle East are set on non-alignment. Why should these peoples not have their way? And why is their will not respected?
>
> (cited in Makdissi 2002: 549)

In Washington, the Egyptian decision to turn to the Soviet Union produced an 'us vs. them' dichotomy, with significant policy implications. The prevailing, if simplistic, political logic dictated that if Nasser was a communist, then the United States would do well to consider his enemy, Israel, as a friend.

1967: THE SIX-DAY WAR

As the 1960s unfolded Nasser's Egypt became more firmly entrenched in the Soviet camp. In the Arab world, the idea of pan-Arab nationalism, or pan-Arabism, became increasingly prominent. Influenced by socialism, pan-Arabism sought to unify the Arab world and focused on the ideal of a shared Arab destiny. The socialist flavour of this movement and its allegiance to Moscow led to a frosty reception from the United States. By the mid-1960s, Nasser was at the peak of his power and his role as undisputed leader of the Arab world heightened his sense of Egypt's invincibility. Regional tensions had been escalating throughout the decade, with Israel and its neighbours engaging in border skirmishes and low-level hostilities. In May 1967, the situation reached a climax as Nasser ordered the withdrawal of the United Nations Emergency Forces that had functioned as a security buffer between Israel and Egypt since 1957 (Krasno 2004: 232). Then, on 22 May, Egypt declared that it intended to blockade Israeli goods from shipment through the Straits of Tiran. Both acts were clearly provocative. Simultaneously, Syria increased its border clashes with Israel in the north, and Arab rhetoric regarding the imminent destruction of Israel intensified.

In late May, Egypt moved tanks into the Sinai, complete with press coverage that was transmitted throughout the Arab world. Different academics identify various levels of Soviet involvement in the lead-up to this war, with most theories centring on inaccurate Soviet reports to Cairo on 13 May that Israel had concentrated its troops around the Syrian border. This report, indicating that Israel was planning to attack an aligned Arab state, intensified the Egyptian bluster and contributed to Nasser's decision to reinforce his troop strength in the Sinai (Mutawi 2002: 93). Soviet misinformation and the ramping up of public and international tension were perhaps designed to create uncertainty in the region and increase the opportunities for involvement and, in the event of a costly

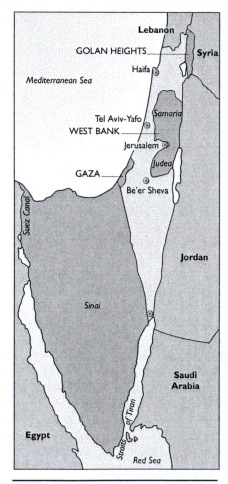

Map 3.1 Post-1967 borders.

BOX 3.2

The **Golan Heights** is an elevated landmass between Syria and Israel. It became Syrian territory in 1941, but was occupied by the Israeli Defence Forces (IDF) in the 1967 war. However, because of its strategic importance, the Golan has been a point of contention among regional states since 1948. The UN established a buffer zone around it after the 1973 conflict, but Israel unilaterally annexed the areas of the Golan under its control in 1981. The annexation is viewed as illegal by many in the region and the international community, including the UN Security Council. At various times, including in 2000 and 2007, Israel has raised the future of the Golan Heights in an attempt to draw Syria to the negotiating table.

war, further entrench Egypt's dependence on Moscow. Drawing attention to the pervasive currents of the Cold War, Ahron Bregman sees the Soviet role as critical to the initiation of this conflict, stating that Moscow simultaneously constrained the Egyptians by refusing to replenish their arsenal in the event of an Arab first strike (2000: 54).

On the ground, Israel perceived itself as increasingly besieged. The political and military leadership reacted to the combination of confrontational Arab rhetoric, the removal of the United Nations troops and the closure of the waterway with increasing unease. Many academics suggest that Egyptian moves in this period were posturing, more aimed at the domestic and broader Arab audience than meant as a clear threat to Israel (Mutawi 2002: 94). For Israel, accepting this interpretation of Egyptian intent was seen as risky. Egypt further inflamed the situation by signing mutual defence pacts with other Arab states (Jordan on 30 May 1967, and Iraq on 4 June 1967). Despite calls for caution from the United States, Israeli leaders viewed conflict as imminent and, concerned that the state could not survive either an Arab first strike or a protracted conflict, launched a pre-emptive assault. On 5 June 1967, conflict began, and a mere six days later Israel had accomplished one of the twentieth century's most stunning military victories, a victory that would alter the political landscape of the Middle East.

At the close of the Six-Day War, Israel was an occupying military power. It was responsible for the West Bank, the Sinai and the Golan Heights, and the more than 1 million Palestinians who lived in those regions. Territorially, Israel had increased its size by six times. This war is understood by Israeli and most Western sources as a war of *anticipatory self-defence*. However, in Arab and Muslim societies in the Middle East this was seen as evidence of Israel's aggressive regional stance.

Israel's swift victory can be attributed to numerous factors. Israeli intelligence played a significant role and was henceforth relied upon as a central component of Israel's military doctrine. The relative ambivalence of the international community assisted the Israeli military planners, who needed to take little action to convince the Israeli public that they faced a moment of existential choice. In the words of Abba Eban, Israelis perceived 1967 in stark terms: 'defend the national existence or lose it for all time' (Eban 1988: 22). Decisive military leadership was also of great importance. Despite the regional awareness of imminent conflict, Arab leaders, especially Nasser, appeared unprepared for an Israeli attack and responded to the outbreak of war in a confused and disorganized manner. One of the most important political outcomes of this war was Israel's capture of Jerusalem. Most sources indicate that the capture of Jerusalem did not figure strongly in the Israeli Defence Force's war plans. However, when Jordan entered the conflict Israel was presented with the opportunity to claim the city. This development propelled Jerusalem, with all of its religious significance, to the very forefront of Israeli and Palestinian politics.

For the Arabs, this was a costly defeat, with thousands dead and the pride of Arab nationalism in tatters. Moreover, the Arab states lost swaths of territory, and the Palestinian Arabs became condemned to live under direct Israeli military occupation. Nasser's prestige was destroyed and the balance of power in the Middle East altered. Many Arab sources suggest that the Israeli victory in 1967 forced the Arab world to belatedly acknowledge Israel's permanence in the region. This conflict also had a profound impact in Washington. Several Arab states, including Egypt, Syria and Iraq, cut formal ties with the United States, alleging interference in support of Israel. Much of this was political bluster, as in reality Washington retained diplomatic ties with Cairo and Damascus and intensified its relationship with Jordan (Raphel 1988). In contrast, Moscow cut all ties with Israel, an act that effectively left the United States as the only external power in contact with both the Israeli and Arab camps.

In Washington, Israel's willingness to comply with calls for restraint in the early months of 1967, as well as the speed of a victory that had not required United States intervention, greatly enhanced the post-war stature of Israel as an important American ally (Bar-Siman-Tov 1987: 143–4). In the coming years, the Israeli–US relationship strengthened dramatically. Since this took place during the Cold War, the relationship was given extra impetus by the Soviet willingness to replenish the Arab war arsenal. The Soviet involvement led to Washington taking the position of Israel's major supplier and thus assuring itself of the role of moderator in the regional balance of power (Spiegel 1988: 118). The ramifications of the 1967 war have been far reaching. This conflict had struck a strong chord in American society: the miraculous nature of the victory by the supposed underdog of

Israel, the deeply engaged pride and activism of the Jewish community and the eschatological Christian associations related to the return of Jerusalem to Jewish control led to a significant increase in Israel's public profile in the United States. However, 1967 also had a polarizing effect on the United States. The conservatives rallied to Israel's cause, but the Palestinian national movement attracted support from American liberals (although not to the same levels seen in Europe). In the aftermath of 1967 the politics of the Arab–Israeli conflict were firmly in the forefront of the American political scene.

For the Palestinians, 1967 was yet another disaster. Having endured repressive Arab rule, the Palestinians were now subjected to Israeli military occupation. The effects of this military defeat were far-reaching for Palestinian political activism. An increasingly assertive Palestinian national movement began to move away from a unified 'Arab' position and to claim independence in the struggle against Israel. The Palestine Liberation Organization (PLO) had been established by Nasser in 1964, largely as a token gesture of Arab political activism in support of the Palestinian cause. Indeed, Anat Kurz argues that the Arab decision to form a distinct Palestinian political entity was actually an attempt to co-opt and restrain increasingly pro-activist elements within the Palestinian nationalist movement, such as the Arafat-founded underground faction Fatah. However, as Kurz opines, it may well have been the 'Arab-sponsored institutionalization of this concept [which] triggered Fatah's decision to make its existence publicly known and to exercise its formal strategy of violence' (2005: 37). Thus, following the disaster of 1967, the PLO became more strident in its political approach and liberal in its use of violence. In many ways, the PLO leaders indigenized the responsibility for the liberation of Palestine. In terms of political psychology, it is interesting to

BOX 3.3

The **Palestine Liberation Organization** (PLO) was established by the Arab League in 1964 after a proposal from Egypt's President Nasser. The organization was conceived as a body dedicated to the cause of Palestinian national liberation and drew strongly on the structure of the Fatah group. The PLO, a secular-nationalist organization, was most closely associated with Yasser Arafat. The PLO became more militant as a result of the crushing Arab defeat in 1967, and its leaders began to pursue a dedicated agenda of agitation, including the use of political and military tactics against Israel. The PLO leadership was exiled from the Middle East in the early 1980s and was based in Tunis until it was reconstituted as the Palestinian Authority under the Oslo Peace Accords in 1993.

> ### BOX 3.4
>
> The **Fatah** movement was established by Palestinians working in Kuwait and the Gulf states in the late 1950s. The group was committed to the liberation of Palestine and moved away from the broader pan-Arab movement to focus on national self-determination. Yasser Arafat was a key force in the establishment of Fatah, which became the dominant faction in the PLO. Over the course of its history, Fatah has produced numerous armed splinter groups. In the Oslo Accords of 1993, the Fatah leadership transformed into the Palestinian Authority. Fatah was defeated in the 2005 elections by HAMAS, and the June 2007 split between the two organizations has left Fatah as the recognized leadership in the West Bank.

note the resonance of similar themes in the Arab and Israeli camps. After decades of humiliating battlefield defeats, the concept of the 'new Arab man' became embodied in the imagery of the determined Palestinian fighter (Sinora 1988). The notion of the revolutionary Palestinian, tired of waiting for distant Arab deliverance and willing to rise up against dispossession, has some emotive parallels with the concept of the 'new Jew', triumphing after 'centuries of powerlessness, persecution and humiliation' (Shlaim 2001: 79), a concept that was forged on the battlefields of 1948–49.

On 22 November 1967, the UN Security Council adopted Resolution 242 in response to the Six-Day War. This proved to be a controversial document and to this day remains unimplemented. The resolution led to vigorous debate and varied interpretations. It called for 'withdrawal of Israeli armed forces from territories occupied in the recent conflict'. However, the exact territories from which Israel was expected to withdraw were not explicitly stipulated, leaving room for differing interpretations. The resolution linked the question of withdrawal to other matters arising from this conflict, calling for

> termination of all claims or states of belligerency and respect for and acknowledgement of the sovereignty, territorial integrity and political independence of every State in the area and their right to live in peace within secure and recognized boundaries free from threats or acts of force while affirming the need for a just settlement for the refugee problem.
>
> (United Nations Security Council 1967)

To the Arab states, this resolution was intended to enforce a complete withdrawal of Israel from the territories taken during the war. However, to Israel and its increasingly close ally the United States, the call for withdrawal was to be read in conjunction with the assertion of the right of a state to security. As US President Lyndon Johnson affirmed on 10 September 1968,

> We are not the ones to say where other nations should draw lines between them that will assure each the greatest security. It is clear, however, that a return to the situation of 4 June 1967 will not bring peace. There must be secure and there must be recognized borders. Some such lines must be agreed to by the neighbors involved.
>
> (cited in Rostow 1975: 284)

The difficulties associated with achieving a resolution's safe passage through the Security Council were evident in this situation, and the result was a resolution that did not meaningfully compel Israel to return its wartime acquisitions. The importance of this document should not be underestimated as it still forms an integral part of peace negotiations today, with withdrawal the focus of supporters of the Palestinians but the question of withdrawal still linked to the right to security in Israeli and US discourse.

The aftermath of 1967 also marked an ideological turning point in the Arab–Israeli conflict. With this victory, minority elements in Israel, the Arab world, and even the United States increasingly exhibited the tendency to view events in the Middle East through the paradigm of divine intervention. For the Muslim world, 1967 marked a moment of intense reassessment, with some organizations positing that the Middle East's acceptance of Western ideologies, such as secular nationalism, was to blame for the crushing losses on the battlefield. An important manifestation of this ideological re-evaluation was the emergence and consolidation of political Islam, a movement that is explored in the following chapter. Underscoring the symbiotic elements of this conflict, a similar trend occurred within Israel, where some individuals construed the victory as a divine reward for the Jewish people (Rubenstein 1984: 98–126). The

BOX 3.5

The **Non-Proliferation Treaty (NPT)** was signed in 1968 by the United States, the United Kingdom and 59 other countries. It aimed at limiting the proliferation of nuclear weapons and called on nuclear powers not to assist non-nuclear states in the development or trade of such technology. France and China did not ratify the treaty until 1992 and some regional power-brokers, such as Israel and Pakistan, have never signed it.

re-establishment of the Jewish people's sovereignty in the land of Israel is, in some Christian theologies, a precondition for the Second Coming. Consequently, this trend was also mirrored in the United States, where the Christian Right began to publicly expound the theory that Israel was on a divinely sanctioned and directed path. This intertwining of religion and politics served only to further inflame the situation on the ground.

Egypt's unwillingness to accept the new status quo led to the lengthy 'war of attrition'. This conflict was fought sporadically between 1968 and 1970 without a clear victor. The major outcome of these hostilities was the increasingly close relationship between Egypt and the Soviet Union, which provided high-tech equipment such as surface-to-air missiles (SAM-3s) and MiG-21 fighters, complete with Soviet crews, to assist Egypt in its attacks on Israel (Bregman 2003: 132). The deepening Soviet–Egyptian ties were an important factor in the strengthening of Israeli–US relations. But Israel was not content to rely on international alliances for security and sought self-sufficiency in its national defence doctrine. Tel Aviv forged ahead with its own defence programme in this period and subsequently refused to sign the Non-Proliferation Treaty (NPT) of 1968. This raised the spectre of nuclear conflict in the region. It also triggered the first clear 'double standard' in US foreign policy as it related to the Arab–Israeli conflict. Washington demanded explanations for the refusal to sign the treaty, but was satisfied with the response that Israel would not be the first to introduce nuclear weapons to the region – that is, that the state would not publicly declare or test weapons unless another state did so first. From the Arab perspective, Israel was receiving special treatment and the United States was turning a blind eye to a flagrant breach of international law.

1973: THE YOM KIPPUR/RAMADAN WAR

As Israel focused on the military doctrine of *active deterrence*, the Arab states began to mobilize once again. Determined to break the status quo established in the aftermath of 1967, the Arab leaders began planning a surprise attack. In this period, Israel relied on a strategy known as the Conception, which was largely based on the problematic information of a Mossad informant who was acting as a double agent for Egyptian President Anwar Sadat (Bregman 2000: 74). The Conception held that Egypt would not attack Israel unless Cairo obtained Scud missiles and high-tech fighter planes. In the context of détente, the Soviet Union was unwilling to supply weaponry of this calibre to its Arab client for use against a state aligned with Washington. The overall Israeli interpretation of Egyptian military planning may have been correct, but this did not stop President Sadat's plans for a 'limited war' to break the status quo.

On Yom Kippur, the Jewish Day of Atonement, a combined assault by Egypt and Syria caught Israel by surprise. The misplaced belief that the Arab states were willing to accept the status quo indefinitely may have contributed to Israel's failure to adequately predict conflict in this instance. As a result, Israel scrambled to repel a well-planned and well-executed attack. Although the Israeli government knew of the attack in the hours before 2PM on 6 October 1973, a mixture of indecisive leadership, poor coordination and a simple lack of time prevented an effective initial defence. Arab advancements in war planning added to the surprise, as Israel's highly valued intelligence services had failed to fully register the implications of Arab troop movements. The initial assault was effective, and Israel scrambled to repel the invading armies. After a tense beginning, the Israeli Defence Force (IDF) was able to regain parity on the field and the conflict proved to be another Israeli victory, albeit on a level far removed from the stunning result of 1967.

However, Israel was well served by some of the outcomes of this conflict. The Yom Kippur War helped consolidate Israel's valuable international alliances. It also firmly placed the Arab–Israeli conflict within the dynamics of the Cold War rivalry. The United States could not allow its most significant regional ally to be overwhelmed by a Soviet-backed assault. Despite initial hesitation, Washington launched a massive airlift of military hardware on 13 October 1973. US policy-makers were faced with a tense situation in the lead-up to this decision. After the first few days of war, Israel's actual 'capacity for self-defence' was being seriously tested, while the Soviet Union kept up its tempo of military aid to Egypt and Syria (Bar-Siman-Tov 1987: 205–7). In a way the situation on the ground literally forced the US decision. The influential US Under Secretary of State Henry Kissinger admitted as much when he observed that the US policy was largely reduced to 'support for Israel and for the status quo' (Shlaim 2000: 321). The reinforcements proved decisive and Israel managed to recover from its initial position of vulnerability and, in the military sense, record another decisive victory. However, the political outcomes were more complex, with Kissinger calling the end of the 1973 war a 'strategic defeat' for Israel (Bar-Siman-Tov 1987: 206). The delay of military aid hurt Israel and implied Washington's willingness to formulate policy to ensure its role vis-à-vis the Arabs. However, when an Israeli victory became inevitable the Arab world turned to another form of pressure to achieve its territorial aims.

The 1973 war led to the politicization of the oil trade. Led by Saudi Arabia, the Organization of Petroleum Exporting Countries (OPEC) placed an embargo on the Western countries and Israel. This was the first time that oil was used as a geo-strategic tool. An implied self-confidence governed this bold step. Arab leaders must have been pondering the extent to which this economic muscle might achieve results where brute force had repeatedly failed. But this plan was too ambitious and its consequences were serious. Israel was not going to give up territory captured in the fighting because of economic imperatives. If the objective of the oil embargo was to force an Israeli withdrawal from the territories occupied in 1967, the strategy was a complete failure. But the 1973 oil embargo did achieve an unintended and extremely negative consequence for the Arab world. It demonstrated to the US administration that the Arab states would go to political and economic extremes to pursue their objectives, a revelation that increasingly situated Israel as the leading rational player in the region. Thus the oil embargo, designed and implemented to affect Israel's regional behaviour, merely brought Israel and the United States even closer.

The oil embargo caused major price increases and contributed to a worldwide energy crisis. It also confirmed the economic and strategic importance of the Middle East to American policy-makers. It irrevocably changed Washington's view of the region, and past attempts at balancing regional relationships gave way to a clearer pro-Israeli line. Even after oil shipments resumed – the embargo was lifted in March 1974 – the policy continued to have serious global economic impacts, even precipitating the economic slump of 1974. In addition, the Gulf states emerged as stronger regional power-brokers, having enriched themselves through the embargo process.

In Israel the trend towards a theologically derived interpretation of events was only strengthened by the close call of 1973. The religious settler movement, led by the ultra-nationalist Gush Emunim, solidified in this period.[1] The Likud Party was also formed as elements within Israeli society took a more hardline approach towards the need to populate the Occupied Territories. This was justified on either theological or geo-strategic grounds. Despite the reality of another military defeat, the events of 1973 were viewed within the Arab world as a restoration, or partial restoration, of Arab pride. Indeed, if viewed as a 'limited war' aimed at propelling the resolution of the Arab–Israeli conflict to the forefront of international

BOX 3.6

Gush Emunim was an Israeli political movement that emerged in the wake of the 1967 war and was consolidated in the aftermath of the 1973 conflict. It was an ultra-nationalist religious movement that encouraged Israelis to move into the newly occupied territories and establish settlements throughout the biblical land of Israel. This was seen as enacting God's will and bringing about the messianic age. The Gush Emunim was recognized as a political organization. However, fringe elements of the movement operated as extra-legal force and were involved in acts of violence against Palestinians.

BOX 3.7

The **Camp David Accords** were a series of agreements concluded in September 1978 that led to the signing of the Egyptian–Israeli peace treaty of 26 March 1979. Egypt was frozen out of the Arab world for pursuing unilateral peace with Israel, and the architect of the Accords, Egyptian President Anwar Sadat, was assassinated by the Egyptian Islamic Jihad movement in 1982.

relations, the 1973 war was indeed a success.[2] Post-war negotiations were initially undertaken in an atmosphere of parity; however, as Israel regained its self-assurance through the 1970s, this slowly changed.

The United States, particularly in the aftermath of the oil crisis, was clearly aligned with Israel and was centrally involved in attempting to create a 'peace in the Middle East'. As part of this agenda the 1978 Camp David Accords were signed between Israel and Egypt, a treaty that marked the beginnings of 'cold peace' between the two former combatants.[3] From the Israeli perspective, the return of the Sinai, including the forced evacuation of the settler community at Yamit, was a taste of things to come. Initially touted as the start of regional peace, Camp David largely failed to trigger a wave of peace deals. The Egyptian President Anwar Sadat was assassinated by the Islamist group Egyptian Islamic Jihad for his role in the Accords, and Egypt was frozen out of Arab politics until the 1990s. The increasing bond between Israel and its superpower backer was formalized on 30 November 1981 with the first signing of an Israeli–US strategic cooperation agreement against Soviet influence. The agreement was contracted despite (or perhaps because of) an international drama in June 1981 in which the Israeli Air Force launched an air raid against a nuclear facility in southern Iraq. Israel's willingness to act as a regional policeman, although best understood as based on self-interest, clearly aided the US agenda in the Middle East.

1982: THE LEBANON WAR

The next Arab–Israeli war under consideration here is perhaps the most controversial. The Lebanon war was a divisive conflict that brought widespread international condemnation of Israel. The context for this conflict was the brutal civil war that had raged in Lebanon between the country's Christian and Muslim militias since 1975. The civil conflict was heavily influenced by outside forces, from Syria's deployment into Lebanon in the late 1970s to Israel's willingness to spend US$150 million

BOX 3.8

The **Yamit settlement** was a settler outpost in the Sinai Desert. Peace accords signed after the 1973 war between Israel and Egypt dictated that Israel was to return the Sinai, captured in the 1967 conflict, to Egypt. The Israeli government set the date for evacuation as 23 April 1982. Amid mass media coverage, the planned evacuation was met with some protests within the settlement. These local protesters were reinforced by a group of ultra-nationalist settlers who travelled to the site to protest the government's actions. Tensions rose between the settlers and the IDF, and Israel watched as the situation peaked. In the end, Yamit was evacuated without injury, but an important precedent was set regarding the possibility of settler defiance of orders to withdraw from the Occupied Territories.

between 1975 and 1977 arming the Lebanese Maronite Christians (Black and Morris 1996: 581).

The invasion of Lebanon was planned by Israel as a response to the activities of the PLO. In the wake of the 1967 defeat, PLO activism became increasingly troublesome for Arab states. Jordan in particular was faced with a restless Palestinian population, a large majority of whom were refugees. PLO agitation in Jordan and armed incursions into Israel threatened Jordan's domestic stability and risked Israeli retaliation. Tension reached boiling point in September 1970 when the Jordanian government moved to crack down on PLO training camps. Following a bloody conflict between Jordanian soldiers and PLO militia in this month, known henceforth as 'Black September', the PLO fighting wing was expelled from Jordan and moved to southern Lebanon. Yasser Arafat, the chairman of the PLO, was committed to keeping the pressure on Israel and southern Lebanon offered the geographical proximity for continued armed incursions into Israel. As a result, cross-border raids became a frequent occurrence in the 1970s. In 1978, Israel briefly invaded Lebanon's Bekka Valley, in Operation Litani, in order to uproot the militants. However, international pressure and the arrival of the United Nations forced a retreat. This did not resolve tensions, as the UN forces proved ineffective in preventing PLO cross-border attacks on Israel.

In this climate of ongoing incursions and attacks against Israeli civilians, Israel required only a pretext for a new offensive. The attempted assassination of Israel's ambassador to the United Kingdom by a Palestinian group provided one. In this context, it did not matter that the Abu Nidal faction, which had attempted the assassination, was a rival offshoot Palestinian faction that rejected Arafat's leadership. As a result, two powerful historical figures were brought into a head-on confrontation in the unfortunate arena of war-torn Lebanon. The Israeli Defence Minister Ariel Sharon was in charge of planning and executing the military operation. This was devised as a military assault on and occupation of southern Lebanon with the aims of breaking the back of Palestinian nationalism and securing Israel's northern borders. The ambitious plan was initially presented to the Israeli Cabinet as a 'Litani-type operation, namely a short and small scale invasion directed against the PLO only' (Bregman 2000: 105). As the conflict unfolded, however, the significant Israeli ground force advanced and laid siege to the Muslim quarter of Beirut for ten weeks. This expansive agenda gave rise to suspicions about Israel's strategic objectives. The relationship between Bachir El-Gemayal, an ambitious Christian Maronite leader, and the authorities in Tel Aviv had been a poorly kept secret in Lebanese political circles. From Israel's perspective, the installation of a pro-Israeli Christian leadership at the expense of Muslim representation would advance Tel Aviv's geo-strategic position.

This conflict is often retrospectively understood as a war between 'greater Israel and greater Syria'. It is a difficult conflict to analyse as the relationships between Lebanese factions changed constantly and external players, such as Syria, supported different factions at different times. It is important to note that in this period, both Israel and Syria were flexing their regional muscles and attempting to redesign the region, and especially the destabilized and devastated Lebanon, to suit their own interests. Despite the usual US calls for restraint, elements in the Israeli military leadership were clearly committed to this conflict. In contrast to previous battles, the war in Lebanon was seen as a war of choice rather than necessity, and it proved deeply unpopular with the Israeli public. However, as Bregman points out, although 1982 'broke the national consensus on defence', it was not Israel's first war of choice, as the wars in 1956 and, to some extent, 1967 had also been undertaken on Israel's terms (2000: 115–16).

Much of the planning and design of the 1982 invasion of Lebanon was conducted in the murky world of intelligence and counter-intelligence, and the alliances between civil war-hardened Lebanese militias and the Israeli state proved disastrous. The siege of Beirut sparked international condemnation. It is also presented by some observers as the final nail in the coffin of pan-Arab unity, since the Arab states offered little assistance to Lebanon as Israel's army surrounded Beirut. More powerfully, Arab inaction revealed the increasingly unpopular status of the PLO. Despite international attempts as mediation, Saudi Arabia, Egypt and the Gulf states all refused to offer refuge to the deeply politicized PLO fighters. Eventually the PLO – or its remnants –were evacuated to Tunisia under a US-sponsored deal, an operation that saw nearly 11,000 people relocated.[4] The departure of the fighting men of the PLO, a force that had deeply destabilized Lebanon for over a decade, set the scene for a gruesome final chapter in this ill-fated conflict.

The infamous events at Sabra and Shatila would prove to be a lasting stain on Israel's international reputation. Sabra and Shatila were two Palestinian refugee camps under the jurisdiction of the Israeli Defence Force. The departure of the armed PLO fighters left these communities vulnerable in a context marked by a desire for retribution. During the siege of Beirut, Israeli forces allowed the Phalange, a Lebanese Christian militia, into the camps, resulting in a massacre of Palestinian men, women and children. The death toll estimates range wildly, from several hundred to over 2,500. News of the massacre triggered mass protests by hundreds of thousands of Israelis, confirming the fundamentally unpopular nature of this conflict. Israel held its military accountable and established the Kahane Commission to investigate the massacres. Relying on the concept of reasonable foresight, the investigation found that the IDF was 'indirectly responsible' for the deaths.

The 1982 war had lasting ramifications for Israel. Internationally, its relationship with the United States was compromised as Israel, in its determination to steer its own course, revealed itself as unwilling to acquiesce to political pressure from Washington. The ill-fated Reagan Peace Initiative of 1982 is an example of the increasing frustration of the United States. This somewhat confused document explicitly denies Israeli sovereignty over the Occupied Territories but simultaneously refuses to offer US support for an independent Palestinian state. As Jamal Nasser points out, under the Reagan administration the 'rejection of Palestinian self-determination became the official policy of the United States' (1991: 159). President Reagan's plan, which was rejected by both the Arabs and the Israelis, also called for an absolute freeze on Israeli settlements. Charles D. Smith contends that the Reagan Initiative, while denying Israeli claims to sovereignty, accepted Tel Aviv's agenda of sidelining the PLO (2004: 369). This contradicted Arab political will, which, in its rhetoric at least, had affirmed the PLO as the legitimate representative of the Palestinian people since the Rabat Conference of 1974. The Reagan Initiative set the tone of US policy for years to come. Palestinian 'autonomy' or 'self-rule' was to be supported, but Israel's security was to be the pivotal concern. As Smith continues, it 'publicly disapproved of Israeli intentions for the West Bank, yet defined terms in ways which backed Israel's positions. In such circumstances the United States did not appear as the honest broker it claimed to be'.

The 1982 war also had potent effects on Israel's domestic politics. In Israeli academic circles, the conflict of 1982 and the shattering of the national consensus on defence created a climate in which the Revisionist or 'new' historians could emerge. As explored earlier, these academics controversially re-examined Israel's foundational myths.[5] The conflict also divided the usually united Israeli public on the necessity of armed conflict and challenged popular notions of Israel's exercise of military power as defensive and legitimate. Despite a departure from the central regions of Lebanon, Israel remained as occupying force in the south of the country. This decision dragged the IDF into a sporadic guerrilla conflict with the Lebanese Hezbollah, a group that emerged to challenge the dominant Lebanese Shia organization Amal. Hezbollah was formed as a resistance movement to the Israeli occupation and drew on Iranian inspirations.[6] In its militant campaign, Hezbollah employed suicide bombers, a development that grew to become a tragic feature of the Palestinian resistance. This organization engaged Israel throughout the folowing decades and proved an intractable enemy. In a regional first, Israel withdrew from Lebanon on 25 May 2000, without a peace accord or concessions from Hezbollah. This entangled relationship set the scene for contemporary regional conflict that, in 2007, appears far from over.

The 1982 Operation Peace for Galilee was a significant page in Israel's military history. Domestically, the image of the Israeli solider as a symbol of power was weakened due to the political turmoil surrounding their deployment in a fragile neighbouring state. In some ways, this war can be identified as a turning point in Israeli political history, where battles were no longer clear-cut, where defence of the Zionist dream became, even in the popular psyche, entangled with the oppression and exclusion of Palestinians.

2006: THE JULY WAR

The IDF withdrawal from southern Lebanon in May 2000 did not mark the end of hostilities between Israel and the Shia militias, which had solidified in response to the occupation of the south. The Israeli withdrawal constituted a significant opportunity for the militias, which for nearly two decades had

BOX 3.9

Hezbollah is a Shia political organization that formed in southern Lebanon during the early 1980s. Its ideology of resistance draws strongly on the doctrines of the Iranian Revolution. The group emerged to resist Israel's military occupation (1983–2000). Hezbollah is backed financially, to unclear levels, by Syria and Iran. These states support Hezbollah for ideological and strategic reasons. In recent years Hezbollah has entered the political mainstream and now has a considerable presence in the largely dysfunctional Lebanese parliament.

BOX 3.10

HAMAS is an acronym that stands for Harakat al-Muqawamah al-Islamiyyah (Islamic Resistance Movement). This Palestinian nationalist organization, formed by the late Sheikh Ahmad Yasin, emerged from the broader Muslim Brotherhood in the first Palestinian Intifada of 1987. HAMAS committed itself to an anti-occupation agenda and employed terrorist tactics in its struggle against Israel. The organization maintains both militant and non-militant wings and has been closely involved in the provision of basic services in the economically stricken Palestinian territories. HAMAS came to power in the democratic elections of January 2006, and communal violence in June 2007 saw the organization take effective control of the Gaza Strip.

legitimized their presence by the need to confront Israel. In this political context, the 2000 withdrawal did not mean a rejection of armed action by Hezbollah, which continued to launch sporadic small-scale rocket attacks against Israel's northern communities. On 12 July 2006, a 34-day conflict erupted that, once again, engulfed the state of Lebanon. Tensions had been simmering between the two parties throughout the early years of the twenty-first century. The interplay between regional actors is important here. In the months leading up to the initiation of this conflict, Israel faced an increase in HAMAS activity in the Gaza Strip, which included the taking hostage of IDF reservists. In July, Hezbollah, amid a campaign of Katyusha rocket attacks against northern Israel, launched a cross-border raid and captured two Israeli soldiers. Several more IDF soldiers died in an unsuccessful rescue attempt. Israel responded with air strikes against Hezbollah targets and civilian infrastructure and a new conflict opened in the Middle East.

An Israeli air and naval blockade preceded a ground invasion of southern Lebanon. The conflict dragged on for over a month with an increasingly horrified international community appealing for a cease-fire. In this war, Israel drew the ire of the international community once again, launching a military campaign that included 'more than 7000 air strikes, the deaths of 1183 people and the displacement of a further 970,000' (Amnesty International 2006). The damage to Lebanon was staggering, with 120 bridges destroyed and the total damage bill amounting to approximately US$3.5 billon. The impact of this conflict on Israel was also significant, with the deaths of 43 civilians and 117 soldiers, and the temporary displacement of 300,000 to 500,000 civilians. It does bear mentioning that Israel's ability to protect its citizens through a system of shelters and evacuations played a significant role in this comparatively limited civilian toll.

The international reaction to the conflict revealed much about the balance of power in the international system. The United States, supported by its allies the United Kingdom and Australia, linked this conflict to the broader 'war on terror' and endorsed Israel's right to self-defence. Other voices pointed out that Israel's conflict was with the Shia Hezbollah, yet it was the people of Lebanon who were paying the price. The political schisms in the Arab world, and the increasing fear of Shia activism, led many Arab states to criticize both Hezbollah's provocative actions and Israel's response. The UN-endorsed cease-fire went into effect on 14 August 2006, and Israel's naval blockade of Lebanon was lifted on 8 September. There was no clear victor in the July War of 2006. Israel did not succeed in eradicating Hezbollah; indeed it added prestige and publicity to the organization's regional standing.

CONCLUSION

The short history of the state of Israel is characterized by war. Arab–Israeli conflicts, however, are based not on primordial hatred but on temporal issues such as territorial concerns, access to waterways, strategic planning and, finally, the personal agendas of politicians. Although they are often underscored by the ever-present reality of competing Israeli and Palestinian claim to the same land, it is the broader issues mentioned above that have been at the heart of many of the region's wars.

Since 1967 Israel has been an occupying power. In the aftermath of 1967, cautious Israelis warned that occupation or annexation was tantamount to 'national suicide' (Eban 1988: 27), harming both the Palestinian people and the moral fabric of Israel. However, as the years passed and the Palestinian resistance became more intractable, the increasing right-wing

BOX 3.11

Shia Islam is a stream of Islam. It is differentiated from the Sunni stream by its interpretation of the legitimacy of succession following the death of the Prophet Muhammad. Shia Muslims believe that the chain of succession should be determined by dynastic tradition, with the position of Caliph passing to the descendants of the Prophet through the person of his son-in-law and cousin Ali. When Ali assumed the position of Caliph in 656 he became the fourth Caliph to succeed the Prophet Muhammad. By his murder in 661, Ali had presided over the cleaving of Islam into Sunni and Shia divisions and, as a result, is recognized as the first Shia Imam.

tendency in Israeli politics prevailed in Tel Aviv's policy formulation. The period 1967–82 also witnessed the rise of the PLO as both a political and militaristic expression of the Palestinian desire for self-determination. Palestinians offered widespread support to the PLO in this period. The PLO's war of attrition against Israel, which commenced following the 1967 war, in addition to the organization's diplomatic presence, led to its quickly gaining recognition as the representative of the Palestinian community. Yet, as the 1982 war demonstrated, this position did not assure the organization of international support or sanctuary in the Arab world. As Nasser has suggested, perhaps 'the most striking characteristic of the PLO . . . has been its ability to survive and develop in the face of massive Israeli and Arab attacks upon it' (1991: 210).

As has been seen in this chapter, superpower influence and patronage assisted or intensified many regional conflicts in the twentieth century. The origins of the Israeli–US alliance, now a feature of Middle Eastern international relations, emerge as rooted in, and as a byproduct of, Cold War logic. As some of the Arab states, in particular Egypt, turned to the Soviet Union, the Israeli–US alliance only intensified. Locked within this Cold War mindset, the United States increasingly committed itself to Israel and its agenda in the region. By the 1990s the sole remaining superpower was seen actively as pro-Israel by *choice*. The US ability to act as a peace-broker and its agenda in the Arab world had thus become viewed with open distrust.

Despite early US attempts to temper the Israeli connection in order to cultivate Arab alliances, the decisive moment in Washington's view of the region was the 1973 oil embargo. This can perhaps be seen as the final chapter in a distinct period of conflict that stretched from 1967 to 1973. The effects of surprise attacks, attrition and strategic versus military victories combined to have a powerful impact on the political psychology of the region. This risky Arab initiative failed and revealed the dangers inherent in threatening the economic interests of the United States. Instead of encouraging the superpower to apply political pressure upon Israel, the embargo essentially convinced US policy-makers that the Arab world could, and if the opportunity existed *would,* seek to harm it economically. This consequently pushed Washington deeper into an alliance with Israel. By 2007, the US position was one of blanket support for Israeli policy in the region. In addition, the Arab public paid the price for OPEC's challenge to the United States. Besides persuading the Americans to support Israel, the embargo encouraged Washington to develop its ties with the often autocratic leaderships of oil-rich Gulf sheikhdoms. This trend developed into a programme of US support for authoritarian regimes in the Middle East – the Islamist backlash against which will be considered in the following chapter.

NOTES

1 On the settler movement, see Sprinzak (1991, 1999).
2 For an Arab account of the 1973 war, see El Badri *et al.* (1978).
3 For a detailed exploration of the Camp David Accords, see Quandt (2001: 205–45).
4 For a full exploration of the impact of the 1983 conflict on the PLO, see Sahliyeh (1986).
5 See the seminal texts on these topics by the 'new historians': Benny Morris (Israel's role in the creating the refugee crisis), Ilan Pappe (Britain's role in the closing months of the Mandate), Avi Shlaim (debunking the 'David and Goliath' myth) and Simha Flapan (the basis of Arab–Israeli relations in the pre-state and early state periods).
6 For a complete exploration of Hezbollah, see Qassem (2005).

REFERENCES

Amnesty International (2006) 'Israel/Lebanon: Deliberate Destruction or "Collateral Damage"? Israeli Attacks on Civilian Infrastructure', 23 August, available at http://web.amnesty.org/library/index/ENGMDE180072006.

Bar-Siman-Tov, Yaaov (1987) *Israel, the Superpowers and the War in the Middle East* (London: Praeger).

Black, Ian and Morris, Benny (1996) *Israel's Secret Wars: A History of Israel's Intelligence Services* (Cambridge: Cambridge University Press).

Bregman, Ahron (2000) *Israel's Wars, 1947–1993* (London: Routledge).

Bregman, Ahron (2003) *A History of Israel* (London: Palgrave Macmillan).

Choueiri, Youssef M. (2000) *Arab Nationalism: A History. Nation and State in the Arab World* (London: Blackwell).

Eban, Abba (1988) 'Israel's Dilemmas: An Opportunity Squandered' in Stephen Roth (ed.), *The Impact of the Six Day War: A Twenty Year Assessment* (London: Macmillan).

El Badri, Hassan, El Magdoub, Taha and Dia El Din Zohdy, Mohammed (1978) *The Ramadan War, 1973* (New York: Dupuy Associates).

Krasno, Jean E. (2004) 'To End the Scourge of War: The Story of UN Peace Keeping', in Jean E. Krasno (ed.), *United Nations: Confronting the Challenges of a Global Society* (Boulder, CO: Lynne Rienner Publishers).

Kurz, Anat (2005) *Fatah and the Politics of Violence: The Institutionalization of a Popular Struggle* (Brighton: Sussex Academic Press).

McNamara, Robert (2003) *Britain, Nasser and the Balance of Power in the Middle East* (London: Routledge).

Makdissi, Ussama (2002) 'Anti-Americanism in the Arab World: An Interpretation of a Brief History', *Journal of American History*, Vol. 89, No. 2, pp. 538–58.

Mutawi, Samir (2002) *Jordan in the 1967 War* (Cambridge: Cambridge University Press).

Nasser, Jamal R. (1991) *The Palestine Liberation Organization – From Armed Struggle to the Declaration of Independence* (New York: Praeger).

Qassem, Naim (2005) *Hizbullah: The Story from Within*, trans. by Dalia Khalil (London: Saqi).

Quandt, William B. (2001) *Peace Process: American Diplomacy and the Arab–Israeli Conflict since 1967* (Berkeley, CA: University of California Press).

Raphel, Gideon (1988) 'Twenty Years in Retrospect: 1967–1987', in Stephen Roth (ed.), *The Impact of the Six Day War: A Twenty Year Assessment* (London: Macmillan).

Ricker, Laurent (2001) 'The Soviet Union and the Suez Crisis', in David Tal (ed.), *The 1956 War: Collusion and Rivalry in the Middle East* (London: Routledge).

Rostow, Eugene V. (1975) 'The Illegality of the Arab Attack on Israel of October 6, 1973', *American Journal of International Law*, Vol. 69, No. 2, 272–89.

Rubenstein, Amnon (1984) *The Zionist Dream Revisited: From Herzl to Gush Emunim and Back* (New York: Schocken Books).

Sahliyeh, Emile F. (1986) *The PLO after the Lebanon War* (Boulder, CO: Westview Press).

Shlaim, Avi (2000) *The Iron Wall: Israel and the Arab World* (London: Penguin).

Shlaim, Avi (2001) 'Israel and the Arab Coalition in 1948', in Eugene Rogan and Avi Shalaim (eds), *The War for Palestine* (Cambridge: Cambridge University Press).

Sinora, Hanna (1988) 'A Palestinian Perspective', in Stephen Roth (ed.), *The Impact of the Six Day War: A Twenty Year Assessment* (London: Macmillan).

Smith, Charles D. (2004) *Palestine and the Arab–Israeli Conflict* (Boston: Bedford/ St Martins).

Spiegel, Steven (1988) 'American Middle East Policy', in Stephen Roth (ed.), *The Impact of the Six Day War: A Twenty Year Assessment* (London: Macmillan).

Sprinzak, Ehud (1991) *The Ascendance of Israel's Radical Right* (New York: Oxford University Press).

Sprinzak, Ehud (1999) *Brother against Brother: Violence and Extremism in Israeli Politics from Altalena to the Rabin Assassination* (New York: Free Press).

United Nations Security Council (1967) 'UNSC Resolution 242', 22 November, available at www.mideastweb.org/242.htm.

SUGGESTED FURTHER READING

Abul-Husn, Latif (1998) *The Lebanese Conflict: Looking Inward* (Boulder, CO: Lynne Rienner Publishers).

Brecher, Michael, with Benjamin Geist (1980) *Decisions in Crisis: Israel, 1967 and 1973* (Berkeley, CA: University of California Press).

Israel Ministry of Foreign Affairs (no date) 'The July War', www.mfa.gov.il.

Dunstan, Simon (2005) *The Yom Kippur War 1973* (Westport, CT: Praeger).

Kissinger, Henry (2003) *Crisis: The Anatomy of Two Major Foreign Policy Crises* (New York: Simon & Schuster).

Rabovich, Abraham (2004) *The Yom Kippur War: The Epic Encounter that Transformed the Middle East* (New York: Schocken Books).

Roth, Stephan J. (ed.), with Avineri, Shlomo and Rabinovich, Itamar (1998) *The Impact of the Six-Day War: A Twenty-Year Assessment* (Basingstoke: Macmillan, with the Institute of Jewish Affairs).

O'Balance, Edgar (1998) *Civil War in Lebanon, 1975–92* (Basingstoke: Macmillan).

Oren, Michael (2002) *Six Days of War: June 1967 and the Making of the Modern Middle East* (Oxford: Oxford University Press).

SUGGESTED STUDY QUESTIONS

1 How did the Cold War impact upon Middle Eastern politics?

2 What was the influence of superpower involvement in the 1973 Arab–Israeli war?

3 What were the regional and international ramifications of the 1973 Arab–Israeli war?

4 What was the impact of the establishment of the state of Israel on inter-Arab relations?

5 What have been the primary sources of regional conflict in the Middle East?

CHAPTER 4

Islamism and the Iranian Revolution

INTRODUCTION

At the time, few could foresee the dramatic regional and global implications of the revolution that gripped Iran in 1979. Ayatollah Khomeini managed to harness the popular revolutionary anger against Iran's autocratic ruler Reza Shah Pahlavi and bring into existence the first Islamic government of the modern age. The heady mix of religious fervour and nationalism that led to the emergence of the Islamic Republic of Iran remains the most famous and enduring product of the movement known as political Islam, or Islamism.

This chapter will explore the origins of Islamism and the political context of the mid-twentieth-century Middle East. In part, the rise of political Islam can be identified as a response to the devastating impact of events such as the 1967 Arab–Israeli war, the failings and corruption of secular-nationalist Arab governments and the authoritarianism of regional regimes, many of which enjoyed US support.

The 1979 Iranian Revolution was a major turning point in both the politics of the region and in Washington's view of Islam as a political force. The influential synthesis of nationalism and religion that triggered the overthrow of the pro-US regime in Iran had significant ramifications for Washington's foreign policy. The emergence of the overtly anti-American Islamic Republic of Iran reflected the wave of popular discontent with US interference and influence throughout the region. In order to explore these issues, this chapter will provide a brief account of Islam and its politicization in the mid-twentieth century before exploring the specific circumstances that led to its utilization as a revolutionary political doctrine.

HISTORICAL BACKGROUND

Islam is a monotheistic belief system that is understood by Muslims as the culmination of the series of revelations that began with the biblical figure of Abraham.[1] The holy book of Islam, the Qur'an, was revealed by God to the Prophet Muhammad (570–632 CE). The Qur'an sets out the foundations of the Sharia, often translated as law but more correctly interpreted as the approved code of Muslim behaviour. The Sharia is primarily based on the Qur'an and the Sunnah (the tradition, custom or practices of the Prophet). In the contemporary context, the attempt to implement the Sharia is a contentious issue because it is closely linked to the formation of an Islamic state. In Islamic history, political power was won and lost through force. This is not unique, as many empires rose and fell in premodern times. The significance of this history, however, is in the political ideas that emerged from the classical period, notably the notion of physical jihad for the faith. This heritage has influenced contemporary Islamic thought and in some circles political ascendency has been closely tied to the concept of jihad.

In the contemporary era, the concept of jihad and its place in the Islamic tradition has consumed academics, politicians and the media. In the Qur'an, the concept of jihad is described in numerous contexts and it can be interpreted in two distinct ways (Bonney 2004). The term can refer to a personal, internal struggle against unbelief, or to a public or communal striving to implement Islamic norms, which could culminate in an armed struggle. It is important to bear in mind that throughout Islamic history a militarized understanding of the concept of jihad has competed with other, non-militant interpretations. Modernist thinkers have displayed a

BOX 4.1

In textual Islam, the duty of **jihad** can be fulfilled by the heart, the tongue, the hand, or the sword. The non-violent interpretations of jihad have always functioned in tandem with the notion of jihad as armed action for the faith or the community. In this way, the concept allows for numerous interpretations and applications. In modernist Islam, the focus is clearly upon non-militaristic interpretations. In the mid-twentieth century, the notion of jihad was reformulated by organizations and individuals as part of a broader political resistance to foreign domination in the Muslim world.

tendency to focus on non-militaristic interpretations, asserting that the 'lesser' jihad of physical, often military, action is not as important as the 'greater' jihad of 'spiritual, political, social, economic and intellectual forms of struggle' (Sadiki 1995: 20).

This debate is pertinent to the political upheavals of the twentieth century. The concept of militant jihad was adopted by those seeking the supremacy of what they claimed to be the 'true' Islam. As a result, Islamists embraced a militant interpretation of jihad as the ultimate force for the sovereignty of God. The political movement known as Islamism emerged in the mid-twentieth century in a context of growing frustration with the shortcomings of secular nationalism in the Muslim world. It was also deeply affected by the regional struggle to redefine politics and society as the Middle East emerged from its colonial past. In this way, Islamism emerged as an expression of revolutionary desire for change (Akbarzadeh and Saeed 2003: 11). Islamism is a political movement that instrumentalizes Islam as a doctrine of political action. In the mid-twentieth century, this movement was often labelled Islamic 'fundamentalism', a term that originated in the context of American Christianity (Denoeux 2002). This designation is misleading, as it implies a focus on the 'fundamentals' of a faith. Muslims widely agree upon and adhere to the fundamentals of the faith, known as the Five Pillars: recognition of God, prayer, fasting, charity and the pilgrimage to Mecca. By contrast, the term *Islamism* more correctly implies a movement – a political movement that claims to act with the religion of Islam as its core. Islamism, however, is not a unified movement, and different groups employ significantly diverse interpretations, aims and methods. Although it draws on the rich intellectual and theological history of Islamic civilization, this movement has been influenced and informed by various socio-political experiences in the Middle East and throughout the Muslim world, especially in the early and mid-twentieth century.

As has been explored, the experience of Western colonialism was traumatic in the Middle East. The defeat and occupation of Arab lands, the creation of new states and the imposition of new systems of governance all created a serious rupture in the political development of the region. As a social response to these changes, secularization crept into the societies of the Middle East or, as in the case of Turkey and Iran, it was forced upon them from above by pro-Western regimes. For some Muslims, these rapid changes were unwelcome, as they were seen as leading the community away from its own traditions. Intellectuals and activists cast about for a response, a political programme suited to and more representative of the Muslim experience. At the core of the Islamist movement is a sense of reactive pride. Although there are major variations in interpretation, objectives and methodology, Islamism essentially hinges on the desire for the reorganization of Muslim societies, and the lives of Muslim individuals, so that they conform to the directives of the Islamic faith.

In the 'revival' period of the 1950s to 1970s, the modern Islamist movement was pioneered by thinkers such as the Muslim Brotherhood-affiliated thinker Sayyid Qutb and the Iranian Ayatollah Ruhollah Khomeini.[2] These men drew on a pre-existing tradition of Islamic political thought and adapted the doctrines of their faith to form the basis of revolutionary socio-political movements. A core aspect of the movement in this period was its responsive and reactive nature. Islamism did not emerge in an intellectual or ideological vacuum and, although it is an indigenous response to the experience of the Muslim world, it was greatly affected by the political trends that swept the world at this time. In this way, Islamism can be understood as a movement partly anchored in the Islamic tradition but that is also highly reactive and responsive to external stimuli. Its major theorists drew on the ancient traditions of Islam to formulate a response to the realities of the early and mid-twentieth-century Middle East. Importantly, although the life and the experience of the Prophet is venerated and held as the ultimate blueprint for society, only a small minority of activists advocate a 'return' to the early years of Islamic history. Yvonne Haddad asserts that most Islamist organizations seek to 'Islamize modernity' rather than return to an idealized past (1992: 272). Islamism is therefore a modern political movement born of the historical experience of the mid-twentieth century.

State secularization played a central role in the rise of political Islam. This is most evident in the history of organizations like the Muslim Brotherhood, an Egyptian organization that was pivotal in the development of Islamism. The Muslim Brotherhood was founded in 1928 by a school teacher, Hasan al-Banna. Initially, this organization was not established as a force for radical change; rather it followed an 'evolutionary path of preaching and socio-political action' (Esposito 1999a: 140). The Muslim Brotherhood leadership advocated a return to Islamic authenticity in the face of increasing secularization in Egyptian society. However, as the Muslim Brotherhood spread throughout the region, its doctrine of grassroots activism was often interpreted, or utilized, as a challenge to the ruling elite. Although conceived of as an apolitical organization committed to the Islamization of society through education, splinter factions of the Muslim Brotherhood increasingly understood the role of the organization as a political one. This trend was made stronger after Hasan al-Banna was assassinated by the state in 1949.

The most influential theorist of the Muslim Brotherhood was Sayyid Qutb, who joined the organization in 1951.[3] Qutb was a well-educated man who spent a period of time in the United States at the behest of the Egyptian government. Observers often focus on his negative experiences in the United States as the trigger for his hardline views. However, Qutb's thought was clearly a response to the role of Arab/Muslim leaders vis-à-vis their own societies rather than a reaction to the relationship between

Muslims and the West. The radicalization of Qutb's views during his decade-long incarceration in Nasser's jails supports this interpretation. During this period, Qutb's worldview hardened considerably and his belief in Islam as a revolutionary political doctrine crystallized. In this way, Qutb's thinking was clearly and definitively a product of, and reaction to, his historical epoch, the period of Arab nationalism.

Qutb authored several pivotal texts that are now seen as blueprints for Islamist action. The most influential major work was the 1960 publication *Milestones* (Qutb 1978). Following a long period of incarceration, Qutb was executed by the Egyptian state in 1966. In the late 1960s, Egypt proved a fertile ground for the Islamist critique of the state, as it was ruled by a repressive secular-nationalist regime. Moreover, the regime was faltering in its ability to provide socio-economic prosperity and a clear regional agenda, especially in relation to Israel. Islamists responded by questioning the role and legitimacy of the state's leadership, and they were subsequently persecuted. This repression led to an ever more radical interpretation of the political potential of Islam as a counter to the secular-nationalist project.

Qutb emphasized the universality of Islam and its application to all Muslim societies (Khatab 2004: 217). This helps explain why his work gained prominence in many diverse areas throughout the Muslim world. Qutb was in some ways a religious theorist, but it was his political context that most strongly shaped his thinking. In the broader socio-political sphere, Qutb's interpretation of Islam as a political doctrine capable of achieving major social revolution coincided with the failure of secular-nationalist regimes to fulfil popular expectations. This can be most clearly seen in the aftermath of the Arab defeat in the 1967 war with Israel. This

BOX 4.2

Arab nationalism and **pan-Arabism** are two interlinked concepts. Pan-Arabism refers to the desire for unification of the Arabs under a single political structure on the basis of their shared history, language and culture. Many leaders, including Egypt's Nasser and the founders of the Ba'th Party, used the rhetoric of pan-Arabism. However, the national divisions of the Middle East have meant that state-based nationalism has often triumphed and leaders have acted according to political pragmatism and opportunism rather than in accordance with a broader vision of Arab unity. Arab nationalism is therefore a nationalist ideology that calls for the acknowledgement of the shared concerns of Arab peoples, but it does not necessarily endorse the creation of a single regional state. Both ideologies developed in resistance to colonial domination and sought varying forms of Arab self-determination.

war proved a catalyst for widespread disillusionment with the secular-nationalist promises of prosperity. In a linked development, the imposition of secular forms of governance in the Middle East and the embrace of secular social norms by sections of the elite were seen by many as evidence of a Western conspiracy against Islam. Concepts such as nationalism, socialism and liberalism were thus rejected by Islamists as corrupt and imported ideologies, unsuitable to Arab society and unnecessary because an indigenous political code, that of Islam, already existed. In this way, a refocusing of communal life on Islamic tenets was seen as the panacea to the decline of the region in the face of Western intervention.

Mohammad Ayoob asserts that Islamist organizations, despite the use of 'an Islamic rhetoric that transcends political boundaries', are usually tied to their national contexts, with a basic objective of bringing systems of existing governance into line with Islamic norms (2004: 2). In the early to mid-twentieth century, Islamism was focused on internal reform, as the pressure brought to bear on secular-nationalist Arab leaders attests. It is sometimes understood that Islamists wish to create a pan-Islamic state, governed by Islamic law. The reality has proven more complex. Islamism is a highly adaptable, diffuse movement capable of great diversity. Yet it is usually linked closely to the specific challenges that affect its socio-economic and geographical context of activity. Although the Muslim Brotherhood served as a major *regional* catalyst for change, its numerous offshoots focused on specific locations. Organizations such as Egyptian Islamic Jihad and the Palestinian group HAMAS have continued to act within the territorial confines of Egypt and the Occupied Territories. Although focused on location-specific goals, such as the struggle against Israel, such offshoot groups draw on the broader Muslim Brotherhood tradition. Only a tiny minority of organizations, such as Hizb al-Tahrir, advocate a return to a supra-national entity. This organization is one of the few to overtly reject the division of Muslims by adoption of the state system (Farouki 1996). The vast majority of organizations seek the local application of Sharia or the Islamization of the existing state.

It is interesting to note that Islamism is sustained by educated and middle-class individuals. Historically speaking, the ranks of the Islamist movement swelled when a generation of educated university graduates attempted to climb the socio-economic ladder, only to discover that the ruling elite had no interest in sharing the spoils of power. The authoritarian and closed societies of Egypt, Iran and Pakistan, to name a few, were too slow to modernize the workforce by absorbing the growing class of technocrats and thus to allow the promise of prosperity to extend beyond the circle of the rich families connected to the ruling elite. This closed system was a source of great disillusionment among upwardly mobile groups. It was not so much absolute power that inspired the increasingly wide embrace of Islamism as it was a perception of poverty and the absence of opportunity for growth and societal change. The middle classes were most affected by this process, and they have proven the most fertile ground for Islamist recruitment. The Islamist response to corruption and nepotism has therefore been a return to Islam. 'Islam is the solution' became a common retort in societies where avenues to development and progression appeared to be closed. As Manuel Castells points out, in such contexts Islamism became the oppositional doctrine to 'capitalism, to socialism, and to nationalism, Arab or otherwise, which are (in the view of Islamists) all failing ideologies of the post-colonial order' (2004: 17). Thus, it is not surprising that the early organizations frequently rejected corruption, nepotism and the pro-Western orientation of secular regimes in the region.

Islamism is one of the major communal responses to a period in which the question of collective and personal identity was explored in the Middle East. This search for identity was sparked by the failure of secular nationalism, the legacy of Western colonialism, economic domination and the repeated military defeat of Arab states in wars against Israel. It is perhaps instructive to consider not what Islamism aims to achieve but what it aims to confront: much of the appeal of Islamism in the Middle East is linked to the central rejection of foreign interference in Arab/Muslim affairs. This position has emphasized the widely held image of Islamism as the great enemy of the 'West'. However, Islamism has historically acted as a double challenge. Certainly, many Islamist organizations define themselves in opposition to the West, and particularly the United States, especially as the latter's foreign policy has become ever more interventionist in the region, but Islamism has also functioned as a challenge to secularizing trends in Muslim societies. There are many examples of this tension between Islamism and secular impulses in Muslim societies, the most enduring of which is the Islamic Revolution in Iran.

THE IRANIAN REVOLUTION

The Iranian Revolution of 1979 constituted a turning point in the political history of the Middle East. It also marked a vital moment in Washington's role in, and perception of, the region. The modern state of Iran was established in 1935; prior to this time the region was known as Persia. In the mid-twentieth century, the Iranian people were in the midst of embracing the democratic process. Public elections led to the accession to power of a nationalist government under the leadership of Mohammed Mossedeq. In line with the experience of many post-colonial leaders, Mossedeq moved to nationalize the Iranian oil industry and free the state from Western economic influence. This action, seen as cutting the West out of the lucrative oil market, was coupled with fears in Washington

BOX 4.3

Mohammed Mossedeq (1882–1967) was the democratically elected Prime Minister of Iran from 1951 to 1953. An ardent nationalist, Mossedeq rejected foreign intervention in Iranian affairs and was a key player in the nationalization of the Iranian oil industry. In the midst of a troubled period in Iranian politics, Mossedeq was overthrown by a US- and UK-backed military coup. The part played by the CIA in the coup, code-named Operation Ajax, is often seen as the first clear example of American intervention in Middle Eastern politics.

regarding Mossedeq's apparent socialist leanings. These concerns led to a coup in 1953, supported by the Central Intelligence Agency (CIA), that overthrew his government and reinstalled the pro-US Muhammad Reza Shah of the Pahlavi dynasty as the King of Iran (Abrahamian 2001). British intelligence agencies were directly involved in planning the coup, with the explicit endorsement of the United States. Thus, the 1953 coup came to be seen in the Middle East as a clear example of direct foreign interference by Great Powers. It was a blatant violation of Iranian national sovereignty, carried out to protect the economic and political interest of the United States and the United Kingdom. This aggressive behaviour left a lasting impression in Iran and in the broader Middle East. Interestingly, the gradual decline of the United Kingdom, coinciding with the global ascendancy of the United States, has over time coloured the collective memory of the coup, with emphasis now placed on Washington as its architect. This perception was cemented as the newly reinstalled Pahlavi dynasty granted the United States a 40 per cent share in the Iranian oil consortium (Keddie 2003: 132). From this point on, the Pahlavi regime became closely aligned with Washington.

The overall context of the early Cold War undoubtedly influenced Washington's decision-making process. The 1953 coup can be seen as an early application of the 1947 Truman doctrine, which held that unless the United States moved decisively, the Soviet Union would gain influence in the oil-rich region. According to Tony Junt and Denis Lacorne, involvement in the coup 'seriously tarnished the reputation of the US and transformed the American ally into the disloyal and deceitful friend' (2005: 4). Following the events of 1953, the public image of the United States suffered a blow in Iran as Washington offered complete support to the authoritarian Pahlavi regime, while merely 'rationalizing or ignoring the tremendous popular disaffection' with this regime (Makdissi 2002: 548).

Secure in his superpower alliance, the Shah embarked on a series of repressive measures. The state's security apparatus, especially the notorious SAVAK, enforced the Shah's rigid grip on power. However,

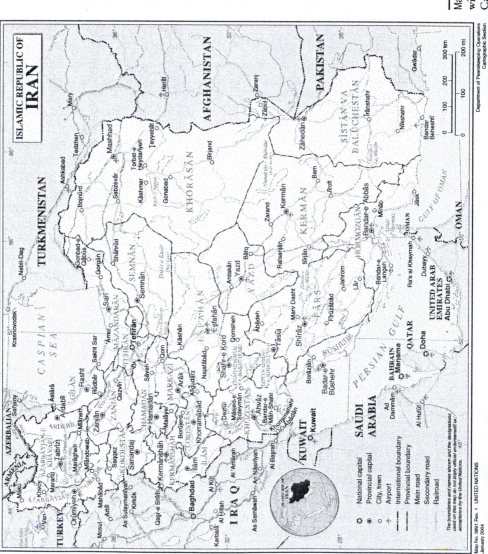

Map 4.1 Iran. Reproduced with permission from the UN Cartographic Section.

popular Iranian discontent was seething. The Shah's regime enacted the White Revolution, a top-down policy of aggressive secularization. These measures were significant: for example, the Shah removed the traditional Islamic calendar and replaced it with a royalist one. As Ervand Abrahamian points out, 'few contemporary regimes have been so foolhardy as to undermine their country's religious calendar' (1999: 26). Although broadly unpopular, these actions were in the end perhaps not as damaging as was the widespread perception that the Shah was a US puppet. In a fiercely nationalist country, the idea of a leadership beholden to external influences was profoundly destabilizing. The Shah imported millions of dollars' worth of high-tech weaponry and US military personnel to operate it. This made his dependence on American aid highly visible and a source of antagonism for many Iranians.

As late as New Year's Eve in 1978, US President Jimmy Carter lavishly praised 'the great leadership of the Shah', which, he insisted, had turned Iran into 'an island of stability in one of the more troubled areas of the world' (quoted in Makdissi 2002: 548). But nothing could have been further from the truth. The Carter administration's support for the Shah can be interpreted through the prisms of both economic and Cold War strategy. After the Shah's return to power, the United States gained a significant foothold in Iran's oil industry. Moreover, in what would become a defining feature of US policy in the twentieth century, Washington demonstrated its preference for status quo leaderships, in order to simultaneously enhance its economic objectives and ensure that the Soviet Union did not make inroads in the region. The willingness of Washington to rely on the Shah's reports of popular support for the regime left the United States completely unprepared for the groundswell of public support for the exiled cleric Ayatollah Khomeini. The Islamic movement, with Khomeini at its helm, harnessed popular discontent against the Pahlavi regime, and revolution was soon at hand. In February 1979 the monarchy was replaced with the Islamic Republic. By 1 April 1979, a referendum had confirmed this dramatic move, establishing the first modern Islamic state.

Khomeini, the central figure in this dramatic shift in regional politics, had been born in 1902 and had trained as a traditional Islamic cleric. His opposition to the Pahlavi regime in the early 1960s led to his exile in Iraq, where he continued to preach an empowered version of Islam. Drawing on the Shia tradition of defying 'unjust' authority, Khomeini used Islam as a political tool for mobilizing the population against the regime, which he dismissed as corrupt and illegitimate. Khomeini developed his Islamic revolutionary ideas further to aim at a novel concept: the supremacy of jurisprudence (*vilayat-i faqih*). In this model, the *faqih*, or the jurisprudent or jurist, sits at the top of the state. The *faqih* is the ultimate decision-maker. The *vilayat-i faqih* is a clear departure from earlier Shia political philosophy, which did not require a unitary source of leadership but acknowledged multiplicity of authority. Indeed, as Dale Eickelman and James Piscatori point out, Khomeini's vision of *vilayat-i faqih* was regarded by many 'as an extraordinary, even heterodox, position' (1996: 49). In this way, Khomeini demonstrated the adaptable nature of political Islam, a movement that was capable of change to accommodate the political needs of its time and place. The need to contextualize Khomeini's ideas within the state of Iran is further underscored by the fact that Khomeini's formulation of this system of governance was also very different to the thinking of Sunni activists such as Sayyid Qutb. In their tradition, there was no reservation of a privileged position for the Islamic clergy in the idealized Islamic state. Henry Munson suggests that nationalism played a vital role in Khomeini's perspective, and that the cleric was 'in fact passionately attached to the nation of Iran, despite his opposition to nationalism as ideology' (2003: 43). Moreover, on a more pragmatic level, Khomeini's own intentions for the role of the clerics in the new Islamic Republic may well have played a significant part in this formulation.

As the clamour for revolutionary change intensified, Khomeini emerged as an embodiment of a new future. His public image was that of a committed activist, and he was seen as anti-Western, nationalist, deeply pious and austere, in contrast to the evident wealth and luxurious lifestyle of the ruling pro-US Iranian elite. Although Khomeini's charismatic power was considerable, the situation in Iran in the late 1970s also explains the dynamics of the Revolution. Dissatisfaction with the Shah caused people to spill onto the streets, and thousands died in public protests. The Shah's government continued its two-pronged approach of crushing dissent and reassuring its American backers that it remained in control of the deteriorating situation. As a result, Washington was completely unprepared when Khomeini swept into power and a sophisticated US-supplied state machinery fell directly into the hands of a religious cleric who had built his political career on an anti-Western stance.

In Washington, 1979 was increasingly becoming understood as a watershed year. The Middle East appeared to be in a state of flux, with the established stalwarts and allies crumbling in the face of domestic agitation for change. To the region's young Muslims, the establishment of the new government in Iran seemed to portend a period of great promise in which Islam would be an emergent power on the world stage. More importantly, the Revolution was seen throughout the region as an indigenous response to external involvement. Underscoring the adaptability of this movement, political Islam, as it was employed in the lead-up to Revolution, was about grassroots politics and people power, not violence. Khomeini's triumphant return from exile in Paris in February 1979 brought for the first time in modern history an Islamic theocracy to power in the region. The Revolution had a vehemently anti-US tone, and Khomeini exploited this element:

America is the number-one enemy of the deprived and oppressed people of the world. . . . It exploits the oppressed people of the world by means of the large-scale propaganda campaigns that are coordinated for it by international Zionism. By means of its hidden and treacherous agents, it sucks the blood of the defenseless people as if it alone, together with its satellites, had the right to live in this world. Iran has tried to sever all its relations with this Great Satan . . .

(Khomeini 1985: 304–5)

Washington was still attempting to digest these changes when a further disaster erupted. Emboldened by the Revolution, a group of Iranian students stormed the US embassy in Tehran and took 56 US citizens hostage. In a hostage crisis that dragged on for 444 days, the various regional perceptions of the United States were revealed. The powerful interventionist tendencies of the United States had played a significant part in uniting the Iranian population in defiance against the Shah and precipitating the Revolution. However, with the hostage crisis, this image was now contradicted by an appearance of vulnerability and ineptitude and a subsequent inability to over-awe the determined proponents of Islamic political revolution. The ramifications of this situation were significant and international in nature. President Carter's administration descended into chaos as it was unable to secure the release of the US citizens, a failure that tarnished the Democratic president's reputation at home and abroad.[4] In the Cold War period the ability to project an image of power was all-important, and as this crisis continued the Carter administration appeared increasingly impotent. President Carter attempted economic measures to secure the release of the hostages, halting oil imports from Iran and freezing Iranian assets in the United States. At the same time, he began several diplomatic initiatives, all of which proved fruitless. On 24 April 1980, US forces attempted a rescue mission that failed, killing eight US marines. This military bungle dealt yet another crushing blow to the Carter administration's public profile. The failure to resolve the crisis contributed to the election of the Republican candidate Ronald Reagan, who had campaigned on a tough security platform. The dealings in this period between the Republican Party and Tehran have been widely questioned. The so-called 'October Surprise' theory suggests that the Republican Party negotiated directly with Tehran to gain political advantage over the embattled Carter administration (Sick 1991). This was a deeply challenging time for the United States in terms of its role on the world stage, and the impact of this period in Iran–US relations cannot be overstated.

As is often the case with political developments in the Middle East, the influence of this period spread much more widely than Washington's halls of power. In their homes, the American public watched televised images of thousands of distant Iranians protesting violently against the

United States. The context of this popular discontent was often ignored by a media and political elite both unaware and unwilling to acknowledge the influence of history in the Iranian stance. In the American cities and heartlands, the political context of Western interference and the repressive rule of the Pahlavi dynasty were completely overlooked as people took in the imagery of Iranians demanding a return to what seemed an archaic system of governance. A deep mistrust on both sides only grew throughout the next 30 years. Deep-seated American fears regarding political Islam's challenge to the United States were fed by consecutive administrations that were concerned with protecting the status quo in the oil-rich Persian Gulf. The hostage crisis and the Iranian regime's unwillingness to compromise humiliated the United States on the world stage. A deep schism developed between Iran and the international community. Imam Khomeini's *fatwa* (Islamic legal ruling) calling for the author Salman Rushdie's death in the mid-1980s did not help the public and political perception of Iran as a profoundly threatening presence.

The Shia revolution in Iran, although it was always unlikely to translate into a regional revolution, clearly served as an inspiration to Islamic organizations throughout the region. Iranian expansionist rhetoric coupled with a lack of understanding regarding the Shia orientation of the Iranian Revolution led to exaggerated concerns in Washington that Islamic revolution was about to sweep the Middle East. Despite the language of universal revolution, however, Khomeini was in fact a fervent nationalist, a political trait that became more pronounced as his regime faced the task of state governance. Moreover, the expansionist mindset in Tehran was

BOX 4.4

The **Rushdie affair** refers to the events following the 1988 publication of the novel *The Satanic Verses* by Salman Rushdie. Although a work of fiction, this text was based upon the experiences of characters clearly drawn from the Islamic tradition. The publication of the book sparked protests throughout the Muslim world and, particularly, in the United Kingdom. In Britain, the book itself and the state's unwillingness to extend British blasphemy laws to prevent its publication and distribution provided a catalyst for a broader expression of discontent by some sections of the British Muslim community. In essence, this was a domestic issue related to the experience of British Muslims with the internal political processes of the United Kingdom. In February 1989 the saga developed an international angle as, driven by theological and public relations considerations, Iran's Ayatollah Khomeini issued a controversial *fatwa* condemning Rushdie and those involved in the publication of the text to death.

checked as Iran became embroiled in a prolonged battle with its neighbour Iraq. In addition to this devastating war, the new regime had recurrent disagreements with Iraq, Saudi Arabia, the United Arab Emirates, Egypt and Jordan. These regional power-brokers were deeply unsettled by the Revolution, which served as an inspiration to groups and individuals seeking to subvert the status quo across the Middle East. For example, Saudi Arabia saw Iran as a serious threat because of the Iranian regime's frequent calls for a Shia uprising in the Gulf region. Throughout the 1980s, these two states engaged in a virtual funding war, extending influence and aid to organizations and individuals in the Muslim world and beyond. Indeed, the Saudi desire to counter the doctrinal appeal of the Islamic Revolution is, in part, responsible for the determination with which the Saudis propagated their Wahhabi creed to all corners of the Muslim world.

In the post-revolutionary chaos, factions fought bitterly to direct and control the future of Iran. Khomeini emerged as the only leader with the political stature to harness and direct the new political system. As a result, Khomeini and his followers centralized power in their own hands. As Khomeini's grip on Iranian politics became stronger, so did the push to Islamize society. Women who had taken the veil as a revolutionary political statement against the Western orientation of the Shah found themselves forced by law to wear it (Afary and Anderson 2005: 113). Such laws were enforced by the Revolutionary Guards, formed in May 1979. The Revolutionary Guards were committed to the vision articulated by Khomeini and were brutal in enforcing Islamic law. For many Iranians, the Revolutionary Guards were the Islamic version of the much-feared SAVAK. The idealism of the Revolution appeared to give way as the leadership's determination to maintain societal control became stronger. Schools and universities, for example, were repeatedly closed and purged of non-Islamic elements, always with reference to the need for vigilance against Western influences.

THE SHIA DIMENSION

It is important to explore the Shia dimension of the Iranian Revolution. At the time it happened, the Shia nature of this uprising was often overlooked. The Shia-specific nature of the revolution helps explain why the Iranian regime's attempts to 'export the revolution' were largely unsuccessful.

The Shia community constitutes roughly 15 per cent of the Muslim world. The Shia stream of Islam is theologically and historically distinct from the majority Sunni stream. The theological differences centre on the concept of legitimate rule of the early Islamic community.[5] The Shia tradition holds that the family of the Prophet Muhammad were the rightful successors after his death, whereas the Sunni tradition emphasizes the importance of community selection of the Prophet's successors. The Shia believe that the twelve descendants of the Prophet Muhammad carried the divine inspiration of Muhammad; they are understood as having been privy to esoteric knowledge. This knowledge enabled them to pass enlightened judgements that were considered by their followers as divinely influenced. Throughout history, the Shia community has maintained an established hierarchy of leaders. This is extremely important to understanding the Islamic politics of the Iranian Revolution. While popular discontent with the Shah was an overwhelming temporal issue, Khomeini was able to draw on deep-seated theological traditions to frame his revolutionary worldview.

The overthrow of the region's staunchest US ally was without question a major blow to Washington's agenda in the Middle East. Iran's economic relationship with the United States was also of prime importance to the Western power, especially in the aftermath of the Arab oil boycott of the mid-1970s. In Washington, Iran's move towards an Islamic frame of reference and a leadership that quickly became virulently anti-Israel and anti-US was interpreted as the potential start of a revolutionary wave of Shia activism that could lead directly to the destabilization of the oil-rich Gulf. Essentially, in Washington there were concerns that the revolutionary events in Iran were just a beginning. This fear perspective was heightened by the demographic placement of the Shia community in many parts of the Middle East, especially in the oil-rich Gulf countries. For example, Iraq has a Shia majority (65 per cent of the population), as does Bahrain (70 per cent), and significant Shia minorities live in states such as Kuwait (30 per cent), Pakistan (20 per cent), Syria (15–20 per cent), the United Arab Emirates (16 per cent) and Saudi Arabia (10–15 per cent). As the Revolution consolidated its grip on power, the formulation of new patterns of governance also posed a serious challenge to Western norms. The Iranian constitution affirmed that

> Absolute sovereignty over the world and man belongs to God, and it is He who has made man master of his own social destiny. No one can deprive man of this divine right, nor subordinate it to the vested interests of a particular individual or group.
>
> ('Islamic Republic of Iran Constitution').

The constitution also explicitly adopted the principle of *vilayat-i faqih*, the governance of the Islamic jurist. The new constitution of Iran clearly reflected the Shia belief system and also revealed the leadership's determination to structure a modern society on the basis of Islam. This commitment has survived a bloody conflict with neighbouring Iraq (as will be explored in Chapter 6) and a hostile relationship with the United States.

CONCLUSION

This chapter has focused on the emergence of Islamism and the seminal moment of the Islamic Revolution in Iran. The politics of the Middle East was, and continues to be, profoundly affected by the events of 1979. As explored, Islamism's appeal is often greatly affected by local issues and challenges faced by Muslim communities. As the case of Iran demonstrates, Islamism has often acted as a vehicle for the expression of indigenous discontent with Western interference, failed or failing systems of national leadership, secularization and economic decline. In societies under authoritarian rule there is often little political space for the expression of dissent. This is particularly true of the Cold War-era Middle East, in which the United States, caught in a bipolar mindset, encouraged the suppression of any forces that appeared to be natural allies of the Soviet Union – that is, left-leaning parties. An unintended consequence of this policy was the empowering of Islam as the only form through which dissent could be articulated. The employment of the language of Islam in the expression of political dissent had, as demonstrated in Iran in the late 1970s, cultural and historical currency in the Middle East. A return to Islam was presented as empowering in societies that were still being rehabilitated from the colonial period and in which communal identity was increasingly conflicted. Seen in this way, political Islam or Islamism can be conceived of as a form of 'identity politics' in a region that is in a state of political flux.

Although Islamic revolutions did not sweep the region, the issues that underpinned Iranian discontent did. Islamist alternatives sprang up in states throughout the Middle East, inspired by the events in Iran and responding to the issues of political stagnation and failure that pervaded the region. Moreover, in Egypt, Iraq, Jordan and Lebanon the expression of dissent remained difficult and dangerous, and the repression of oppositional political parties became a feature of regional politics. In such a climate, community structures and networks, such as mosques, assumed a vital political role. The Islamic tendency towards the blurring of distinctions between the public and private realm became even more pronounced as preachers gained power within society and religious figures provided through their piety a contrast to the opulence of the national, often foreign-backed, leadership. The expression of political dissent through the language of Islam, especially through the language of politicized Islam, made sense to many in the Muslim world. Islam provided an indigenous socio-political code, while secularism, socialism, capitalism and Western doctrines were all open to critique as both imported doctrines aimed at the containment and division of the Arab/Muslim world and as ideologies that had failed to provide prosperity and success for the people of the region.

NOTES

1 Several excellent general texts on Islamic history exist: see Lapidus (2002) and Esposito (1999b, 2005).
2 For a detailed history of Qutb, see Musallam (2005). For an exploration of Ayatollah Khomeini, see Kurzman (2004).
3 A comprehensive account of Qutb's life can be found in Musallam (2005).
4 For a detailed exploration of the impact of the hostage crisis, see Bowden (2006).
5 For an exploration of the origins of the split, see Rogerson (2006).

REFERENCES

Abrahamian, Ervand (1999) *Radical Islam: The Iranian Mojahedin* (London: IB Tauris).

Abrahamian, Ervand (2001) 'The 1953 Coup in Iran', in *Science and Society*, Vol. 65, No. 2, pp. 182–216.

Afary, Janet and Anderson, Kevin B. (2005) *Foucault and the Iranian Revolution: Gender and the Seductions of Islamism* (Chicago: University of Chicago Press).

Akbarzadeh, Shahram and Saeed, Abdullah (2003) 'Islam and Politics', in Shahram Akbarzadeh and Abdullah Saeed (eds), *Islam and Political Legitimacy* (London: Routledge).

Ayoob, Mohammad (2004) 'Political Islam: Image and Reality' *World Policy Journal*, Vol. 21, No. 3, pp. 1–14.

Bonney, Richard (2004) *Jihad from the Qur'an to bin Laden* (London: Palgrave Macmillan).

Bowden, Mark (2006) *Guests of the Ayatollah: The First Battle in America's War with Militant Islam* (New York: Atlantic Monthly Press).

Castells, Manuel (2004) *The Power of Identity* (London: Blackwell).

Denoeux, Guilain (2002) 'The Forgotten Swamp: Navigating Political Islam', *Middle East Policy*, Vol. 9, No. 2, pp. 56–81.

Eickelman, Dale F. and Piscatori, James P. (1996) *Muslim Politics* (Princeton, NJ: Princeton University Press).

Esposito, John (1999a) *The Islamic Threat: Myth or Reality?* (Oxford: Oxford University Press).

Esposito, John (ed.) (1999b) *The Oxford History of Islam* (New York: Oxford University Press).

Esposito, John (2005) *Islam: The Straight Path* (New York: Oxford University Press).

Farouki, Suha Taji (1996) *A Fundamental Quest: Hizb al-Tahrir and the Search for the Islamic Caliphate* (London: Grey Seal).

Haddad, Yvonne (1992) 'Islamists and the Problem of Israel: The 1967 Awakening', *The Middle East Journal*, Vol. 46, No. 2, pp. 266–85.

'Islamic Republic of Iran Constitution' (1979), Article 56, available at www.iranonline.com/iran/iran-info/Government/constitution.html.

Junt, Tony and Lacorne, Denis (2005) 'The Banality of Anti-Americanism', in Tony Junt and Denis Lacome (eds.), *With Us Or Against Us? Studies in Global Anti-Americanism* (New York: Palgrave Macmillan).

Keddie, Nikki (2003) *Modern Iran: Roots and Results of Revolutions* (New Haven, CT: Yale University Press).

Khatab, Sayed (2004) 'Arabism and Islamism in Sayyid Qutb's Thought on Nationalism', *The Muslim World*, Vol. 94, No. 2, pp. 217–44.

Khomeini, Ruholla (1985) *Islam and Revolution: Writings and Declarations*, trans. by Hamid Alga (London: Mizan Press).

Kurzman, Charles (2004) *The Unthinkable Revolution in Iran* (Cambridge, MA: Harvard University Press).

Lapidus, Ira (2002) *A History of Islamic Societies* (New York: Cambridge University Press).

Makdissi, Ussama (2002) 'Anti-Americanism in the Arab World: An Interpretation of a Brief History', *Journal of American History*, Vol. 89, No. 2, pp. 538–58.

Munson, Henry (2003) 'Islam, Nationalism and the Resentment of Foreign Domination', *Middle East Policy*, Vol. 10, No. 3, pp. 40–54.

Musallam, Adnan A. (2005) *From Secularism to Jihad: Sayyid Qutb and the Foundations of Radical Islamism* (Westport, CT: Praeger).

Qutb, Sayed (1978) *Milestones* (Beirut: Holy Koran Publishing House).

Rogerson, Barnaby (2006) *The Heirs of the Prophet Muhammad and the Roots of the Sunni–Shia Schism* (London: Little, Brown).

Sadiki, Larbi (1995) 'Al-la Nidam: An Arab View of the New World (Dis)order', *Arab Studies Quarterly*, Vol. 17, No. 3, pp. 1–22.

Sick, Gary (1991) *October Surprise: America's Hostages in Iran and the Election of Ronald Reagan* (New York: Random House).

SUGGESTED FURTHER READING

Afshar, Haleh (ed.) (1985) *Iran: A Revolution in Turmoil* (London: Macmillan).

Arjoman, Said Amir (ed.) (1988) *Authority and Political Culture in Shi'ism* (Albany, NY: State University of New York Press).

Bakhash, Shaul (1984) *The Reign of the Ayatollahs, Iran and the Islamic Revolution* (New York: Basic Books).

Cronin, Stephanie (ed.) (2004) *Reformers and Revolutionaries in Modern Iran: New Perspectives on the Iranian Left* (New York: RoutledgeCurzon).

Esposito, John L. and Ramazani, R.K. (2001) *Iran at the Crossroads* (New York: Palgrave).

Haddad, Yvonne and Stowasser, Barbara Freyer (2004) *Islamic Law and the Challenges of Modernity* (Lanham, MD: Rowman & Littlefield).

Hoveyda, Fereydoun (2003) *The Shah and the Ayatollah: Iranian Mythology and Islamic Revolution* (Westport, CT: Praeger).

Mir-Hosseini, Ziba and Tapper, Richard (2006) *Islam and Democracy in Iran: Eshkevari and the Quest for Reform* (London: I.B. Taurus).

Mohammadi, Ali (ed.) (2003) *Iran Encountering Globalisation: Problems and Prospects* (New York: RoutledgeCurzon).

Piscatori, James (1990) 'The Rushdie Affair and the Politics of Ambiguity', *International Affairs,* Vol. 66, No. 4, pp. 767–800.

Zubaida, Sami (1989) *Islam, the People and the State: Essays on Political Ideas and Movements in the Middle East* (London: Routledge).

SUGGESTED STUDY QUESTIONS

1 How would you define 'Islamism'?

2 What factors contributed to the emergence of Islamism in the Middle East during the twentieth century?

3 What are some examples of Islamist groups in the Middle East? Do they differ from each other in terms of ideology or practical function, and, if so, how?

4 Has ideology or religion been the major contributing factor to conflict between states in the Middle East?

5 How has the rise of Islamism affected regional and international relations in the modern Middle East?

CHAPTER 5

Proxy War
The Superpowers in Afghanistan

INTRODUCTION

In Washington the impact of the Iranian Revolution of January 1979 had barely subsided when a new crisis erupted. The United States was once again caught by surprise when the Soviet Union invaded Afghanistan on 23 December that year. This constituted a major development in the context of the Cold War, in which Soviet expansionism was seen as a major threat to US regional interests. The subsequent conflict in Afghanistan – between local rebels, known as the Mujahideen, who were funded and armed by a range of states including the United States and Saudi Arabia, and the local communist government and the Soviet forces – decimated the infrastructure of this Central Asian state. The decade-long conflict also laid this fragile state open to a long and divisive civil war following the Soviet withdrawal in 1989.

Washington's involvement and conduct in Afghanistan eventually emerged as a major point of tension in the contradictory relationship between the United States and the forces of international Islamism. By the late 1980s, the United States was acting as a major supporter of elements of the Mujahideen who, by this point, had been reinforced by an influx of Muslim volunteers from outside Afghanistan who had come forward to resist the occupying 'atheist' forces of the Soviet Union. Washington's willingness to utilize the Mujahideen in a proxy war against the Soviet Union greatly affected the regional popular perception of the United States. The short-sighted nature of American foreign policy in this period helped to create the forces and leadership structures of militant Islamism. These forces then emerged as the greatest challenge to US hegemony in the post-Cold War world. This chapter will explore the situation in Afghanistan in order to understand Washington's decision-making process and this conflict's consequences for regional stability and global politics.

HISTORICAL CONTEXT

The history of Afghanistan is complex. The modern state and its internal structure is the product of an ever-changing process of tribal and ethnic loyalties. The focus here will be on contextualizing the impact of the Soviet invasion of Afghanistan on global politics and regional perceptions of the United States. As explored previously, the relationship between political Islam and the United States has its roots in the early Cold War period. By the late 1970s, the Middle East was in a period of unequalled turmoil. Following the events of 1967, the death of Nasser in 1970 and the rise of Islamic alternatives, the relevance of pan-Arabism had subsided. Moreover, the Islamic Revolution in Iran had propelled into the popular mind the potential of politicized Islam to organize society. The United States had followed a policy geared towards maintaining the status quo, but this agenda faced increasingly serious challenges. The surprise loss of a lynchpin ally in the Iranian Shah had shaken Washington's belief in its ability to continue to shape the region in ways that served its own strategic and economic interests. Moreover, within the context of the Cold War, the Soviet decision to invade Afghanistan raised the very real spectre of Soviet domination of the Persian Gulf and its oil supplies. The role of the United States in the Gulf was therefore under threat from two distinct and potentially oppositional forces: communism and political Islam.

In the nineteenth century, Afghanistan's geographical position had made it the lynchpin in the regional balance of power between the colonial powers of Britain and Russia. Afghanistan was made famous by the 'great game' of imperial rivalry, and the country was often cited as the gateway between Asia and the Middle East. This changed with the demise of British colonialism and the shifting of the superpower rivalry fault-line westward. The new configuration of global forces, which effectively divided Europe between Eastern and Western spheres of influence, signalled a decline in Afghanistan's geo-strategic significance. As the tumultuous decade of the 1970s came to a close, the Soviet invasion brought Afghanistan back from the international backwaters and propelled it into the spotlight. Although Soviet action in Afghanistan drew the attention of the international community, it did not seem to trigger a serious rethinking of Afghanistan's intrinsic geo-strategic importance. This fact is underscored by the US decision to divert its attention from the country once the Soviet forces withdrew in 1989. As will be discussed in this chapter, Washington's short attention span with regard to Afghanistan proved highly detrimental to its standing in the Middle East.

Afghanistan borders Iran, Pakistan and the new Central Asian states, which, at this time, composed the southern flank of the Soviet Union. The Islamic Revolution in Iran, a major threat to US interests, also constituted a serious challenge to the regional interests of the Soviet Union. In 1979, Moscow was concerned about the possibility of an unchecked spread of religiously inspired destabilization in its Muslim-dominated provinces. Post-revolution Iran had emerged, much to Moscow's dismay, as another axis of power in the tense world of Eurasian politics. Although the embroilment of Iran in a costly war with Iraq, explored in the next chapter, ameliorated Soviet concerns dramatically in the 1980s, in 1979 political Islam appeared poised to expand its influence. With the benefit of hindsight it can be seen that the invasion of Afghanistan was perhaps Moscow's most disastrous Cold War decision. However, it can also be argued that, from a realist perspective in 1979, the Soviet Union may have seen itself as having few viable alternatives.

In April 1978, the People's Democratic Party of Afghanistan (PDPA) came to power following a military coup. This fledgling government faced an immediate and sustained popular backlash from diverse sections of Afghan society. The resistance to the new government was based on a range of issues, including the political ambitions of local leaders and the rejection of the secular orientation of the new regime. Essentially, in as much as it was inspired by ideas of modern centralized government organized along socialist lines, the new government was at odds with the tribal and ethnic traditions of the local people. It is noteworthy that prior to the communist takeover, Afghanistan did not have a centralized state system, and power was dispersed throughout the country with local chiefs exercising near-complete control of their territories. As the government struggled to maintain its grip on power, the rebellion was further assisted by the region's inhospitable terrain and the local knowledge of the fighters. The various rebel factions were reasonably effective in their operations and the communist government began to falter. In addition to the armed rebellion, the situation was further complicated by the unwillingness of the people of Afghanistan to submit to programmes such as forced secularization. William Maley suggests that the PDPA's desire for secularization was aimed at highlighting the link between the new government and the Soviet Union. Thus, as he asserts, it is 'hardly surprising that opposition to the regime was rhetorically articulated in religious terms' (1988: 8). After only a few months in power, the communist regime felt besieged and called for help. On 5 December 1978, the PDPA and the Soviet Union signed a military cooperation agreement, a 'friendship treaty', that both consolidated and formalized the support the communist movement in

Afghanistan had received since the early 1950s. Maley states the level of Soviet economic aid to Afghanistan was significant, with the state receiving US$1.265 billon from Moscow by 1979, an amount that placed it 'behind only India and Egypt' (2002: 21).

The 1978 treaty included a clause asserting the right of the PDPA to call on the Soviet Union for military assistance. Arundhati Roy suggests the expedited signing of this treaty demonstrated Moscow's awareness of the 'tenuous social base of the April revolution' and a subsequent desire to quickly institutionalize the regime (1987: 19). The treaty sounded serious alarm bells in Washington and encouraged American planners to more deeply involve themselves in the domestic politics of Afghanistan. Indeed, there is evidence that the United States, under a programme code-named Operation Cyclone, was already supporting the rebels in the months preceding the Soviet troop deployment (Maley 2002: 78). Reflecting the cyclical nature of the Cold War period, this reactive US interest sparked off greater concern in Moscow that Washington was attempting to destabilize its vital and increasingly vulnerable southern flank.

The battle for influence in Afghanistan intensified, and from June to November 1979 the Soviet Union increased the presence of its military advisors from 700 to 2,000 (Roy 1987: 21). The intensification of engagement clearly signified Moscow's long-term commitment to assist the communist regime in Kabul. In this period, covert US support for anti-communist forces in Afghanistan was channelled through the Pakistani Inter-Services Intelligence (ISI). The decision to use Pakistan as the medium for delivering support to the rebel factions in Afghanistan led to the regionalization of this conflict. As clashes between government forces and the rebels intensified, the United States capitalized on the internal discontent in its efforts to destabilize the fragile communist regime. Cold War logic informed this decision, yet Washington was still committed to a path of relative caution. The Carter administration, which was still deeply embroiled in the hostage crisis in Iran, was unwilling to risk an outright confrontation with the Soviet Union at this time. Therefore, military planners sent low-level weaponry and funds through the Pakistan channel, a method that provided the United States with the key Cold War requirement of plausible deniability. The anti-communist rebellion, increasingly articulated in the language of political Islam – or more correctly in the language of anti-secularization – was successful in gaining support from other actors in the international system, including the Saudi kingdom and Pakistan itself. By late 1979 it became clear that the rebels were succeeding in destabilizing the regime and that the government in Kabul could not retain power without direct Soviet intervention. This situation presented a major and eventually costly political challenge for the Soviet Union. The internationalization of support for the anti-communist rebellion triggered significant discontent in Moscow, and an unwillingness to accept foreign interference in a neighbouring socialist state became increasingly evident. A feature of Soviet politics for some time, this mindset had been articulated explicitly in the Brezhnev doctrine of 1968:

> When external and internal forces hostile to socialism try to turn the development of a given socialist country in the direction of the restoration of the capitalist system . . . this is no longer merely a problem for that country's people, but a common problem, the concern of all socialist countries.
>
> (Brezhnev cited in Ouimet 2003: 67[1])

Given the Cold War imperative that it project an image of power, the Soviet Union could not afford to sit idly by while a fellow communist regime was destabilized, or, worse, overthrown, with American assistance. To do so would have been to draw into question the power and the prestige of the Soviet Union as an ally, and thus to lead other vulnerable Soviet-aligned states to question their orientation. Considering this, Moscow took the decision to intervene directly in Afghanistan. On 23 December 1979, the Soviet Union entered Afghanistan with 40,000 troops. (This figure increased over time but never exceeded Moscow's set cap of 120,000.) This deployment immediately changed the dynamics of the conflict. The Soviet occupation served to raise the profile of the Mujahideen struggle, and Afghanistan was thrust into the centre of Cold War tensions.

REASONS FOR THE SOVIET DECISION

As is the case with other conflicts, interpretations of the decision-making process that led to the Soviet invasion of Afghanistan vary. In the days following the invasion, Moscow justified its deployment in Afghanistan under the terms established in the 1978 'friendship treaty'. But the deployment is largely seen as an invasion. This interpretation rests on the nature of the government in power in Afghanistan and the method of its rise to power. As a communist regime in a religiously conservative state, the government in Kabul was strongly unrepresentative. In addition, its succession to power via a coup did not afford the regime any significant popular legitimacy. Furthermore, after declaring that it had been invited to intervene by the Afghan government, the Soviet army ruthlessly replaced the existing leadership with factions that were more pro-Soviet. Thus, the idea that the Soviet Union was responding to an invitation under the terms of the 1978 treaty is highly dubious. According to Amin Saikal, 'it is in relation to this fact [the killing of the President of Afghanistan] and the Soviets' post-entry behaviour that the Soviet action was nothing less than an invasion' (2004: 195). As Gilles Dorronsoro more explicitly opines, the

Soviet justification problematically 'relied on the verbal appeal made by the Afghan leader Hafizullah Amin before his execution by Soviet Special Forces' (2000: 192). As is suggested by Saikal, the understanding of this event as an invasion was further solidified by the brutal nature of the military campaign waged by the Soviet forces in their attempt to subdue the Afghan rebels.

Academics and political observers have advanced a range of possible factors that may have contributed to the decision-making process in Moscow. As suggested, the Soviet Union may have acted to prevent Islamic-orientated destabilization of its southern, Muslim-dominated regions. The fear of such domestic destabilization may have been enhanced as a result of the Iranian Revolution. Moscow may have also been concerned that another Islamic seizure of power could further destabilize the regional balance and present political Islam as unstoppable (Roy 1987: 27). This theory links into the Soviet need to indirectly contain post-revolutionary Iran. At this stage, Iran appeared to be a well-armed and technologically advanced state that was politically committed to the doctrine of 'exporting the revolution'. This policy posed a serious threat to Soviet interests. The Soviet action can therefore be construed as a warning to proponents of political Islam. The rebels in Afghanistan were increasingly composed along 'Islamic' lines and Moscow could not allow such a force to gather pace on its southern borders. A dominant presence in Afghanistan also provided Moscow with an additional presence on Iran's eastern borders and sent a clear message that the Soviet Union would act to protect its regional role. The interplay of other regional factors may also have been relevant, especially Soviet fears of an increasingly close Chinese–Pakistani relationship aimed at challenging the regional balance of power (Saikal 2004: 196). Finally, the role of the United States was a consideration, as many in Moscow perceived that increased US involvement during the final years of the 1970s signalled Washington's desire to gain a foothold in Afghanistan in order to compensate for the loss of Iran.

Above all, it is evident that the Soviet Union was trapped by its own ideological orientation as expressed in the long-standing Brezhnev doctrine (Galeotti 1995: 11). According to Willard Matthias, intervention in Afghanistan was not popular in Moscow, yet the Politburo felt compelled to move, and it justified the action on the basis of internationalism (2001: 290). Essentially, the Soviet leadership could not afford to remain on the sidelines and watch the region slide towards instability.

There is a large body of literature exploring Moscow's long-term agenda. Some see the invasion as a short-term preoccupation, literally a 'quick fix', aimed at rescuing a friendly and dependent socialist regime from external attack and internal disintegration (Galeotti 1995: 12). Theories of Soviet expansionism with an ultimate objective of securing alternative routes of sea access have been largely discredited. However, the deployment of troops may also have served other interlinked Soviet interests. The United States had sent a generation of soldiers into combat in Vietnam, thereby equipping them with active combat experience. An apparently small-scale conflict, perceived as an 'easy victory', may have appeared to offer Moscow the opportunity to provide its own forces with combat experience while also testing new training methods and weaponry.

From a realist perspective, the dynamics of the Cold War should have worked to keep the Soviet Union in check. However, Moscow may have believed that the United States, still struggling to deal with the loss of Iran and embroiled in the continuing hostage crisis in Tehran, was unlikely to respond definitively, while other regional powers such as Pakistan and China lacked either the will or the resources to react decisively (Collins 1986: 134). Overall, two major sets of factors emerge as central in Moscow's decision-making process: the geo-political and the ideological. Geo-politically, the Soviet rationale is self-evident: Moscow was increasingly alarmed by the unstable, unpredictable situation on its southern border. This dovetailed with a more ideological policy stance, articulated in the Brezhnev doctrine, which held that the Soviet Union had a right and a responsibility to 'counter threats to socialism in any one state of the socialist community' (Maley 2002: 35).

Officially entering Afghanistan on 23 December 1979, the Soviet forces, aided by superior technology, quickly consolidated control of the major urban centres on behalf of the Afghan leadership. However, in the harsh terrain of rural Afghanistan Soviet troops found it difficult to contain the rebels, despite sustained aerial campaigns. In addition, the deployment of Soviet troops had an invigorating and unifying effect on the resistance. Although initially only small bands of Afghans were engaged in active resistance to the local communist government, as Louis Dupree points out, after 24 December, 'virtually the entire Afghan nation resisted the foreign invader' (1988: 27). This corresponds to Maley's perspective that the full-scale rebellion against communist rule in Afghanistan began as a grassroots reaction to occupation (2002: 60).

This war was fought between anti-communist Muslim guerrillas, commonly known as the Mujahideen, and Afghan government and Soviet forces. Soviet aerial dominance placed the superpower in a position to inflict horrific casualities on the under-equipped Mujahideen. Although the figures for the total Soviet deployment vary, most sources estimate that Moscow sent 118,000 troops. This force was sufficient to maintain the status quo but not powerful enough to crush decisively the Mujahideen factions. It is argued that the limited nature of the deployment resulted from domestic political constraints. Some observers see the limited effort as politically expedient, as it provided the Soviet Union with time to achieve several important goals mainly focused on the urban centres: the creation of party organizations and the entrenchment of close cultural, social and economic ties between Afghanistan and the Soviet Union.

The Mujahideen rebellion that had begun in 1978 can perhaps best be understood as an expression of local political aspirations, even though it was often expressed in the language of a religious struggle. Factions were initially organized on a tribal basis. Yet as the conflict progressed, the language of Islam became used as a unifying force for warlord leaders seeking to further their own local, often repressive, agendas. At the time, the conflict was often understood in the West as a battle between the forces of 'freedom' and 'totalitarianism'. This understanding reflects the worldview of the incoming Reagan administration. As US propaganda regarding the role of the Afghan 'freedom fighters' increased, a tendency to apply Western-centric political interpretations to the rebels in Afghanistan became more evident. This was highly problematic, as the normative values of liberal democratic political participation clearly did not underpin the rebellion against the Soviet presence. The situation in Afghanistan was much more closely linked to local issues. Rebel groups may have shared a religion, but few shared a comprehensive worldview. Instead, unity among groups predominantly hinged upon their shared commitment to resist foreign occupation. Old social divisions, ethnic rivalries, Sunni and Shia divisions, rural–urban divides and class issues remained important, and tribal alliances still determined the course of the resistance movement. As the conflict progressed and volunteers from throughout the Muslim world flocked to Afghanistan, the rebel factions increasingly stressed their Islamic credentials in order to legitimize their struggle. As a result, the contrast between the secular, atheist superpower and the Islamic resistance became the overarching image of the Afghan war.

REGIONAL REACTIONS

The Soviet invasion of Afghanistan signalled a major turning point in regional politics. Pakistan emerged from the conflict as an important player in the increasingly internationalized political arena of Central Asia. At the outset of the conflict, Pakistan was the most vulnerable of the region's states to Soviet expansionism. This reality was spotlighted as the invasion brought Soviet troops into close proximity to Pakistan's borders. Therefore, for reasons of self-interest, Pakistan strongly supported the Mujahideen. The call for volunteers to fight the 'godless' Soviets attracted scores of men from throughout the Islamic world. Pakistan acted as the base for this international Mujahideen movement, a situation that greatly enhanced its standing in the Muslim world. Therefore, as Maley surmises, the Soviet invasion 'did not simply confront Pakistan with threats; it also provided it with opportunities' (2002: 70). Pakistan's role was further enhanced through the lower levels of involvement by other regional powers. Iran, by now busy with its own war with Iraq, was restricted in its influence. Tehran was also aware of its own territorial proximity to the Soviet Union and the potential demands of prosecuting a war while consolidating the Revolution.

The repercussions of the conflict filtered through the Muslim world, and states as geographically distant as Saudi Arabia deepened their involvement. A major financier of the Mujahideen, Saudi Arabia used the Afghan conflict as an opportunity to bolster its Islamic leadership pretensions. Simultaneously, the conflict provided the Saudis with the opportunity to strengthen their relationship with the United States, based on the shared need to confront the Soviet Union. Across the region, state responses to this conflict were dominated by the theme of self-interest, a reaction in line with realist conceptions of the political behaviour of states. Further complicating the Afghan conflict, numerous intelligence agencies were active inside the country, principally the ISI, the KGB and the CIA. Local Afghan factions acted as conduits for arms and information in a field of alliances that were constantly changing and often contradictory. Despite these complex political currents, the widespread condemnation of the Soviet invasion created a climate wherein Washington 'could press on with its counter-interventionist strategy with almost global immunity' (Saikal 2004: 199).

THE ROLE OF THE UNITED STATES

Washington, deeply shaken by events in Iran, was not prepared to cede a key Central Asian state to direct Soviet rule. Casting around for an ally, the United States aligned itself with Pakistan and the Mujahideen in an attempt to contain the Soviet Union without risking direct confrontation. Once the Soviet army entered Afghanistan, Afghan rebels began to be presented in American rhetoric as 'freedom fighters'. Although the rebels were clearly fighting for freedom from occupation, they were not striving for the democratic liberalism that the American political imagination linked to this term. This misunderstanding underscores the importance of comprehending cross-cultural differences for foreign policy, especially in this region. Both the public rhetoric about 'assisting freedom fighters' and Afghanistan's proximity to the oil-rich Persian Gulf necessitated a clear US response to the conflict. President Jimmy Carter put it succinctly:

> Let our position be absolutely clear: an attempt by any outside force to gain control of the Persian Gulf region will be regarded as an assault on the vital interests of the United States of America. And such an assault will be repelled by any means necessary, including military force.
>
> (Carter 1980)

Articulated in January 1980, the Carter doctrine formed the political basis for the US decision to sustain the rebels in Afghanistan. At the geopolitical level, Afghanistan was shaping up as a major arena for the Cold War power struggle. On the ground, the impact of this growing conflict on the people of Afghanistan was devastating, with a high civilian death toll and the internal displacement of millions.

CASE STUDY: THE STINGER CONTROVERSY

In Washington, the situation in Afghanistan was viewed with increasing concern. US advisors became alarmed over the seemingly endless destabilization in the region and the potential effect on oil supplies. Acting in accordance with the Cold War paradigm, the United States looked for an opportunity to advance its global ideological struggle against the Soviet Union and counted on global outrage, especially in the Muslim world, to render the region more receptive to American influence. In the last days of the Carter administration this conflict was seen as constituting a serious danger to the regional, even global, balance of power. A White House memorandum by National Security Advisor Zbigniew Brzezinski reveals the level of concern in Washington:

> The Soviets are likely to act decisively, unlike the U.S., which pursued in Vietnam a policy of inoculating the enemy. As a consequence, the Soviets might be able to assert themselves effectively, and [in] world politics nothing succeeds like success, whatever the moral aspects.[2]

Despite the dire warnings reverberating around Washington, overall the United States followed a low-key policy towards the conflict until the mid-1980s. This stance was based on a realist interpretation of the situation: events in Afghanistan had dragged the Soviet Union into a costly and demoralizing war. Planners in Washington were well aware of the effect such conflicts could have on domestic politics. Short of having the Red Army driven out of Afghanistan, keeping the Soviets 'bogged down' in a difficult guerrilla war was the best outcome the United States could wish for. The willingness to adopt a 'wait and see' attitude was evident in the Carter doctrine. President Carter's policy was largely defensive and revealed a clear preoccupation with preventing Soviet control of the Persian Gulf. To avoid a superpower confrontation while ensuring the ongoing ability of the rebellion to occupy the Red Army, the CIA employed an approach that hinged on the provision of covert support. The weapons funnelled to the rebels were largely of Soviet origin (either captured by the Israeli Defence Force in Lebanon in 1982 or bought from China), and Pakistan's ISI was responsible for directing the flow of arms, thus ensuring the United States could not be directly implicated in funding the Mujahideen. The assistance thus offered to the rebels was also comparatively limited. Although it ensured that the fighters were sufficiently well armed to harass, or 'bog down', the Soviet forces, they were not supplied with enough military hardware to mount a serious challenge to the Red Army. In short, Carter's policy towards Afghanistan after the 1978 coup can be understood as a 'policy of moderation' (Hilali 2005: 142).

However, the change of US leadership in 1981 heralded a new era in US foreign policy. The change from a Democratic to a Republican administration set the United States, and thus its response to the conflict in Afghanistan, on a new and more aggressive foreign policy trajectory. Initially, the Reagan administration retained the existing policy and continued a cautious, though expanding, programme of covert support. The new administration, elected partly because of a public perception that Carter had been 'soft' in projecting American power abroad, then resituated the conflict in Afghanistan within a wider policy aimed at toppling communist regimes in the third world through the provision of assistance to domestic opposition. Between 1980 and 1984, Afghan rebels received US$50 million a year, a figure that rose sharply in 1985 when the controversial decision was made to give the Mujahideen much greater support to combat the Soviet presence in Afghanistan. The Reagan doctrine of 1985 clearly articulated the change in US foreign policy and signalled the growing willingness of the United States to interpret its own 'national interest' expansively:

> We must not break faith with those who are risking their lives . . . on every continent, from Afghanistan to Nicaragua . . . to defy Soviet aggression and secure rights which have been ours from birth. Support for freedom fighters is self-defense.
>
> (Reagan 1985)

After intense debate in Washington, the United States declared support for the rebels and commenced the transfer of high-tech, US-made anti-aircraft Stinger missiles to the Mujahideen in 1986. This was an important decision. In supplying US-manufactured arms, Washington was essentially declaring its *overt* involvement in the conflict.

The decision to deploy the Stinger missile was controversial in Washington, largely because it risked escalating the conflict in Afghanistan into an open superpower confrontation. A far superior weapon to those previously given to the Afghan resistance, the Stinger was seen as one of the few weapons capable of breaking Soviet aerial dominance (Walker 1993: 287). The decision to deploy these weapons was not taken lightly. Since the early 1980s, various US figures and Afghan rebel leaders had been agitating for more direct assistance, ideally in the form of the Stinger missile. Washington was initially reluctant to authorize deployment for a number of reasons. Pakistan had baulked at having US-made arms funnelled through its territory for fear it could draw a direct Soviet response, and the US administration was cautious of raising the tempo of the conflict with high-tech weaponry.[3] Furthermore, US military officials were concerned that the deployment of the Stinger missile would provide Soviet forces with the opportunity to capture the weapon and formulate effective counter-measures to it. Despite the massive scale of the CIA involvement in the Afghan conflict, that organization had few operatives on the ground, and would have to rely on the ISI to monitor the deployment of any technologically advanced US-made weapons. This too did not sit well with many in Washington. Thus, accountability, political considerations and operational control were major concerns. Opponents of the Stinger deployment were also concerned that intensification of US support for the Mujahideen would force the Soviets to retaliate by deploying their own high-grade weaponry in other volatile regions such as Central America.

However, changes in the Cold War balance of power, the situation on the ground in Afghanistan and the political climate in Washington increasingly worked to set the scene for a greater US role. At this point, the Cold War balance of power was in a state of flux. The succession to power of Mikhail Gorbachev signalled that a new era had arrived in the Soviet Union's internal politics. The new government's commitment to the costly conflict in Afghanistan was unknown, and the Stinger deployment can be interpreted as a way in which Washington decided to test Moscow's resolve. In addition, in 1985 the Soviet forces, although not raising their troop numbers, intensified their tactical campaign against the Mujahideen. These changes were compounded by the consolidation of the Republican administration's agenda in Washington, where lobbyists effectively stirred up public sentiment behind the Mujahideen cause.

In 1985 President Reagan issued National Security Decision Directive (NSDD) 166, titled *Expanded US Aid to Afghan Guerrillas*. Although this document is still classified, it is widely understood to be a Presidential Directive authorizing 'all means available' to assist the Mujahideen, a decision that transformed the US policy from assisting the rebels to actively seeking a decisive Soviet defeat. Some have argued that this intensified US involvement served only to lengthen the conflict, as the clear engagement of its superpower opponent prevented the Soviet Union from making a hasty, face-saving exit from what had become a stagnant military campaign. Although the impact of the Stinger missile on this crisis has been exaggerated by conservatives eager to link US action and the fall of communism (Kuperman 1999: 219), the evenutal US decision to supply the weapon did affect the balance of power in the air, which led to a shift in the military status quo and a turning of the tide with regard to the effectiveness of the rebel campaign. The financial commitment of the United States peaked in 1987 at US$670 million (Tanner 2002: 266–7). As Soviet losses mounted, troop morale declined and the political climate in

Moscow increasingly worked against the continuation of hostilities. The Soviet presence in Afghanistan had become untenable.

RESOLUTION OF THE AFGHAN CONFLICT

The Gorbachev era heralded significant changes in Soviet politics. Moscow increasingly viewed the continuation of the conflict in Afghanistan as an obstacle to the realization of its newly articulated domestic policies such as *perestroika*. The change in Soviet direction was underscored in February 1988 when the Politburo publicly announced its intention to withdraw troops from Afghanistan. This instance provides an interesting insight into the behaviour of a state in a time of war. It can be argued that internal forces, such as a leadership change, had a much greater role than military actions or the US decision to supply Stinger missiles in bringing this conflict to a close. As Richard Falk has pointed out, the withdrawal of troops was 'consistent with the overall thrust of Gorbachev's leadership . . . perestroika; reducing east–west tensions; and eliminating by unilateral initiative expensive and unsuccessful Soviet commitments overseas' (1989: 144).

As a result of international diplomacy, on 14 April 1988 the Geneva Accords were signed, formally bringing to a close the conflict in Afghanistan. Although the set withdrawal date for Soviet forces of 15 February 1989 was met, many observers criticized the Accords for failing to represent the interests of the Afghan people (Saikal and Maley 1991: 100–17). The Accords were essentially negotiated between Pakistan, as the major backer of the Mujahideen, and the Soviet-backed Afghan regime in Kabul. Popular representation was conspicuously absent.

On reflection, it can be seen that the Soviet Union misjudged the conflict in Afghanistan both in terms of military needs and, perhaps, in terms of the willingness of the United States to commit resources to the conflict and raise the stakes. Although parallels to the American experience in Vietnam have often been drawn, caution needs to be exercised when comparing the two conflicts. In both, the conventionally organized armies of the superpowers struggled to cope with the guerrilla warfare tactics of their opponents; however, the Afghan war was a much smaller affair. The Soviet Union remained within its initial limit of 120,000 troops, as opposed to the much larger American deployment of 500,000 in Vietnam. Although the Afghan conflict was deeply unpopular among the Soviet people,[4] a more repressive society and tighter governmental control of the media ensured that it did not engender the powerful social changes that the United States experienced during the anti-war movement of the 1970s. However, the power of Soviet public displeasure with the war should not be entirely discounted. As Maley points out, even in 'highly autocratic systems, significant public dissatisfaction can . . . constrain' the leadership's actions (2002: 53).

As well as exacting a political price in Moscow, the war in Afghanistan also tested the international institutions. As a result of the Soviet Union's place on the Security Council, the United Nations was largely hamstrung in relation to this conflict. The General Assembly did pass several resolutions condemning the conflict; for example, Resolution 37/37 in 1983 affirmed the sovereign nature of Afghanistan and called for the immediate withdrawal of all foreign troops (UN Resolution 37/37). The fact that resolutions passed in the General Assembly are non-binding, however, severely limits their effectiveness in constraining the actions of major powers. As seen in the case of Afghanistan, resolutions of this character, although an expression of the concern of the international community, have often failed to influence events on the ground.

The human cost of the Afghan war was immense. Although only approximate figures are available, the death toll and damage to Afghanistan's infrastructure was staggering. Death figures vary between 800,000 and 1.24 million – or 9 per cent of the total population (Saikal and Maley 1991: 135–6). In addition the World Health Organization states that 1.5 million Afghani people were left physically disabled by the conflict (cited in Maley 2002: 154). The Soviet cost was also significant. By March 1989 the Soviet Union had amassed 13,833 dead and 49,985 wounded.[5] The stability of the entire region was affected, as around 6 million refugees were driven into surrounding countries during the course of the war (Maley 2002: 154). The financial costs of this conflict, waged in a third world country, were also devastating, with estimates suggesting that US$50 billion in damage was inflicted upon Afghanistan, a figure that equalled one-third to one-half of the country's net worth. The long-term damage to infrastructure was clearly significant, with the majority of paved roads destroyed and over 1 million land mines laid throughout the country.

From Washington's perspective and that of the international community, the subsequent instability and repercussions of this conflict were also important. Following the Soviet withdrawal, the United States increasingly distanced itself from the factions it had armed and supported during the war. Indeed, although US funding peaked at around US$600 million per year, it dropped substantially after the Soviet withdrawal, and ceased completely by 1992 (P. W. Rodman, cited in Saikal 2004: 205). Once the Soviet threat decreased and the Islamized nature of the tribal factions became more evident, US planners realized that unquestioning support of the rebels as proxy ground forces against the Soviet troops had created its own problems. The lack of operational control by Washington over the flow of funds and arms, and the faith placed in Pakistan's ISI, also proved highly problematic. This was illuminated through post-war US concerns regarding the Stinger missiles deployed: a reported 300 of the 1,000 weapons supplied were unaccounted for at the close of the conflict

(Bradsher 1999: 226–7). It was assumed that the weapons were stockpiled in Pakistan, sold on the black market or remained in Afghanistan. By the early 1990s, the CIA was actively attempting to buy back the Stingers on the black market at inflated prices (Kushner 1998: 14).

Most damaging to the United States, the decision to foster international volunteers for the 'Afghan jihad' carried significant costs. Some of the so-called 'Arab Afghans' were funded by the CIA through the ISI; others operated with privately raised resources. Despite academic debates over the relationship between the CIA and Osama bin Laden in this period, what is clear is that the American willingness to fund resistance movements, with little or no oversight, created a cadre of professionally trained, combat-ready Islamists. These men, drawn from throughout the Muslim world, were indoctrinated with the vision of successful Mujahideen action against a superpower, and they became increasingly difficult for their Pakistani 'handlers' to contain. The Afghan experience encouraged individuals, such as Osama bin Laden, and Muslim states, such as Saudi Arabia, Kuwait and Pakistan, to use religious justifications for armed conflict. In this climate, the withdrawal of the Soviet Union became mythologized throughout the Muslim world as an 'Islamic' victory against a secular superpower. This interpretation lent further credence to militant Islamism as an active, energized doctrine through which Islamic political aspirations could be attained. The emergence of several organizations, notably al-Qaeda, provided coherence and structure to this loosely affiliated movement. As Olivier Roy correctly recognized in 1985, the Mujahideen in Afghanistan, although seen by most at the time as participants in an isolated battle for a country on the periphery of the international system, were in fact 'part of the movement of political revivalism which [was] sweeping through the Muslim world' (1990: 215).

BOX 5.1

Muhammad Omar, often referred to as Mullah Omar, emerged as a major political figure in post-Soviet Afghanistan. Omar fought against the Soviet Union during its occupation of Afghanistan. As the local communist rule fell in 1992, Omar established the Taliban, a group whose members were drawn predominantly from Islamic religious schools. Omar was declared the Emir of Afghanistan in April 1996 and served as the de facto head of state between 1996 and 2001. In 1997 he renamed the state the Islamic Emirate of Afghanistan. The reclusive leader had extremely limited contact with the outside world and much of the information related to his life is contested. It is believed that he remains alive and in hiding either in Afghanistan or Pakistan's North-West Frontier Province.

BOX 5.2

The **Pashtun** people are loosely defined by a shared ethno-linguistic heritage. The Pashtuns live in both Afghanistan and Pakistan, and their shared tribal identity acts as a challenge to the national structures of those countries. Pashtuns are predominantly, but not exclusively, Sunni Muslims, and are also bound together by a pre-Islamic cultural code. Many Pashtuns fought against the Red Army during the Soviet occupation of Afghanistan, and the group constituted the backbone of the Taliban.

CONCLUSION

The *jihadi* mindset, propagated through training centres throughout the region, began to spread and gain credibility faster than the United States had foreseen. The Afghan war therefore produced a generation of men convinced that united military action, by Muslims of various ethnicities and nationalities, could defeat Western military-political power. Returning to their home states, many ex-fighters turned their attention to the ruling regimes there, which they viewed as corrupt. Scattered throughout the Muslim world, with their own agendas based on this experience, many veterans of the Afghan war became prominent proponents of Islamist revolution and conflict. The Algerian civil war and the radicalization of the Islamic political opposition in Egypt in the 1990s can both be identified as unforeseen repercussions of this conflict. In this way, the war in Afghanistan contributed to the continued internationalization of militant Islamism.

As a result of its involvement in Afghanistan, the United States inadvertently assisted in the creation of a network of highly trained militants. The dynamics of the conflict made legends of those who had fought with distinction against the Soviets – Mullah Omar and Osama bin Laden being obvious examples. Within Afghanistan the withdrawal of Soviet forces did not signal a return to stability. Pre-existing tribal loyalties remained influential and post-war Afghanistan emerged as a fractious entity, wracked by warlord-based divisions. The ensuing civil war was exacerbated by factional support provided by outside actors, including Pakistan, Saudi Arabia and Iran (Esposito 2001: 13). Further adding to the suffering of the people of Afghanistan, the Taliban emerged in the early 1990s. Drawn largely from the religious schools and orphanages serving Afghan refugees in Pakistan, the Taliban was supported by Saudi Arabia and Pakistan. The Taliban advocated a return to 'pure Islam', a doctrine understood as functioning in opposition to the fighting and factional

BOX 5.3

The **Taliban** (from 'talib', meaning student) was initially a youth party established in the Islamic religious schools of Pakistan and Afghanistan. At the outset it received support from the many Afghans who were disillusioned with the incessant fighting among warlords that characterized the post-Soviet period. However, the predominantly Pashtun organization adhered to a strict, literalistic version of Islamic law. After taking power in 1996, the Taliban applied an extremely repressive social code. The regime also provided sanctuary to Osama bin Laden, raising the ire of the international community. Only three states – Pakistan, Saudi Arabia and the United Arab Emirates – recognized the Taliban's rule of Afghanistan. Inside the country the Taliban was opposed by the Northern Alliance, which relied on Tajik and Uzbek communities. After September 11, 2001, the United States, along with the Northern Alliance, overthrew the Taliban government. However, by relying on cross-border loyalties and tribal alliances, many of the Taliban fighters were able to disperse and regroup, and the international forces in Afghanistan are still engaged in sporadic conflict with reconstituted Taliban forces.

conflict that characterized the early post-war period. Exploiting the lack of social cohesion and the experience of decades of conflict, the group quickly gained strength, and eventually seized power in this devastated country.

To many regional observers, the Taliban was a product of the betrayal of the US government in the post-war period. As the Taliban became more repressive, the United States increasingly condemned its vision for Afghanistan. The irony of this situation was not lost on the Muslim world: in the 1980s, because of an apparent convergence of agendas and the strength of the Cold War mindset, similar groups had been represented by Washington as heroic 'freedom fighters'.

NOTES

1 The Soviet foreign policy stance known as the Brezhnev doctrine was articulated by Leonid Brezhnev at a meeting of the Polish United Workers Party on 13 November 1968. It was the culmination of a series of policy statements made by Soviet officials to justify the Red Army's interventions in satellite states such as Czechoslovakia and Hungary. For a full exploration of the impact of this policy stance, see Ouimet (2003).
2 From 'Memo to President Jimmy Carter on Soviet Intervention in Afghanistan (26 December 1979)', cited in Brzezinski (2002), pp. 108–10.

3 For a detailed analysis of the Stinger missile controversy, see Kuperman (1999: 219–64).
4 For the results of a range of public opinion polls that show the mass dissatisfaction with this conflict, see Maley (2002: 53–4).
5 Figures vary, and other sources place the Soviet death toll much higher. These statistics correlate with the official Soviet numbers and are taken from Saikal (2004: 199).

REFERENCES

Bradsher, Henry (1999) *Afghan Communism and Soviet Intervention* (Oxford: Oxford University Press).

Brzezinski, Zbigniew (2002) 'Reflections on Soviet Intervention in Afghanistan, December 26, 1979', in Barry Rubin and Judith Colp Rubin (eds.), *Anti-American Terrorism and the Middle East* (London: Oxford University Press).

Carter, Jimmy (1980) 'State of the Union Address 1980', 23 January, available at www.jimmycarterlibrary.org/documents/speeches/su80jec.phtml.

Collins, Joseph (1986) *The Soviet Invasion of Afghanistan – A Study of the Use of Force in Soviet Foreign Policy* (Washington DC: Lexington Books).

Dorronsoro, Gilles (2000) *Revolution Unending – Afghanistan: 1979 to the Present*, trans. by John King (London: Hurst & Company).

Dupree, Louis (1988) 'Cultural Changes among the Mujahidin and Muhajerin', in Bo Huldt and Erland Janson (eds), *Afghanistan – The Social, Cultural and Political Impact of the Soviet Invasion* (London: Croom Helm).

Esposito, John (2001) *Unholy War: Terror in the Name of Islam* (Oxford: Oxford University Press).

Falk, Richard (1989) 'The Afghanistan "Settlement" and the Future of World Politics', in Amin Saikal and William Maley (eds), *The Soviet Withdrawal from Afghanistan*, (Cambridge: Cambridge University Press).

Galeotti, Mark (1995) *Afghanistan – The Soviet Union's Last War* (London: Frank Cass).

Hilali, A.Z. (2005) *US–Pakistan Relationship: Soviet Invasion of Afghanistan* (London: Ashgate).

Kuperman, Alan (1999) 'The Stinger Missile and US intervention in Afghanistan', *Political Science Quarterly*, Vol. 114, No. 2, pp. 219–63.

Kushner, Harvey W. (1998) *The Future of Terrorism: Violence in the New Millennium* (London: Sage).

Maley, William (1988) 'Interpreting the Taliban', in William Maley (ed.), *Fundamentalism Reborn? Afghanistan and the Taliban* (London: Hurst & Company).

Maley, William (2002) *The Afghanistan Wars* (New York: Palgrave Macmillan).

Matthias, Willard C. (2001) *America's Strategic Blunders: Intelligence Analysis and National Security Policy, 1936–1991* (University Park: Pennsylvania State University Press).

Ouimet, Matthew (2003) *The Rise and Fall of the Brezhnev Doctrine in Soviet Foreign Policy* (Chapel Hill: University of North Carolina Press).

Reagan, Ronald (1985) 'State of the Union Address', 6 February, available at www.presidency.ucsb.edu/ws/print.php?pid=38069.

Roy, Arundhati (1987) *The Soviet Intervention in Afghanistan – Causes, Consequences and India's Response* (New Delhi: Associated Publishing House).

Roy, Olivier (1990) *Islam and Resistance in Afghanistan* (Cambridge: Cambridge University Press).

Saikal, Amin (2004) *Modern Afghanistan: A History of Struggle and Survival* (London: IB Tauris).

Saikal, Amin and Maley, William (1991) *Regime Change in Afghanistan – Foreign Intervention and the Politics of Legitimacy* (Sydney: Crawford House).

Tanner, Stephen (2002) *Afghanistan: A Military History from Alexander the Great to the Fall of the Taliban* (Cambridge: DaCapo).

United Nations General Assembly (1983) 'The Situation in Afghanistan and Its Implications for International Peace and Security', UN Resolution 37/37, 29 November, available at www.un.org/documents/ga/res/37/a37r037.htm.

Walker, Martin (1993) *The Cold War and the Making of the Modern World* (London: Fourth Estate).

SUGGESTED FURTHER READING

Dupree, Louis (1973) *Afghanistan* (Princeton, NJ: Princeton University Press).

Emadi, Hafizullah (1990) *State, Revolution, and Superpowers in Afghanistan* (New York: Praeger).

Hyman, Anthony (1982) *Afghanistan under Soviet Domination, 1964–81* (London: Macmillan).

Male, Beverley (1982) *Afghanistan: A Reappraisal* (London: Croom Helm).

Marsden, Peter (2002) *The Taliban: War and Religion in Afghanistan* (London: Zed Books).

Matinuddin, Kamal (1999) *The Taliban Phenomenon: Afghanistan 1994–1997* (Karachi: Oxford University Press).

Nojumi, Neamatollah (2002) *The Rise of the Taliban in Afghanistan: Mass Mobilisation in Afghanistan* (New York: Palgrave).

Rashid, Ahmed (2001) *Taliban: The Story of the Afghan Warlords: Including a New Foreword following the September 11 Terrorist Attacks of 2001* (London: Pan).

SUGGESTED STUDY QUESTIONS

1 What was the nature and impact of US involvement in Afghanistan during the era of Soviet occupation?

2 What has been the impact of US support for the Mujahideen during the Soviet invasion of Afghanistan?

3 How was the conflict in Afghanistan indicative of the tensions of the Cold War?

4 What were the major outcomes of the US involvement in Afghanistan?

5 What role has the Afghan war played for stability in the Middle East?

CHAPTER 6

Wars in the Persian Gulf

INTRODUCTION

The Persian Gulf emerged as one of the major battlefields of the late twentieth century. The Gulf's strategic and economic significance was demonstrated as the region was consumed by conflict between local forces in the 1980s and then by global forces in 1991. The international dimension of conflict in the Persian Gulf reveals much about the accession of the United States to the position of sole superpower and its subsequent ability to project hegemonic power in the sphere of international relations. In this chapter, two conflicts will be explored: the Iran–Iraq War and the US-led Operation Desert Storm. These conflicts are explored together as they are intricately linked. Throughout the 1980s and 1990s, the United States played a central role in the arming, advising and finally fighting that consumed the Persian Gulf. The United States, freed from the counter-balancing effect of the bipolar system, pursued an increasingly interventionist regional agenda that was aimed at securing both influence and resources. As a result, Middle Eastern perceptions of the superpower and its intentions in the region were adversely affected.

The Iran–Iraq War of 1980–88 was the longest-running conventional war of the twentieth century. Death toll estimates for this conflict range from 850,000 to 1 million people. Despite this, for most of the war the international community appeared largely ambivalent towards the continued carnage. This altered in 1987 when the United States was drawn into the conflict against Iran. As well as the appalling loss of life, this conflict included the use of chemical weapons against civilians. This war provided the backdrop to some of the most questionable US foreign policy decisions of the late twentieth century. Initially a localized conflict between two neighbouring states, by the late 1980s, the Iran–Iraq War had regional and, as a result of the oil market, international ramifications. The conflict commenced with the Iraqi decision to invade its neighbour, the newly established Islamic Republic of Iran. Exploring this decision by the Iraqi regime, led by Saddam Hussein, is crucial to understanding the regional power plays that characterized this period.

HISTORICAL BACKGROUND

The political relationship between Iran and Iraq ebbed and flowed throughout the twentieth century. Issues of contention revolved around border demarcation, access to waterways and ethnic tensions. Iran and Iraq are both major Middle Eastern states in terms of political influence, resources, population and size. Historically, Iran and Iraq have both played a leading role in the development of the region and maintained close relations with external powers, particularly the United Kingdom and the United States. The outbreak of inter-state conflict between these two states in the 1980s was a result of a specific set of historical and political tensions that were brought to the fore by the catalyst of the Islamic Revolution in Iran.

The state of Iraq was established in 1921 and gained formal independence from British Mandate rule in October 1932. It was the first Arab state to emerge from colonial domination.[1] However, formal independence did not mean that Iraq was free of external influence and interference. Tensions with the United Kingdom over Iraq's apparently pro-Axis orientation during the Second World War peaked with the brief flare-up known as the Anglo–Iraqi War of 1941, in which British forces quickly subdued the Iraqi rebellion (Davis 2005: 70). As a result of this brief conflict, Iraq remained under direct British occupation until the close of the world war. The Hashemite royal family took power in Iraq in 1945 with the explicit approval of the British Crown. Under the British-backed Hashemites, Iraq remained closely aligned with the United Kingdom. This was most evident in the signing of the Baghdad Pact in 1955.

The Baghdad Pact tied Iraq, Pakistan, Turkey and Iran to the United Kingdom in a mutual defence and economic cooperation treaty. This was clearly an anti-Soviet grouping. However, this external security treaty could not mask the highly fractious and tense nature of Iraqi politics. Iraqi society was deeply fractured along sectarian and ethnic lines. These fault-lines continue to haunt Iraq today. Since the 1930s, various sectarian and ethnic groups had challenged the authority of Baghdad, usually seeking greater representation or autonomy. This is a direct outcome of Iraq's geo-social structure, in which Sunni, Shia and Kurdish communities live in different regions of the state. During the twentieth century, the inter-sectarian tensions inside Iraq were often muted by the actions of repressive and authoritarian state leaders. In the post-2003 period, the relationship between Iraq's Sunni and Shia communities has degenerated into a state of open conflict, as explored in Chapter 8. The catalyst for this disintegration was a combustive mix of factors related to external occupation, geo-politics and the dynamics of Iraq's political system. Yet, historically, the most restive population in Iraq has been the Kurds.

Iraq's Kurdish community constitutes approximately 20 per cent of the state's total population and has traditionally been centred in the oil-rich north. Kurdish agitation for autonomous rule has long been a feature of Iraq's history. Indeed, Sa'ad Jawad notes that, aided by British and Turkish meddling, Iraqi Kurds 'were in almost continuous revolt between 1919 and 1947' (1982: 47). In 1920, the post-war Treaty of Sèvres promised the Kurdish people independence in the region of the defunct Ottoman Empire known as Kurdistan. Despite this promise, the regional powers of Iran, Turkey and Iraq absorbed the lands of Kurdistan, repressing the Kurdish nationalist endeavour with varying degrees of brutality. This proved to be an ongoing source of tension, and the denial of Kurdish aspirations for self-determination has been a feature of Iraq's political history since the colonial period.

In the late 1950s, political turmoil in Iraq intensified, and by 1958 it was evident that the ruling regime in Baghdad was failing. Cleveland reports that corruption and economic mismanagement characterized Iraq's situation, with less than 1 per cent of the population in control of over 55 per cent of all private land (2000: 318). In July 1958 a violent coup, led by Brigadier General Abd al-Karim Qasim, resulted in the deaths of the royal family and the establishment of a new political order in Iraq. Qasim attempted to chart a new course for Iraq and withdrew from the

BOX 6.1

The **Kurds** are an ethnic group who traditionally occupy a tract of land that encompasses parts of Turkey, Iraq, Syria and Iran. Estimates place the Kurdish population at somewhere between 27 million and 35 million, making the Kurdish people a very significant ethnic group in Middle Eastern politics. The Kurds have been embroiled in various inter-state and intra-state conflicts in the twentieth and the twenty-first centuries, especially in Turkey and Iraq, as the established state structures have resisted moves towards Kurdish independence or autonomy.

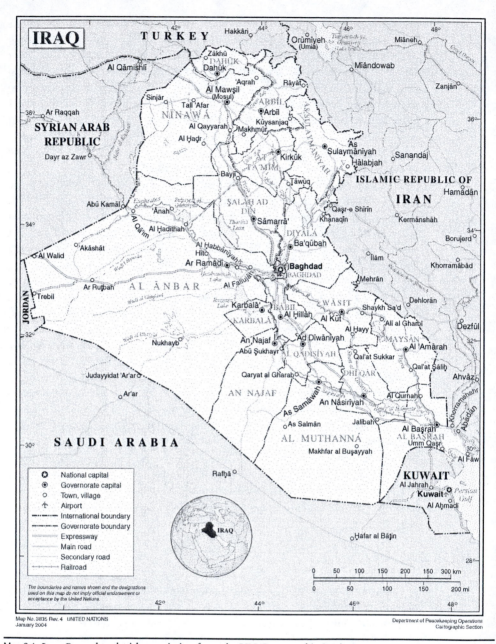

Map 6.1 Iraq. Reproduced with permission from the UN Cartographic Section.

Baghdad Pact, subsequently tilting the state towards the Soviet Union. This heralded a period of significant unrest in Iraq marked by a series of coups and counter-coups, during which time the secular-nationalist Ba'th

Party attained and then lost power. In 1968, a final coup brought the Ba'thists to power once again.

The Ba'th Party had been established in 1947 as a transnational movement for Arab renewal. In 1966 it split into two major wings: the Syrian and Iraqi branches. Its major focus was Arab nationalism, emphasizing the unifying factors of shared history, culture and language. The party's doctrine was also informed by socialism, anti-imperialism and militarism (Rezun 1992: 5). Ba'thism has proved a potent force in Arab politics, especially when utilized by state leaders. However, throughout the late twentieth century, the movement also suffered from internal divisions and infighting (Ajami 1992: 48–60). The Ba'th Party, similar to other strands in Arab politics, radicalized as a result of the Arab defeat in the war of 1967 (Baram 1991: 18). Throughout the region, Israel's victory was interpreted as proof of the failings of existing Arab governments. In Iraq, the Ba'th Party took advantage of this mood and public disenchantment with the ruling regime to rationalize the coup and consolidate its own position in power.

As the Iraqi Ba'th Party strengthened its control of the state, power became centralized in the hands of an ambitious leader, Saddam Hussein. By 1979 Saddam had taken over the party, and in the following years he emerged as a ruthless and determined dictator. An instance of the interplay between secular nationalism and Islamic politics in the Middle East can be observed by an investigation of Saddam's political career. Despite his clear secular-nationalist orientation, Saddam did seek Islamic legitimacy when it was politically expedient. Indeed, Saddam rewrote his own family tree

BOX 6.2

Saddam Hussein was the President of Iraq from 1979 to 2003, when he was ousted from power by the US-led coalition forces. Born in 1937 and raised a Sunni, he rose through the ranks of power to become the leader of the secular Ba'th Party in 1979. He quickly consolidated his repressive control over the government and military. From 1980 to 1988, Saddam led Iraq in a war against the Islamic Republic of Iran. In 1990, he ordered the Iraqi military to invade Kuwait. For more than a decade following the Gulf War, the United States, through the United Nations, imposed crippling sanctions on Iraq and kept the state militarily contained. However, after the September 11, 2001, terrorist attacks and the transformation in US foreign policy that resulted, George W. Bush led an international coalition to war against Iraq, without UN Security Council approval. On 14 December 2003, Saddam was captured. He was later tried for war crimes, including the massacre of Iraqi Shias and Kurds. On 5 November 2006 he was found guilty, and on 30 December 2006, Saddam Hussein was hanged.

in order to link his lineage to the family of the Prophet in an attempt to provide his regime with Islamic credence (Rezun 1992: 20). As is the case with numerous twentieth-century Arab politicians, Saddam's personal history is sketchy and contested.

Saddam Hussein was born in a poor rural region near the Sunni-dominated town of Tikrit in 1937. He became active in politics at an early age and was involved in a assassination attempt against Iraq's military leader Qasim in 1959. Saddam fled to Egypt in the aftermath of the failed assassination and returned to Baghdad in 1963 when the Ba'th Party first took power. The Ba'thists were overthrown in 1964 and Saddam was imprisoned until 1968. This period of incarceration served to sharpen his ideological orientation. Saddam Hussein's rise to power and repressive rule is best understood in the context of the fractious ethnic composition of the state of Iraq. As Ephraim Karsh and Inari Ratusi assert, Saddam did 'not set the rules of the game in [the] cruel system' of Iraqi politics, but he has 'been its most savage and able player' (Karsh and Ratusi 1991: 4). Saddam's rule over Iraq was highly autocratic and characterized by the persecution of the Shia majority and of the Kurds, and by the suppression of all political opposition.

Saddam led his state into three major wars: the 1980s Iran–Iraq War, the 1991 Gulf War and the 2003 US-led invasion. Until his death in late 2006 he remained an important and divisive figure in Arab politics. After his consolidation of power in the late 1970s, Saddam faced a nervous Arab world. The ramifications of Iran's revolution were still unclear and the small Arab kingdoms of the Persian Gulf felt vulnerable to Shia revolution. Iraq was thus able to assume a leading role as the Gulf's physical and ideological buffer against Tehran. Iran and Iraq, by virtue of geography, political orientation and size, are two of the region's major power-brokers. Therefore, the relationship between these two states has been vital to the broader stability of the region. The political tensions that led to modern Iraq's first major war have their roots in disputes over waterways, resources and territory.

IRAN–IRAQ TENSION

On 6 March 1975 Iran and Iraq negotiated a settlement called the Algiers Agreement. This agreement was aimed at resolving two long-standing points of tension between the states: the right of access to the Shatt al-Arab waterway and Iranian support of Iraqi Kurdish opposition to Baghdad. Under the terms of the agreement, Iraq, in order to elicit a promise that Iran would discontinue support for the restive Kurds, agreed to a border on the thalweg (deep-water line) of the Shatt al-Arab waterway. This provision accepted Iran's demand for shared use of this vital passage. As Karsh points out, considering Iraq's long-standing claim of sovereignty over the waterway, such a concession, made by Baghdad to ensure both internal and frontier stability, was extensive (Karsh 2002: 8). Largely unsatisfactory to the Iraqi regime, the Algiers Agreement clearly revealed the regime's need to restrict external support to the Kurds. Although it was an unpopular settlement, the agreement was reflective of the relationship between the Shah's Iran and Ba'thist Iraq – tense but functioning, especially on issues of security.

This careful cooperation changed with the establishment of the Islamic Republic in 1979. Initially, Iraq was cautiously welcoming of the new government in Tehran. However, the newly empowered Ayatollah Khomeini soon emerged as a vocal critic of Baghdad. Khomeini had spent part of his exile in Najaf, Iraq, where he had witnessed repression of the Shia at the hands of Iraqi's dominant Sunni minority and the Ba'th Party. As Khomeini consolidated his power in Iran, he began to turn his attention to the question of how best to 'export the revolution'.

Khomeini's increasing stranglehold on power was mirrored in Iraq. On 16 July 1979, Saddam Hussein became President of Iraq and quickly turned the state into a dictatorship. This move merely formalized his role as the ultimate decision-maker in Iraqi politics, a position he had actually held since the mid-1970s (Tripp 2000: 215). The interplay of these two personalities had a significant impact on the evolution of the conflict between the neighbouring states. Hoping to capitalize on the change in Iran's leadership, Iraqi Kurdish factions approached the Iranians for support. Khomeini intensified his rhetoric on the need for Shia revolution throughout the Gulf region. He singled out Iraq's Ba'th regime as corrupt, called for its overthrow, signalled his rejection of the pre-existing Iran–Iraq relationship and violated the terms of the 1975 Algiers Agreement by recommencing assistance to restive Kurdish factions inside Iraq (Musallam 1996: 81). In response, the regime in Baghdad moved against Iraq's Shia community. The arrest of the prominent Shia leader Muhammad al-Sadr by Ba'thist forces added to the increasing sense of sectarian destabilization inside Iraq. Tensions between Iraq and Iran continued to escalate as both leaderships used ethnic, religious and sectarian differences to solidify their bases of support. By October 1979, violent resistance to Saddam had become a popular idea among significant proportions of Iraq's Shia majority. This constituted a dangerous moment for Saddam Hussein's regime and the Ba'th Party.

The increasingly tense state of affairs was being watched with interest in Washington. The United States was still reeling from the unexpected shock of the Islamic Revolution in Iran. As indicated by the Carter doctrine of 1980, Washington was committed to the maintenance of the status quo in the oil-rich Gulf region. Moreover, the United States was seeking a way to contain the new regional wildcard of Iran and lessen the appeal of its revolutionary rhetoric. Considering this, the increasing paranoia in Baghdad was not an unwelcome development. Saddam's regime began to publicly agitate for 'Arab' unity, a clear signal that Baghdad was expecting a conflict with the Persian state. Although issues of religious and ethnic difference played little part in the actual decision to engage in conflict, they provided a strong propaganda tool for the Iraqi regime. Focusing on the Persian and Shia character of Iran, Baghdad portrayed its neighbour as a threat to the entire Gulf region and positioned itself as the willing champion of vulnerable Arab regimes.

Saddam Hussein's perception of his domestic position may have played a key role in his decision to go to war. Since the establishment of Iraq, and especially since the accession to power of the predominantly Sunni Ba'th Party, members of Iraq's Shia community had seen themselves as a repressed majority. The Shia now appeared to pose a significant challenge to the Baghdad regime, which was composed in accordance with Saddam Hussein's own Sunni tribal alliances. F. Gregory Gause suggests that Saddam's perception of Iran's determination to destabilize his regime *from within* was the trigger for this conflict (2002: 47–70).

Despite a history of poor relations with the United States, largely as a result of Iraq's condemnation of Israel, Saddam Hussein initially sought to protect his leadership with a move towards Washington. He increasingly positioned himself as a potential US ally in the region, condemning the Soviet invasion of Afghanistan and focusing on the ability of his secular nationalist state to act as a buffer between Iran and the Gulf. This balancing act between solidifying his control of Iraq's internal political situation and containing neighbourhood tensions was difficult. For example, Baghdad's decision in mid-April to execute the influential Shia cleric Muhammad al-Sadr and expel thousands of Shia Muslims may have entrenched Saddam Hussein's hold on power inside Iraq, but it further inflamed public opinion in Iran. In turn, Saddam became convinced the Islamic Republic was whipping up dissent inside Iraq. Baghdad may have believed that Iran, still recovering from the chaos of the Revolution, would be unable to withstand an attack at this juncture. On 22 September 1980 Saddam evidently decided to bring the simmering tensions to a boil and launched an attack on Iran.

The Iraqi assessment of Iran's military weakness in the wake of the Islamic Revolution proved grossly miscalculated. The Iranian population mobilized to repel the invading army. The imagery of the Revolution was utilized by the regime in Tehran to give the conflict strong religious and nationalist overtones. Despite early Iraqi gains, by 1982 the war had transformed into an entrenched war of attrition. At this point, with Iranian territory free of Iraqi soldiers, Tehran could have declared a limited victory. However, each leadership appeared committed to the destruction of the other. The war continued for eight years – making it the longest conventional war of the twentieth century. Reflecting on conflicts, Samir al-Khalil has suggested that the 'absence of military strategy, when shared by both sides, leads to gruelling slogging matches in which nothing is more expendable than human life' (1989: 281). This description seems apt.

As the conflict continued, the fusion of Shia-inspired traditions of martyrdom with a fervent sense of Iranian nationalism created a military culture of self-assured superiority that proved difficult for the Iraqi forces to counter. This disadvantage on the battlefield, added to the smaller size and capacity of Iraq, in turn intensified Baghdad's need for regional assistance. Although the fighting remained contained, Arab concerns about Iranian expansionism triggered a political regionalization of this conflict. The major parties involved were the exposed Gulf states, and their response to the conflict was initially guarded but ultimately governed by geo-strategic considerations. Despite worries about the nature and regional intentions of Saddam Hussein's own regime, most Arab states decided that the containment of Iran was the overriding concern (Rezun 1992: 31). Saudi Arabia, geographically and doctrinally the state with the most to fear from Iranian expansion, strongly supported Iraq, allowing the use of its air bases and ports and providing billions of dollars in funding (Abir 1993: 125–44).

The willingness of external actors to provide the financial and military resources by which the conflict could be continued had disastrous effects. A conflict on this scale was devastating to the societies of both Iraq and Iran, with 1.3 million men placed on active duty; this number constituted one-half of Iraqi and one-sixth of Iranian men of military age. The Iran–Iraq War was also marked by the use of chemical weapons. In addition to using cyanide gas against Iranian troops on the front line, Baghdad wielded this deadly weapon against Iraqis. As described previously, the Kurdish population had been systemically suppressed by the regime in Baghdad. The Kurds' separatist aspirations made them a target for a regime looking to consolidate its stranglehold on power. The Anfal campaign of 1987–88, a program of systematic violence against Iraqi Kurds, has been described by some as a strategy of ethnic cleansing. The most infamous incident took place in February 1988 in the Kurdish village of Halabjah, where up to 5,000 civilians died as a result of the use of poison gas. Despite the negative international response, Baghdad continued its offensive against its own Kurdish citizens, accusing the Kurds of treason by acting as a 'fifth column' in support of the Iranian army.

Alongside the targeting of factions seen as disloyal to Baghdad, the broader civilian and military toll of the conflict mounted as both sides proved unwilling to compromise. Attempts at resolution failed as both states demonstrated their intransigence. Iran insisted on Iraqi admission of guilt, the removal of Saddam and war reparations as preconditions to peace negotiations. These unrealistic demands effectively demonstrated

Tehran's determination to perpetuate the conflict. Iraq, also trapped in the war, attempted to force the enemy to the negotiating table by inflicting massive civilian casualties. As the smaller nation, Iraq traded on its geographical position to garner regional support, focusing on the notion of Iraq as a physical buffer for the Gulf states. This tactic was successful and Iraq was loaned billons of dollars. By the close of the conflict Iraq's war debts topped US$80 billion, at least half of which was owed to the Gulf states (Freedman and Karsh 1993: 39). As we shall see, Iraq's inability to repay these loans led directly to the Iraqi decision to invade Kuwait in August 1990.

The United Nations and the international community, although issuing strong calls for an end to the conflict, appeared largely unable to influence events. This was despite the protracted nature of the conflict and international awareness of the use of weapons of mass destruction, namely chemical weapons. The lack of concerted international effort can perhaps be ascribed to the fact that the impact of the war was contained within the region. Despite differences in size and resources, external assistance made Iran and Iraq well-matched adversaries, and neither state was able to gain a decisive advantage. This situation, although costly in terms of human life, basically ensured that the conflict did not spread and entangle other states in the region. The international community was, however, concerned with trade routes in the Persian Gulf, particularly with regard to oil shipment, so an Iranian decision in 1987 to threaten the flow of oil through the Gulf put US interests at risk. This threat signalled that the conflict was about to spill over, and would affect not only the region but potentially the global economy. The international community, fearful of the repercussions, thus stepped up the pressure for peace. The danger of direct superpower involvement in particular triggered an immediate response by the United Nations; the Security Council issued Resolution 598 in 1987, calling for an immediate cease-fire, and in August 1988 Iran and Iraq agreed to one. Spanning a significant decade in the Cold War, the Iran–Iraq War proved particularly susceptible to the influences of the two superpowers.

THE SUPERPOWERS' INVOLVEMENT

Washington's response to the Iraqi invasion of Iran in 1980 was affected by numerous factors. American public and political opinion on the Iranian Revolution was overtly negative, and the impact of the continuing hostage crisis in Tehran should not be underestimated. The inability of the Carter administration to secure the release of US hostages was seen as a humiliation to the United States in the global arena, and this strongly influenced Washington's perspective on US alliances in the Gulf. Moreover, Washington was concerned about the relationships between

Iran and regional groups such as the Hezbollah in Lebanon. These factors combined to persuade the US decision-makers that supporting Iraq was the best available means for containing Iran.

The Soviet Union also faced a series of choices about how to respond to the war between Iran and Iraq, and its decision-making process was influenced by numerous, often conflicting, considerations. In the 1960s and 1970s, Iraq's anti-Israel – and thus by extension anti-US – rhetoric had positioned it as a natural Soviet ally. Therefore, by 1980, Moscow had an entrenched commitment to Iraq's territorial unity and stability. However, as was evident in Soviet decisions with regard to Afghanistan, Moscow was keenly aware of the ramifications of the Iranian Revolution. The removal of the pro-US Shah in Iran suggested to Moscow that a new alliance could be formed with Tehran, a development that would guarantee Washington's displeasure. Yet simultaneously Moscow was concerned that a decisive Iranian victory over Iraq would only increase the prestige of political Islam and potentially destabilize the southern areas of the Soviet Union. With these geo-political realities in mind, Moscow elected to sustain Iraq. However, the increasingly close relationship between Baghdad and Washington gave the Soviet Union reason to pause. This convoluted web of strategic considerations led to the Soviet decision to arm both sides in the conflict. Moscow's involvement and interest in the war between Iraq and Iran, meanwhile, was limited by its heavy engagement in Afghanistan in this period. By the close of the Iran–Iraq War in 1988, the Soviet Union, strongly committed to the new economic policies of *perestroika* and *glasnost*, was a declining influence in regional affairs.

The US strategy in the region was even more convoluted and, ultimately, more problematic. Prior to the outbreak of hostilities in 1980, the United States had had a tense and unfriendly relationship with Ba'thist Iraq. Baghdad's condemnation of Israel played a major role in Washington's negative view of the state, and Iraq had broken all official diplomatic ties with the United States in the aftermath of the 1967 Arab defeat. However, the shock of the Islamic Revolution in Iran, the potential for Shia destabilization of the Gulf and the ongoing political humiliation of the hostage crisis critically influenced Washington's regional policy. One manifestation of the change in US policy was its increasing support for Iraq. Publicly, Washington adhered to a policy of neutrality, but it increasingly supplied Baghdad with weapons and information (Pauly 2005: 29). The United States pursued two interlinked objectives: checking Soviet influence and, as an increasing focus, preventing an Iranian victory in the Gulf. In the first years of conflict, there was little spillover from this conflict, so the United States saw no need to intervene directly. As the war began to favour Iran, the Reagan administration grew concerned that Iraq might collapse, leaving Iran in a position of unrivalled regional power. Seen in this way, the entry of the United States into this conflict was both an active choice and a result of the evolution of the war itself.

The dilemma for US policy began to deepen in 1983 when Iraq threatened to intensify its attacks on Iranian oil facilities and shipping. Iran responded by threatening to close the Gulf altogether. The introduction of oil as a tactical weapon triggered a more active superpower involvement. Washington slowly cultivated its relationship with Baghdad. Donald Rumsfeld, a private citizen and confidant of the Reagan administration at the time, visited Baghdad in order to smooth out the Iraq–US relationship. As a confidence-building gesture, Baghdad toned down its anti-Israeli stance and condemned terrorism. By 1984, Iraq and the United States had resumed full diplomatic contacts, and a steady flow of military hardware, information and intelligence had begun (Rezun 1992: 39). As mentioned, during this period embattled Iraq was also receiving support from the Soviet Union. The continuation of the conflict, or at least Iraq's continued willingness to fight the war, can in part be attributed to the support it received from the two superpowers.

The emerging Iraq–US relationship was not without its hiccups. A public relations disaster for the Reagan administration occurred in the mid-1980s: the Iran–Contra scandal, which greatly affected the regional perception of the United States. Although the United States was seemingly committed to an Iraqi victory in the Gulf, it began to sell arms to Iran. This decision appears to have been taken by rogue elements within the White House and the National Security Council without the authorization of the US Congress. (Much of the documentation relating to this foreign policy escapade was destroyed or remains classified.[2]) The intricacies of the US political system, and the failure of that system's checks and balances, were largely lost on a Middle Eastern audience increasingly aware that the United States was arming two regional states in a costly war of growing brutality.

The apparent rationale behind the sale of arms to Iran was based on

BOX 6.3

Donald Rumsfeld (born 1932) has played a major role in the formulation and implementation of US foreign policy in the second half of the twentieth century. In 1975 to 1977, Rumsfeld served as Gerald Ford's Secretary of Defense. In the 1980s, Rumsfeld was a confidant of the first Bush administration and served as Special Envoy to the Middle East from November 1983 to May 1984. In this period, Rumsfeld had extensive dealing with Saddam Hussein's regime. From 2001 to 2006 Rumsfeld again served as the Secretary of Defense, this time under George W. Bush. Rumsfeld was publicly seen as a major architect of the 'war on terror', a perspective that eventually led to his departure from public political life.

two types of exchange: arms for money and arms for influence. Just as this incident in US foreign policy involved several geographic regions, it had significant repercussions for the perception of the United States and President Reagan around the globe. Following the socialist-orientated Sandinista revolution in Nicaragua in 1979, which ended the pro-US rule of the Somoza dynasty, Washington commenced an extensive programme to arm and train an opposition movement. The Contras were funded by the Reagan administration to launch a coup against the revolutionary government. But this overt intervention in the internal affairs of another state was deemed illegal by the US Congress when it passed the 1984 Boland Amendment, legislation aimed at preventing US assistance to the Contras. Details of what followed remains shrouded in mystery, but it is clear that certain members the US administration would not abandon their client in Nicaragua. Public records of the period suggest that these 'rogue elements' saw arms sales to Iran as a covert way to raise the funds necessary for supporting the Contras. This was a clear contravention of US law. The Iran–Contra affair proved to be a major embarrassment for the United States, further damaging its standing in Central America and the Middle East.

The arms sales to Iran were not simply a fund-raising exercise. They were also aimed at exploring a covert way in which to win influence in Iran and Lebanon. In the 1980s, the Shia-orientated Hezbollah militia in Lebanon was taking increasingly bold steps against US troops stationed in Lebanon as part of an international peace-keeping force. Hostage-taking in Lebanon was on the rise and Washington had no effective channels of communication with the militia organization. However, Hezbollah was effectively backed by Iran and this offered a window of opportunity to the United States. The Iranian regime needed arms. Sunk in the costly and drawn-out battle with Iraq, it required military hardware to continue the conflict. As the bulk of Iran's military equipment had been US-supplied during the Shah's reign, a supply of American-made spare parts was critical. Under this rogue policy, government elements provided limited shipments in an attempt to improve relations with the Iranian regime. Initially Israel acted as the middleman in this relationship, but by 1986 representatives of the United States were dealing directly with Iranian arms dealers in an attempt to influence the regime and, by extension, Hezbollah. This relationship became public, amid much international outcry, in November 1986. Irrespective of the motivations, the predominant regional interpretation was that the United States was cynically arming two Middle Eastern states in order to prolong a costly regional conflict. This scandal was extremely damaging to the United States in the Middle East.

The United States was drawn ever more deeply into the Iran–Iraq conflict and eventually played a decisive role in its conclusion. In the aftermath of the Iran–Contra scandal, the United States took a more direct and interventionist role. This can be understood largely as a result of the increasing danger that the conflict presented to the production and transportation of oil. As one of the major oil-producing states, Kuwait played an important role in drawing the United States into active involvement in the closing years of the war. Kuwait had much to fear from an Iranian victory. Its own territory could be easily threatened, and, given its own sizeable Shia minority, it also feared the influence of Iranian revolutionary rhetoric. As the situation in Iraq became dire, Kuwait decided it was time to involve the superpowers in the conflict in order to secure protection and support. Kuwait used its importance to the international oil market to foster its relationship with the United States to compensate for its vulnerable geo-political position.

Kuwait had made the decision to carry Iraqi oil to facilitate Iraq's revenue-raising during the war. These tankers became increasingly targeted by Tehran, a development that threatened Kuwait's economic position. Washington viewed Kuwait's appeals for the protection of shipping lines in the Persian Gulf as an opportunity to increase the US presence in the region and perhaps hoped to make amends after the revelations of the Iran–Contra scandal. Washington therefore launched Operation Earnest Will, under which Kuwaiti tankers were reflagged and protected by US Special Forces (Cordesman 1997: 8–9). This operation offered the vessels significant protection, as targeting a ship bearing the US flag would have brought about an escalation of the conflict that Iran was unwilling to countenance. Washington's willingness to be publicly identified as aiding Iraq increased in the following months. The close relationship between Washington and Baghdad was not without its mishaps, however, as the accidental bombing of the USS *Stark* by an Iraqi Mirage fighter on 17 May 1988 shows. However, overall the Kuwait–US alliance was positive for Iraq, which had been trying to involve the superpowers directly for years.

The battle between Iran and Iraq was now a regional conflict being played out in the all-important waters of the Persian Gulf. A catalyst for the full commitment of the US military occurred when the USS *Samuel Roberts* was severely damaged by a newly laid Iranian mine on 14 April 1988. The United States retaliated with Operation Praying Mantis, the largest US naval engagement since the Second World War. US Special Forces seized and destroyed Iranian oil platforms and sank several Iranian vessels, an act that marked a serious escalation of the conflict and made a direct Iranian–US sea conflict seem imminent. Concerns abounded as to the true nature and scope of the US military presence in the Gulf. As there was no congressional approval for conflict with Iran, questions regarding the Reagan administration's foreign policy and its accountability were raised once more. The Iran–US sea tensions galvanized the international community and led many leaders throughout the world to pressure Iran and Iraq to accept Security Council Resolution 598. The accidental shooting down of Iran Air Flight 655 on 3 July 1988 by a US frigate may well have been a decisive moment for the cessation of this conflict. The increased role of the United States and its willingness to deploy military forces against Iran probably pushed Tehran towards a cease-fire. Iran unconditionally accepted UN Resolution 598 on 18 July 1988, and in August 1990 a formal peace deal between Iran and Iraq was reached.

The US decision to involve itself in this conflict against Iran was to have long-term implications. The political dynamics of the region, coupled with the perceived threat posed by Iran's revolutionary stance, drew Washington deeper into the conflict. Despite the reality of a costly stalemate, Iraq constructed the outcome of the war as a victory and appeared to view the United States as an ally willing to accept its regional agenda. This perception would prove drastically mistaken only a short time later when Iraq made the fateful decision to recoup its war losses by occupying the tiny oil-rich kingdom of Kuwait.

AFTER THE IRAN–IRAQ WAR

After serving as vice president in the Reagan administration, George H. W. Bush was sworn in as the 41st American President in 1989. During his years under Reagan, Bush had remained comparatively quiet on foreign policy issues and thus began his tenure free from the damaging fallout of the Iran–Contra scandal. Initially, the incoming Bush administration followed the pre-existing doctrine of 'constructive engagement' in its Middle East policy. Economic incentives, such as an agricultural credits scheme, were used to lure Saddam Hussein into Washington's sphere of influence and moderate his political behaviour in the region. The conventional approach to Iraq as a buffer against an expansionist Iran was retained by Washington, and the Bush team continued to pursue positive relations with Baghdad.

The decision to use economic incentives to gain influence with the Iraqi dictator seemed like a logical choice for Washington. The close of the Iran–Iraq War in 1988 had led to a regional stalemate. Iraq, although now a strongly armed state, had sunk into excessive debt. Throughout the eight-year conflict, Baghdad had relied heavily on regional aid, especially from the Gulf states, which had felt threatened by the expansionist rhetoric of Tehran's clerical regime. The political mood in the region was for change. The Soviet Union, humbled by its foray into Afghanistan, was declining in regional influence, and the bipolar environment of the Cold War period was coming to an end.

Despite the increased intimacy of the relationship between Iraq and the United States during the 1980s, by the end of the decade Baghdad's public image was suffering a downturn in the United States. The media and sections of the Washington establishment showed increasing signs of distrust of Saddam Hussein. Publicity had surrounded Iraq's use of chemical weapons against the Kurds, and this led to calls for sanctions against the Iraqi regime. This agenda was fought off by both the Reagan and Bush Republican administrations, which subscribed to the philosophy of regional containment and the need to maintain a friendly buffer against Iran. The Bush administration believed that the war with Iran and the economic devastation it had caused Iraq had moderated Baghdad's behaviour, drawn Iraq into the circle of US-backed Gulf states and linked Saddam Hussein to the West. Essentially, Washington's foreign policy decision-making in this period demonstrated a willingness to accept Saddam Hussein's totalitarian regime in exchange for predictable foreign policy behaviour. Support for the status quo in the region, even if it meant accepting totalitarian regimes such as that of Saddam Hussein, characterized Washington's approach to the Middle East.

REGIONAL TENSIONS: WATER AND OIL

Against the backdrop of US determination to draw Saddam closer into the fold and Iraq's continued financial desperation, Baghdad's relations with its neighbours soured dramatically. The relationship between Iraq and its neighbour Kuwait was one of tension based on history. Like the majority of regional states, Kuwait was a colonial creation, a pocket of land carved out of Iraq and given to the al-Sabah family as recompense for their support of the British. To Iraqis this colonial 'line in the sand' was seen as largely illegitimate, and Kuwait was often referred to in the state's public discourse as a province of Iraq. This situation had been undoubtedly exacerbated by the discovery of bountiful oil reserves within the kingdom, a development that had enriched its small population. These historic tensions became more pronounced at a time of such economic hardship for Iraq. In the aftermath of the Iran–Iraq War, Baghdad raised concerns that Kuwait was manipulating its borders to maximize its access to various oilfields that straddled the contested border, most notably the Rumiela field. In addition, Baghdad accused Kuwait and the United Arab Emirates of exceeding their OPEC-set oil production levels and thus hindering Iraq's post-war economic recovery (Finlan 2003: 25). These economic concerns were matched with other territorial tensions. During the 1980s Iraq had requested that the al-Sabah family hand over control of the strategic islands of Warba and Bubiyan in the Shatt al-Arab waterway. Kuwait had refused. The interplay of tensions over national identity, borders, economics and oil set the stage for a regional showdown over Iraq's position in the Arab world.

The potential for conflict between Iraq and Kuwait did not go unnoticed in the region. Jordan, a long-time ally of Iraq and a regional state that often sought the middle ground between its volatile neighbours, sent delegations to Baghdad to facilitate negotiations between Kuwait, Iraq and Saudi Arabia over the repayment of Iraq's war debts and extension of further credits in the hope of reducing tensions. However, Baghdad's response was one of strident rejection. The Iraqi regime felt its war debts should be forgiven as it had 'defended' the Gulf from Iranian expansionism. Saudi Arabia, a wealthy state whose interests were not served by regional conflict, complied. Kuwait, perhaps emboldened by Iraq's dire financial situation, refused to negotiate unless Iraq repaid its war debt and recognized all of Kuwait's borders. This was an opportunistic political move by Kuwait, as border recognition was a major point of historical contention. When Kuwait announced its independence in 1961, General Qasim, then leader of Iraq, had made a formal claim to the country (Musallam 1996: 90). This was rebuffed by the quick deployment of both British and Arab troops, and although Iraq officially recognized the independence of Kuwait in 1963, the border demarcations had been a source of ongoing tension. Considering this, Kuwait may have seen the call for post-war negotiations as an opportunity to resolve the long-standing border issue.

This period of regional tension coincided with a spate of incidents that thrust the regime in Baghdad into the international limelight. On 10 March 1990 a British-Iranian journalist, Farzad Bazoft, was condemned to death in Baghdad on espionage charges. Western appeals for clemency were ignored and Bazoft was executed on 15 March (Ghareeb and Khadduri 2001: 99). Only two weeks later, British officials confiscated a shipment of US-made nuclear triggers headed for Iraq. This discovery led to fears that Iraq was intent on developing a nuclear weapons programme and resulted in significant media attention. These developments raised the profile of Iraq in the Western public consciousness and caused a significant media backlash over the authoritarian nature of the regime.

Reflecting his understanding of the relationship between the media and the state, Saddam Hussein perceived this media attention as censure from Washington and became agitated. US Ambassador April Glaspie, who emerged as a controversial figure in this crisis, intervened and assured the

BOX 6.4

The **Organization of Petroleum Exporting Countries (OPEC)** is a non-governmental organization that seeks to secure and promote the interests of oil-producing states and to provide stability in the international oil market. In the late 1970s, the OPEC-led oil embargo introduced the notion of 'oil as a weapon'. Since this time, OPEC has moved firmly away from this approach, instead working to stabilize oil production and export.

government of Iraq that the United States did not question the legitimacy of the Baghdad regime. However, by April 1990 it was clear that the policy of 'constructive engagement' was having little effect on Baghdad's aggressiveness, and the Bush administration suspended its assistance schemes. This unequivocal display of US government displeasure triggered a wave of confrontational rhetoric from Baghdad. Saddam Hussein initially focused his outrage on the US ally Israel:

> By God, if the Israelis try anything against us, we'll see to it that half their country is destroyed by fire. . . . Whoever threatens us with atomic bombs will be exterminated with chemical weapons.
>
> (cited in Cockburn and Cockburn 2002: 84)

Such rhetoric revealed Baghdad's political paranoia and the ongoing regional belief that Israel, with American and British backing, could act as a striking arm for the West in the Middle East. In addition, Saddam's hostile language contributed to Western suspicions about Iraq's weapons programme and heightened concerns regarding the dictator's willingness to deploy advanced weaponry in the region.

However, Washington's attention was focused elsewhere in this period as, with the fall of communism, the entire global order was changing. At the time, the consensus among US policy-makers was that Iraq's confrontational posture was merely a display of strength aimed at creating a favourable climate for negotiations regarding border issues and enhancing its economic position. It was in this climate that the Bush administration elected not to react to Baghdad's troop deployments along the Iraq–Kuwait border. These dangerous moves were accompanied by an ever more hostile stream of rhetoric from Baghdad. Washington's failure to respond, either through the international media or by a symbolic rejoinder such as moving warships to the Persian Gulf, is seen by many as having contributed to Saddam's mistaken belief that he retained American support or that Washington would endorse a reconfiguring of the region's borders. Moreover, a meeting conducted by US Ambassador Glaspie on 25 July 1990 with senior Ba'th Party officials, including Saddam Hussein, has been the subject of much controversy. The meeting was retrospectively used by Baghdad as proof of a so-called American 'green light' in relation to Iraq's war plans for Kuwait. Historians now question whether Glaspie, and thus the United States, 'inadvertently gave Saddam a green light or merely failed to show a red one' (Finlan 2003: 26).

The tense situation peaked in July as inter-Arab meetings reached a diplomatic impasse. Negotiations between Kuwait, Saudi Arabia and Iraq stalled as a now desperate Iraqi delegation insisted on a major financial aid package totalling US$10 billion from its neighbours. Kuwaiti officials, believing themselves secure in their alliances with the West, goaded the

Iraqi delegation by offering US$9 billion, a move that served to raise the ire of a disgruntled and increasingly paranoid Baghdad. Driven by a mix of economic need, determination to reassert its political pride and miscalculation of American intentions, Iraq responded by invading Kuwait on 2 August 1990. The Kuwaiti royal family fled to Saudi Arabia and Arab attempts to convince the Iraqi forces to withdraw failed. The international community responded strongly to this breach of Kuwait's sovereignty. The UN Security Council immediately issued Resolution 660, calling for Iraq's complete and unconditional withdrawal from Kuwait (Conte 2005: 117). The United States froze all Iraqi funds and banned trade with and travel to Iraq by US citizens. US Secretary of State James Baker embarked on a series of major tours of diplomacy aimed at resolving the crisis. The European Union placed a boycott on Iraqi and Kuwaiti oil and banned the sale of weapons. Within days, the Security Council intervened again by issuing Resolution 661 (6 August 1990), which placed mandatory arms and economic sanctions on Iraq.

As it became clear that the United States was willing to confront Iraq militarily, the Arab states faced a series of stark choices: (a) take the decision to act regionally and confront Saddam Hussein, only recently the champion and defender of the Arab world; (b) confront Saddam Hussein in alliance with the United States and thus by extension Israel; or (c) support Saddam Hussein. For most Arab leaders this decision concerned more than the fate of the Iraqi regime and the sovereignty of Kuwait. For states intimately involved in the Arab–Israeli conflict, such as Syria, the choice was existential. Syria's position was predicated on the need to reject occupation per se in order to validate its stand against Israel's role in the Palestinian territories. Most damaging for the Arab world, it quickly became evident that disunity would plague any and all attempts at regional initiatives. Saudi Arabia and Egypt, the two most powerful states in the Arab League, lobbied for the condemnation of the Iraqi occupation of Kuwait and called for immediate withdrawal of Iraqi forces. Yet the fractured nature of the Arab League made such a resolute position impossible. Seven member states, including Jordan, abstained from endorsing such a declaration. Reflecting the Arab leaderships' anxiety about international outrage against Saddam Hussein, and its repercussions, the final Arab League declaration issued on 3 August 1990 included a clause urging against 'any foreign intervention or attempt to intervene in Arab affairs'. Yet the die was cast, and four days later, on 7 August 1990 and at the request of the al-Saud royals, US forces deployed in Saudi Arabia. The effects of this challenge to the regional status quo rippled throughout the broader Middle East. For example, Turkey came under intense US pressure to close Iraq's pipelines in order to apply economic pressure on the regime, a request it agreed to after a significant bequest from the Gulf states (Kuniholm 1991: 37–8).

This was a vital turning point in Middle Eastern politics, the effects of which linger to this day. Saudi Arabia's decision to invite the US deployment proved divisive within the kingdom and triggered protests from individuals such as Osama bin Laden, who warned the royal family against relying on American assistance (Cordesman 2003: 211). Bin Laden advocated an indigenous defence plan, offering to activate the 'Arab Afghans' of al-Qaeda against the Iraqi army (Minter 2003: 14). For bin Laden, the al-Saud decision to invite US forces to the holy land of Islam proved a radicalizing turning point and marked the beginning of his campaign against the Arab leaderships.

From Washington's perspective, Iraq controlled 10 per cent of the world's oil reserves and with the occupation of Kuwait had added significantly to its resources (Hill 1994: 186). The prospect of further expansion into Saudi Arabia was daunting, as it would have serious economic implications for the major oil consumers. A sense of the Saudis' vulnerability and its own desire to gain a foothold in the Persian Gulf region contributed to this divisive geo-strategic decision on the part of the United States. Unlike most Arab states, Saudi Arabia had never experienced colonial rule. The decision by the Saudi royal family to invite American forces into the birthplace of Islam reverberated throughout the Muslim world and drove a wedge between the Arab leadership and the Arab streets.

OPERATION DESERT STORM

Under the initial phase, named Operation Desert Shield, the United States deployed 200,000 troops armed with light defensive weaponry. On 8 November 1990 President Bush declared the build-up for the liberation campaign was under way and authorized the deployment of another 200,000 soldiers. The backdrop to this military response was a programme of regional economic incentives and coercive US diplomacy aimed at securing a broad-based international military coalition to confront Saddam Hussein. It has been argued that Saddam's government may well have been intending only a brief occupation of its southern neighbour in order to redraw the borders. Whatever his intentions, the regime in Baghdad paid dearly for this foreign policy adventure.

The momentum for war gained pace when the UN Security Council issued what amounted to an authorization for conflict with the passing of Resolution 678 on 29 December 1990. This resolution ordered Iraq to comply fully with all earlier UN resolutions regarding its position in Kuwait. It further authorized member states 'to *use all necessary means* to uphold and implement resolution 660 . . . and restore international peace and security in the region' (United Nations Security Council 1990; emphasis added). Aware that a military confrontation was now inevitable, and that other Arab states were aligning themselves with the United States, Saddam attempted to widen the gap between the Arab street and Arab leadership. Saddam attempted to present himself once again as an Arab champion by focusing on the willingness of the Arab leaders to align themselves with Israel's primary ally and on his own determination to stand up to the West. Moreover, he attempted to link his stance to the Palestinian issue through a focus on the relationship between Israel and the United States. This rhetoric struck a chord in Arab communities throughout the world and revealed many of the tensions inherent in Arab politics.

Saddam Hussein's decision to invade Kuwait had been marked by several major miscalculations. First, Saddam assumed Saudi Arabia, given its historical and theological prominence in the Arab world, would not approach the United States for help. Baghdad also overestimated the continued influence of the Soviet Union, assuming that Moscow would resist a US military build-up so close to its territory. The belief that Kuwait was expendable to the United States was also deeply mistaken. Finally, and perhaps most importantly, Saddam misinterpreted the nature of his own relationship with Washington. The regime in Baghdad, by its own foreign policy choices based on economic imperative and political miscalculation, brought the might of the US war machine down upon itself. However, the United States was not alone in this conflict. This first war in the unipolar world was marked by a sense of global multilateralism. By the time that Operation Desert Storm commenced in January 1991, 28 countries had sent 750,000 troops to liberate Kuwait.

The US-led coalition began an aerial campaign on 17 January 1991. In response, Iraq launched Scud missiles against Saudi Arabia and Israel in an attempt to draw Israel into the war and splinter the Arab alliance (Donaldson 1996: 173). This tactic failed. The humbling of Saddam Hussein was clearly in Israel's national interest and Tel Aviv was aware that its active participation in the war would present Baghdad with a public relations triumph and endanger the coalition. Ninety-three Scud missiles landed on Israeli soil, yet in a testament to the strength of both national self-interest in policy formulation and the Israel–US alliance in this period, Israel, widely known for its hardline military responses, refrained from being drawn into the conflict.

This war had major implications for the Palestine Liberation Organization. Saddam Hussein's willingness to act as a financial backer for the PLO, the popularity of his attacks against Israel and his determination to cast himself as a champion of the Palestinian cause forced PLO Chairman Yasser Arafat's hand, and the PLO congratulated Saddam for taking the first step in the liberation of Palestine. This misstep by Arafat would have major political ramifications throughout the 1990s, including the financial devastation of hundreds of thousands of Palestinian workers and their families when they were expelled from Kuwait and Saudi Arabia in the post-war period (Rezun 1992: 99–100). Moreover, as a punitive measure, the Gulf states suspended their US$133 million in annual contributions to the Palestinian organizations, financial pressure that greatly curtailed the effectiveness of the PLO (Karsh 2003: 52).

Western media, such as CNN, broadcast the coalition air strikes throughout the West and the Arab world. The intensity of this campaign was unprecedented and was clearly aimed at crushing the Iraqi infrastructure. Coalition jets flew thousands of missions and dropped more bombs than had been dropped in the entire Second World War. The air campaign was followed by the ground war, which commenced on 24 February 1991. Three days later, US forces entered the Kuwaiti capital. The cost to the Iraqi army was considerable, and, although the highly politicized nature of such statistics makes the true figure impossible to ascertain, it is usually placed at around 100,000 troops (Mueller 1994: 123). The final phase in the war became a point of controversy in the international and US media. The successful coalition-building undertaken by the United States and the supportive stance of the United Nations became increasingly endangered in the final stages of the conflict. As the Iraqi troops retreated along Kuwait's main highway, US forces bombarded them with an unrelenting aerial assault. The high rate of casualties inflicted on an army in retreat and disarray provoked the international media to dub the road the 'Highway of Death'. Negative coverage of the US prosecution of the conflict was rightly identified as damaging to the moral high ground taken by Washington in liberating Kuwait and to the ability of the United States to work effectively with the Arab world after the war (Yetiv 1997: 41). Therefore it was decided to terminate the war at midnight on 28 February, 100 hours after the ground war commenced. President Bush declared that the mandate offered by Resolution 660 had been fulfilled, Kuwait had been liberated and the status quo restored. However, this decision was criticized by many, especially in Saudi Arabia, as it allowed Saddam Hussein to remain in power and Iraq to retain military hardware that it then used on Iraqi Kurds and Shia after the war. Saudi military leaders had advocated a continuation of the conflict, and US and Arab military leaders on the ground believed that an additional 24 to 48 hours would have dealt the Iraqi regime, and especially the Republican Guards, a decisive blow (Yetiv 1997: 44).

The post-war confusion became even more pronounced in the aftermath of a televised speech in late March 1991 in which President Bush called for the rising up of the Iraqi people and military to force Saddam Hussein out of power. Widely interpreted as a call for revolution, the rhetoric from Washington did not match US actions on the ground, where cease-fire negotiations had allowed the defeated Iraq to retain its military capabilities. This enabled the weakened regime to deploy its remaining air power against the uprisings that occurred in the Shia south and the Kurdish north. US policy in relation to Iraq's military capability and refusal to come to the aid of the popular uprising that Washington had invited were widely seen as a serious betrayal. Hundreds of thousands of Iraqi Shia and Kurds were killed. In the north of the country, up to 2.5 million people were displaced by the end of April (Farouk-Sluglett and Sluglett 2001: 289). Michael Gunter suggests that the US decision-making process in this matter was based on several fears: regional destabilization in the advent of the 'Lebanization' of Iraq, the provision of a model for Kurdish independence that would anger Turkey, the possibility that Saddam would put down the rebellion and an 'unwanted, perpetual US commitment' (1992: 54).

Finally, in the face of an impending humanitarian disaster, especially in the Kurdish areas, American, British and French warplanes were ordered to enforce 'no-fly zones' in the north and south of the country. These no-fly zones were patrolled throughout the 1990s and led commentators to observe that a virtual, if undeclared, war continued between Iraq and the Western allies throughout the decade. In addition to the no-fly zones, the international community placed a series of restrictive sanctions on the defeated state of Iraq to ensure the destruction of Baghdad's weapons capabilities. UN Resolution 687 called for the destruction of all illegal weaponry, such as bacteriological, chemical and nuclear weapons. The 1990s were fraught with accusations of Iraqi failure to comply with this resolution and Baghdad's counter-claims of innocence. The devastating effects of the UN sanctions on Iraq have been documented by numerous human rights organizations that assert the brunt of these intensive sanctions was borne by the civilian population of the country.

OUTCOMES OF DESERT STORM

Despite the brutal post-war repression of rebellion in Iraq and international concerns regarding Washington's decision to leave the Iraqi dictator in power, President Bush emerged from the conflict with a greater than 80 per cent approval rating.[3] The Desert Storm coalition had decisively won a popular war and signalled the beginning of the 'new world order', a global system in which the primacy of the United States, now the lone superpower, was assured. The US presence in the Middle East was also entrenched through the failure of the Arab states to contain Saddam Hussein without US assistance. In addition, the continuation of the Iraqi regime had cemented the role of the United States as the Gulf's protector. This outcome led some to postulate that Washington, although publicly mindful of the limits of the mandate established by Resolution 660, was using the lingering threat of Saddam Hussein as leverage to ensure that the oil-rich Persian Gulf remained dependent on the United States for its security.

This conflict inflicted yet another critical blow to Arab unity. The inconceivable had happened: Arab states had sided with the United States against another Arab state. This development was clearly a manifestation of the state-based political system and of the concerns of the Arab leadership with self-preservation. The process by which this had occurred added vigour to the Islamist critique of the existing Arab states as deeply corrupt. This perspective was strengthened by the continued presence of US soldiers on the holiest land in Islamic civilization. As the 1990s progressed, the gap between the Arab street and the Arab leadership periodically re-emerged as a key destabilizing factor in the region.

At the international level, the 1991 Gulf War signalled the end of the Cold War. Despite the occasional tensions it had engendered, it was the first example of rapprochement between Moscow and Washington. On reflection, these first tentative steps by the new lone superpower were marked by multilateral considerations and coalition-building as the United States adapted to the new system in which it was free from the restraining influence of a peer competitor. However, as the decade progressed, Washington's self-assurance – and willingness to interpret its national interest expansively – grew.

CONCLUSION

As the first and second conflicts in the Persian Gulf demonstrate, this region is of the utmost economic and strategic importance to external powers. As the long and costly Iran–Iraq War raged, the United States, cynically operating under the philosophy enshrined in the anti-communist Reagan doctrine, clearly sought to better its own strategic position in the region. This was, however, a pattern mirrored by many states in the international system. The costs of such decision-making were carried by the civilian populations of Iraq and Iran.

As the global system moved into a unipolar phase, the power and prestige of the United States increased. Washington's willingness to foster global support for the launching of a war to 'liberate' Kuwait from occupation was seen as an example of clear hypocrisy in a region marked by the post-1967 Israeli occupation of the Palestinian territories. To many Arabs, Kuwait's oil wealth and position appeared to be the basis upon which its sovereignty was respected by the international community. Moreover, it was oil, rather than a political commitment to respecting the fate of the region, that was seen as integral to Washington's decision to carry out a military liberation. This discrepancy in the US response to two cases of occupation strengthened Arab distaste for US regional policy. The two Gulf conflicts constitute a vital phase in the history of Arab–US relations. Although

Operation Desert Storm was a highly successful military campaign, the Islamist backlash against the US presence in the region emerged as a major unforeseen consequence of the new superpower's regional agenda.

NOTES

1 Saudi Arabia was the first Arab state to be formally recognized, but it was not a product of the colonial period.
2 For a primary source account, see Walsh (1997).
3 WSJ.com analysis of Gallup Presidential Popularity poll conducted during G.H.W. Bush's tenure, in 'How The Presidents Stack Up', available at http://online.wsj.com/public/resources/documents/info-presapp0605–31.html.

REFERENCES

Abir, Mordechi (1993) *Saudi Arabia Government, Society and the Gulf Crisis* (London: Routledge).

Ajami, Fouad (1992) *The Arab Predicament: Arab Political Thought and Practice since 1967* (Cambridge: Cambridge University Press).

al-Khalil, Samir (pseud. of Kanan Makiya) (1989) *Republic of Fear – The Politics of Modern Iraq* (Berkeley: University of California Press).

Baram, Amatzia (1991) *Culture, History and Ideology in the Formation of Ba'thist Iraq, 1968–89* (New York: St Martins).

Cleveland, William (2000) *A History of the Modern Middle East* (Boulder, CO: Westview Press).

Cockburn, Andrew and Cockburn, Patrick (2002) *Saddam Hussein: An American Obsession* (London: Verso).

Conte, Alex (2005) *Security in the 21st Century: The United Nations, Afghanistan and Iraq* (London: Ashgate).

Cordesman, Anthony (1997) *Recovery and Security after the Gulf War* (Boulder, CO: Westview Press).

Cordesman, Anthony (2003) *Saudi Arabia Enters the Twenty-First Century: The Military and International Security Dimensions* (New York: Praeger/ Greenwood).

Davis, Eric (2005) *Memories of State: Religion, History and Collective Identity in Modern Iraq* (Berkeley: University of California Press).

Donaldson, Gary (1996) *America at War since 1945: Politics and Diplomacy in Korea, Vietnam and the Gulf War* (New York: Praeger/Greenwood).

Farouk-Sluglett, Marion and Sluglett, Peter (2001) *Iraq Since 1958 – From Revolution to Dictatorship* (London: IB Tauris).

Finlan, Alastair (2003) *The Gulf War 1991* (London: Osprey).

Freedman, Lawrence and Karsh, Ephraim (1993) *The Gulf Conflict 1990–1991* (Princeton, NJ: Princeton University Press).

Gause, Gregory F. III (2002) 'Iraq's Decisions to Go to War, 1980 and 1990', *The Middle East Journal*, Vol. 56, No. 1, pp. 47–70.

Ghareeb, Edmund and Khadduri, Majid (2001) *War in the Gulf 1990–1991: The Iraq-Kuwait Conflict and Its Implications* (London: Oxford University Press).

Gunter, Michael (1992) *The Kurds of Iraq – Tragedy and Hope* (New York: St Martins Press).

Hill, Enid (1994) 'Rhetoric, Politics and Policy in the United States', in Tareq Ismael and Jacqueline Ismael (eds), *The Gulf War and the New World Order: International Relations of the Middle East* (Miami: University Press of Florida).

Jawad, Sa'ad (1982) 'Recent Developments in the Kurdish Issue', in Tim Niblock (ed.), *Iraq: The Contemporary State* (London: Croom Helm).

Karsh, Ephraim (2002) *The Iran–Iraq War: A Military Analysis 1980–1988* (London: Osprey).

Karsh, Ephraim (2003) *Arafat's War: The Man and His Battle for Israeli Conquest* (London: Grove).

Karsh, Ephraim and Ratusi, Inari (1991) *Saddam Hussein – A Political Biography* (London: Brassey's Defence Publishers).

Kuniholm, B. R. (1991) 'Turkey and the West', *Foreign Affairs*, Vol. 70, No. 2, pp. 34–49.

Minter, Richard (2003) *Losing Bin Laden: How Bill Clinton's Failures Unleashed Global Terror* (Washington DC: Regnery).

Mueller, John (1994) *Policy and Opinion in the Gulf War* (Chicago: University of Chicago Press).

Musallam, Musallam Ali (1996) *The Iraqi Invasion of Kuwait – Saddam Hussein, His State and International Power Politics* (London: British Academic Press).

Pauly, Robert J. (2005) *US Foreign Policy and the Persian Gulf: Safeguarding American Interests through Selective Multilateralism* (London: Ashgate).

Rezun, Miron (1992) *Saddam Hussein's Gulf Wars – Ambivalent Stakes in the Middle East* (Westport, CT: Praeger).

Tripp, Charles (2000) *A History of Iraq* (Cambridge: Cambridge University Press).

United Nations Security Council (1990) 'Resolution 678', 29 November, available at http://daccessdds.un.org/doc/RESOLUTION/GEN/NR0/575/28/IMG/NR057528.pdf?OpenElement.

Walsh, Lawrence (1997) *Firewall: The Iran-Contra Conspiracy and Cover-Up* (New York: Norton).

WSJ.com (undated) 'How The Presidents Stack Up', available at http://online.wsj.com/public/resources/documents/info-presapp0605–31.html.

Yetiv, Steve (1997) *The Persian Gulf Crisis* (London: Greenwood).

SUGGESTED FURTHER READING

Amitav, Acharya (1987) *The Gulf War and 'Irangate': American Dilemmas* (Canberra: Strategic and Defence Studies Centre, Australian National University).

Ball, Desmond (1991) *The Intelligence War in the Gulf* (Canberra: Strategic and Defence Studies Centre, Research School of Pacific Studies, Australian National University).

Bulloch, John and Morris, Harvey (1991) *Saddam's War: The Origins of the Kuwait Conflict and the International Response* (London: Faber and Faber).

Miller, Judith and Mylroie, Laurie (1990) *Saddam Hussein and the Crisis in the Gulf* (New York: Times Books).

O'Balance, Edgar (1988) *The Gulf War* (London: Brassey's Defence Publishers).

Schofield, Richard N. (1993) *Kuwait and Iraq: Historical Claims and Territorial Disputes*, second edition (London: Royal Institute of International Affairs).

Sciolino, Elaine (1991) *The Outlaw State: Saddam Hussein's Quest for Power and the Gulf Crisis* (New York: Wiley).

Short, Martin and McDermott, Anthony (1981) *The Kurds*, fourth revised edition (London: Minority Rights Group).

Tarock, Adam (1988) *The Superpowers' Involvement in the Iran–Iraq War* (Commack, NY: Nova Science).

United Nations Department of Public Information (1994) *Resolutions of the United Nations Security Council and Statements by Its President concerning the Situation between Iraq and Kuwait (2 August 1990–16 November 1994)* (New York: United Nations Department of Public Information).

United Nations Department of Public Information (1996) *The United Nations and the Iraq–Kuwait Conflict, 1990–1996, with an Introduction by Boutros-Boutros Ghali* (New York: United Nations Department of Public Information).

Vali, Abbas (ed.) (2003) *Essays on the Origins of Kurdish Nationalism* (Costa Mesa, CA: Mazda).

SUGGESTED STUDY QUESTIONS

1 What was the rationale for, and impact of, superpower involvement in the 1980–88 Iran–Iraq War?

2 What were the major outcomes of Operation Desert Storm?

3 In what ways can the 1991 Gulf War be considered a turning point in Middle Eastern politics?

4 Why did the United States leave Saddam Hussein in power after the 1991 conflict?

CHAPTER 7

Israel and Palestine

The Failure to Find Peace and the Role of
the United States

INTRODUCTION

The conflict between Israel and the Palestinians has proved the most
divisive issue in contemporary Middle Eastern politics. Washington's
role as Israel's primary backer has greatly complicated the Arab–US
relationship. As explored, the United States was not a major player in the
establishment of the state of Israel in 1948. In the early twentieth century
the US role, as seen in the ill-fated King–Crane Commission of 1919, was
characterized by a sense of caution. However, once the Israeli state was
established, Washington became a major financial sponsor. As the century
progressed, Tel Aviv and Washington became increasingly aligned in their
political views. Pivotal moments, such as the 1974 oil embargo, pushed the
two states ever closer. This bonding was influenced by Cold War strategy,
shared political values, the US Israel lobby and, most importantly, by the
changing relationship between the United States and Israel's neighbours.

The relationship between the Israel–US alliance and Arab anti-
Americanism is symbiotic. Arab views of the United States have changed
dramatically since the early twentieth century when Washington was seen
as a natural ally of Arab anti-colonial movements. During the Cold War, as
major regional states such as Egypt and Syria moved towards the Soviets,
Israel emerged as a natural and willing ally of the United States. Although
religious and cultural affinities are often a matter of focus, the Israel–US
alliance can most constructively be understood as a byproduct of the Cold

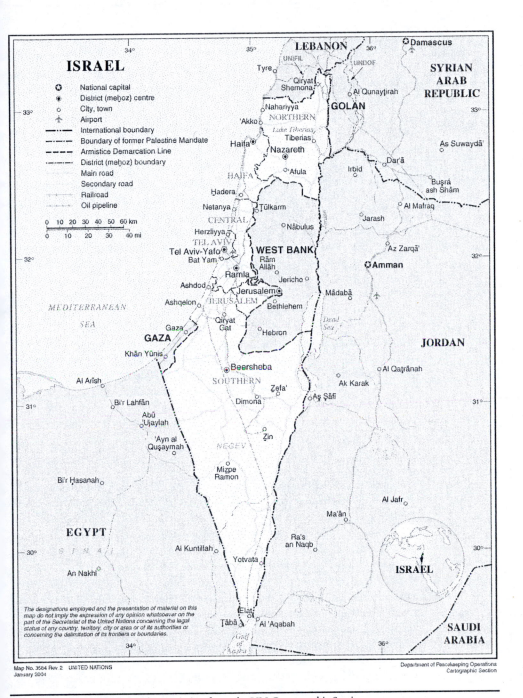

Map 7.1 Israel. Reproduced with permission from the UN Cartographic Section.

BOX 7.1

Yasser Arafat was born in 1929 into a Palestinian family. His birthplace is contested, with different versions of history suggesting Egypt, Gaza and Jerusalem. Arafat became active in post-1948 factional Palestinian politics and violence. He completed his education at Cairo University, and was initially a supporter of Nasser's vision for the Arab world. Along with other Palestinians in exile, Arafat formed Fatah in 1957 in Kuwait. After the defeat of 1967, Arafat became more strongly committed to Palestinian self-determination outside the auspices of pan-Arabism. He was elected Chairman of the Executive Committee of the PLO in February 1969 and proceeded to push the PLO agenda from pan-Arabism to national liberation. Arafat was expelled from Jordan in the 1970 crackdown. He addressed the UN General Assembly on 13 November 1974, wearing a pistol, carrying an olive branch and dressed in a military uniform. He was removed from the region under a US-sponsored deal after the siege of Beirut in the early 1980s. Arafat's major political misstep was his public support for Saddam Hussein in the 1991 Gulf War, which placed him at odds with the international community. After the Oslo Accords, Arafat re-entered the Palestinian territories as the accepted leader of the Palestinian people. In 1994 Arafat received (with Yitzhak Rabin) the Nobel Peace Prize. He then consolidated the Palestinian Authority and was elected President in 1995. From 1995 to 2000 Arafat fulfilled his side of the Oslo bargain in an erratic fashion, and he was frequently accused of corruption and nepotism. Arafat died of an undisclosed illness on 11 November 2004 and was buried, amid much public grieving, in Ramallah.

War period. As explored in Chapter 3, the Israel–US alliance was not cemented until the aftermath of the 1973 Yom Kippur War. Yet, by the late twentieth century, Israel was the primary recipient of US foreign aid and the 'special relationship' between Israel and the United States had become a key feature of Middle Eastern politics. Today, the depth of this strategic friendship cannot be overstated. In 2007, the administration of George W. Bush signed a deal with the Israeli government that represents a 25 per cent increase in military aid to Israel, a rise that will see aid increase from the 2007 level of US$2.4 billion for the year to US$3 billion a year over ten years. The widespread discontent over Tel Aviv's regional policy and, by extension, Washington's ongoing commitment to Israel, is at the very core of the Arab–US relationship.

In the Middle East, this 'special relationship' is seen as one that excludes, if not directly opposes, Arab interests. This perspective is fostered by Washington's historical tendency to endorse heavy-handed Israeli responses to Palestinian calls for statehood. It is against this backdrop

BOX 7.2

Ariel Sharon was born in Palestine in 1928. Sharon was therefore a *sabre* – part of a generation of locally born Jews committed to the founding of the state of Israel. Sharon fought in all of Israel's wars and was the driving force behind the settlement programme in Gaza after the 1967 conflict. Sharon's political career stalled in the 1980s when he was forced to resign after the Kahane Commision found him indirectly responsible for the massacres of Palestinian civilians in the camps of Sabra and Shatila in Lebanon. Sharon returned to politics as housing minister in the 1990s and presided over the biggest building drive in Jewish settlements in the West Bank and Gaza since Israel had occupied the territories in 1967. Sharon went on to become leader of the right-wing Likud Party in opposition in 1999. Like his nemesis Yasser Arafat, Sharon was a fascinating politician, and few public figures tapped into more elements of Israel's national mythology. Sharon won elections in 2001 and 2003 based largely on a single factor: Israelis trusted him to take whatever measures were needed to protect them against the ongoing campaign of Palestinian suicide attacks – even though many blamed him for sparking the Intifada. Sharon suffered a massive stroke in January 2006 and was entirely incapacitated.

that the public assumption by the United States of the role of mediator between Israel and the Palestinians has led Arab public opinion to view the United States as untrustworthy and to identify significant double standards in Washington's policy toward the region. This chapter explores how the Palestinians and the broader Middle East have responded to the role of the United States in the various international peace attempts, especially the pivotal moments of Oslo, Camp David and the Roadmap to Peace. The variation in US reactions to civilian casualties – caused in this conflict by both state action and the tactics of sub-state terrorist organizations – is also of importance in perpetuating popular scepticism.

In recent years, Washington's self-appointed role as the 'honest broker' of the 1990s has degenerated into little more than open endorsements of Israeli policy, a development that has left the peace process stagnating and the Palestinian issue unresolved. The centrality of the Palestinian question to regional stability has been evident in numerous moments in Middle Eastern history: Jordan's Black September of 1970, the Israel–Lebanon war of 1982 and the internal dynamics of Lebanon from 1975 to 2007.

As a result of its critical financial and diplomatic support for Israel, the United States is seen as the only state in the international system with real influence over Tel Aviv. Therefore, Washington's failure to effect real change and resolve the Israeli–Palestinian crisis has greatly affected regional opinions of the United States.

THE FIRST UPRISING: INTIFADA 1987

The status quo established by the sweeping Israeli victory of 1967 was challenged in the Occupied Territories in the late 1980s. The Palestinian population had grown exponentially and the Israeli military occupation permeated every aspect of the individual and communal lives of the community. The PLO, in exile in Tunis since the end of the Lebanon conflict in the early 1980s, had become a distant source of solace for the people of Gaza and the West Bank. The seething discontent with occupation and political stagnation merely required a spark. It was provided by a traffic accident in Gaza on 9 December 1987. This incident triggered a grassroots uprising that rocked Israel and the international community. This uprising is commonly known by its Arabic name: Intifada.

As the state of civil unrest spread to the West Bank it became clear to all observers, Israeli and international, that a new phase in the conflict between Palestinians and Israelis had begun. The traditional Israeli doctrine of absolute military might, which had served the state so well in its wars with the Arab world, was hardly suitable for dealing with a campaign of civil disobedience. First and foremost, this uprising was an expression of anti-occupation sentiment. As Sami Farsoun and Jean Landis point out, the Intifada was similar in conceptualization to other rebellions against occupation (1999: 16). Seen in this way, the Intifada can be understood as a manifestation of the national liberation struggle of the Palestinian people. However, the events of 1987 were also a powerful statement on internal politics. The outburst of discontent constituted a significant challenge to the PLO. Therefore, the first Intifada can be understood as both a challenge to Israel's occupation and an expression of 'frustration at the PLO's failure to stop the occupation and the abuses that occurred within it' (Meir 2001: 65). As the newly empowered Palestinian community took to the streets in rallies, boycotts and protests, a behind-the-scenes struggle for control commenced. The 'inside' leadership was composed of a new generation, born under occupation, which had tired of the political manoeuvrings of the distant PLO hierarchy. However, as the Intifada gained pace, the PLO quickly sought to harness the energy generated by the rebellion and re-establish its claim to the leadership mantle.

For Israel, the Intifada of 1987 was a serious challenge. The Intifada leaders, through both a lack of options and as part of a considered political strategy, encouraged tactics such as boycotts and stone-throwing. Images of Palestinian children armed with stones facing off with Israeli armoured vehicles were beamed throughout the world. Israel's political and military leadership ordered a strong military response, and images of Israeli soldiers beating unarmed Palestinian civilians only intensified international calls for resolution. Inside Israel, the inability of the Israeli Defence Forces to suppress the Intifada reignited the debate over the moral and political costs of occupation. According to Azmay Bizhara, this led to a 'polarization which . . . penetrated all of Israel's political parties' (1999: 217). In the midst of the growing popular unrest and street mobilization, the various Palestinian leadership structures merged into loose coalitions. Over time, the PLO-backed organizations began to gain ground (Milton-Edwards 1999: 145). However, the influence of the Islamic political alternatives was significant, and a complicated power-sharing relationship began to emerge. The PLO, long the accepted representative of the Palestinian community, was being challenged from within. The rise of an Islamic alternative was a key outcome of this shifting of the balance of power in Palestinian politics.

THE EMERGENCE OF HAMAS

The emergence of Islamic groups in the Palestinian political scene was not a new phenomenon. The Muslim Brotherhood had been active in the Palestinian territories for decades. During the height of the PLO years, Israel had supported the Muslim Brotherhood as a counter-weight to the secular-nationalist perspective that was committed to the liberation struggle. As Beverly Milton-Edwards argues, this was a 'classic divide and conquer' tactic (1999: 103). However, in the lead-up to December 1987, the Muslim Brotherhood's traditional prestige in the Occupied Territories was also under challenge from within its own community.

Palestinian Islamic Jihad, a group that had splintered from the Muslim Brotherhood, was officially founded in Gaza in 1980. This faction attracted the backing of regional power-brokers such as Syria and Iran. Palestinian Islamic Jihad functioned as an alternative to the Muslim Brotherhood, which it saw as having failed to challenge the secular-nationalist impulse in Palestinian politics (Abu-Amr 1994: 96). In this way, the faction was yet another long-term legacy of the 1967 defeat of the forces of Arab secular nationalism. This organization blended Palestinian nationalism, traditional Muslim Brotherhood ideology and the more assertive doctrines of revolution that emerged from the Islamic Revolution of 1979 in Iran. Islamic Jihad also drew strongly on the example of the Egyptian Islamic Jihad movement, which was responsible for Anwar Sadat's assassination in the aftermath of the Egypt–Israel Peace Accords of 1978. Inside the Palestinian territories, Islamic Jihad undertook several daring attacks against IDF outposts, and these actions were juxtaposed against the more traditional and quiescent stance of the Muslim Brotherhood. The merging of resistance and religion proved a heady mix, especially among a younger generation that had come of age under Israeli occupation. As popular discontent became entrenched in the Intifada, Islamic Jihad cemented its place within the resistance and attracted many young Muslim Brotherhood supporters who were keen to participate more actively in the rebellion.

Sheikh Yassin, a factional leader of the Muslim Brotherhood and a champion among Palestinian youth, pushed his organization's leadership to declare itself a leading participant in the struggle against Israel. The Muslim Brotherhood elite refused to commit the organization to the Intifada, aware that, should the resistance be crushed, Israel's forgiveness was likely to be limited. However, Yassin's pursuit of his cause resulted in the creation of a new wing of the Muslim Brotherhood, Harakat al-Muqawama al-Islamiyya. This organization was better known by its acronym, HAMAS. With Yassin at the theological helm, HAMAS declared itself through its covenant in 1988 and soon became a major player in Palestinian politics (HAMAS 1988). As noted by Rashad al-Shawwa, mayor of Gaza at the time, the appeal of HAMAS was theological, ideological and situational:

> One must expect these things after twenty years of debilitating occupation. People have lost hope. They are frustrated and don't know what to do. They have turned to religious fundamentalism as their last hope. They have given up hoping that Israel will give them their rights. The Arab states are unable to do anything, and they feel that the PLO, which is their representative, has also failed.
>
> (cited in Hroub 2000: 37)

HAMAS quickly overtook the Muslim Brotherhood in terms of relevance. As the Intifada continued, the traditionally fractious Palestinian political scene became increasingly dominated by two organizations: HAMAS and the PLO. The ideological relationship between the organizations was often tense, yet both leaderships saw the benefits in unity. This is evident in the HAMAS covenant, which was careful to express support for its fellow Palestinian organizations (HAMAS 1988). HAMAS operated both military and welfare wings and thus became central to both the resistance against Israel and the functioning of Palestinian society.

THE OSLO ACCORDS (SEPTEMBER 1993)

The Intifada dragged on for several years and claimed approximately 1,500 Palestinian and 450 Israeli lives. It marked a significant turning point in the Palestinian struggle and was widely supported in the Palestinian Diaspora. Israel attempted to contain and confront the challenge posed by the Palestinian community in various ways. In 1992, for example, Israeli authorities deported 418 HAMAS and Islamic Jihad leaders. Yet, as both

BOX 7.3

The **Oslo Accords**, officially called the **Declaration of Principles on Interim Self-Government Arrangements** or **Declaration of Principles (DOP)**, were the product of negotiations contracted between Israel and the Palestinians that had been brokered by a group of Norwegian academics. The Accords were signed on 13 September 1993 at a ceremony in Washington. The Oslo agreement was not a resolution to the conflict between Israel and the Palestinians, but it represented a dramatic step forward in relations between the two communities. The Accords provided for the creation of the Palestinian Authority and the phased withdrawal of Israeli forces from the Occupied Territories.

Israelis and Palestinians grew increasingly weary of conflict, they joined the international community in a more substantial search for resolution. Rumours began to filter out that Israeli and PLO negotiators had been secretly meeting under the auspices of Norwegian academics in an attempt to lay the foundations for peace. The Oslo Accords, which emerged from this process, were the major political outcome of the 1987 Intifada. Both the Israeli and Palestinian leaderships perceived that there was much to be gained from being at the negotiating table at this particular point in history. Israel's international prestige had been profoundly damaged by the heavy-handed military tactics employed during the Intifada. For the PLO, exiled in North Africa, the dynamic surge in local political leadership meant that its position as the unchallenged representative of the Palestinian cause was no longer secure. Therefore, finding safe passage back into the Territories became an overriding consideration. In addition, Arafat's reputation required some polish after his ill-advised articulation of support for Iraq in the 1991 Gulf War. Polling in both national communities suggest there was strong support for peace in this period.

As the title suggests, the Oslo Accords, or Declaration of Principles, were not a peace agreement. Rather it was a framework: a process through which the participants hoped peace could be achieved. The Oslo Accords laid out a structure of staged steps. This approach to conflict resolution, dubbed 'phased reciprocal negotiation', was intended to build confidence and establish a firm foundation for negotiation on the so-called 'final status' issues: the future of the refugees, Jerusalem and borders. The Oslo Accords, although often vague, implied – or, more importantly, were perceived by the Palestinian community as leading to – a two-state solution. This phased approach, although designed to build confidence, ran the risk of playing the reverse role, as it was vulnerable to derailment by extreme elements on either side. Further problems arose from the composition of the Accords. As Benny Morris has pointed out, a feature of the Oslo process was the use of obscure language that allowed 'two radically opposed visions of what the Accords really meant' (2001: 54).

Washington's role in the Accords was initially limited. However, once the potential of these meetings to resolve one of the greatest political issues of the twentieth century became clear, the Clinton administration seized a central role. As Manuel Hassassian points out, with its entry into the Oslo process, the United States came to play 'the contradictory roles of arbiter, staunch supporter of Israel and promoter of peace and regional stability' (2004: 125). At the time, however, these conflicting trends were submerged, and the Oslo Accords were regarded as a triumph for all involved. The handshake between Yasser Arafat and Yitzhak Rabin on the White House lawn was a defining moment of the Clinton presidency. For the PLO's Arafat, the Oslo Accords signalled a return to the international stage. More importantly, the Accords provided an end to the PLO's exile in North Africa. The organization returned to the Occupied Territories, where it transformed into the Palestinian Authority. Retrospective accounts of the Oslo Accords reveal that all parties had their doubts that the process would bring lasting peace. Indeed, just moments before the historic handshake there were serious concerns that Rabin would refuse to publicly shake Arafat's hand.[1] However, in 1994, Yitzak Rabin and Yasser Arafat shared the Nobel Peace Prize for their efforts, and there was a sense of hope that a new chapter in Israeli–Palestinian relationships had begun.

OSLO'S FAILURE AND THE AL-AQSA INTIFADA

Israel's post-1967 settlement programme in the West Bank and Gaza intensified with the ascendance of Likud in the 1977 Israeli elections. By the 1990s, settlement had become an entrenched feature of the Israeli approach to the disputed territories. The question of settlements, like the other 'final status' issues of borders and Jerusalem, were left out of the Oslo

BOX 7.4

Yitzhak Rabin was born in Palestine on 1 March 1922 and served as a general in the Israeli army and as a politician. Rabin was the Prime Minister of Israel from 1974 to 1977 and again from 1992 until his death in 1995. In 1994, Rabin shared the Nobel Peace Prize with fellow Israeli politician Shimon Peres and the Palestinian leader, Yasser Arafat. As another consequence of his participation in the Oslo Accords, Rabin was targeted and assassinated by Yigal Amir, a right-wing Israeli extremist.

Accords. This is a common criticism of the Accords, as the desire to form some kind of loose agreement overrode the importance of dealing with the issues at the core of the conflict. However, it was agreed that neither party would take steps to change the status of the Occupied Territories before the final negotiations (Hass 2004: 48). This was widely believed to mean a freeze on the expansion and development of settlements. These affirmations did not reflect the situation on the ground, where settler activity continued unabated.

For the Palestinian population, the Oslo Accords and Israel's intention to adhere to either the letter or the spirit of the negotiations were increasingly drawn into question. These state-based measures were, however, only half the problem. The settler community in the West Bank, a minority of extremists who had long operated on the fringe of Israeli law, were also engaging in sporadic acts of violence against the Palestinian community. The cyclical nature of aggression between ultra-nationalist Israeli settlers and the Palestinians among whom they chose to live has been a feature of the conflict from 1970 onwards. This situation peaked in 1994 with a massacre by Baruch Goldstein, a settler in Hebron who opened fire in a mosque, killing at least 29 Palestinians. In turn, Goldstein was beaten to death at the scene of the massacre. Although this was the act of a lone gunman, it shocked the Palestinian and Israeli public alike. Goldstein was portrayed as a crazed fanatic in the Israeli media. However, this interpretation was not uniformly shared. Among sections of the settler communities, Goldstein gained a hero-like status, and his funeral offered an opportunity for public mobilization against the Oslo Accords and the prospect of an Israeli withdrawal from the Occupied Territories. Further complicating matters, the Israeli state found it necessary to allow Goldstein's funeral cortège to pass through the streets of Jerusalem (Ruthven 2005: 162). This was a grave signal, pointing to the strength of the right-wing influence in Israeli politics and the limitations of the Israeli

BOX 7.5

Likud is a right-wing political party that was formed in September 1973, in the aftermath of the 1973 Arab–Israeli war. The fractious Israeli political scene has meant that even when it is not the ruling party in government, Likud has often been a decisive force through 'unity government' arrangements. Likud has traditionally followed a conservative, nationalist ideology and has been known for its tough stance on security matters and relations with the Palestinians. Likud moved further to the right as a result of the Palestinian Intifadas, and in the twenty-first century it has come to be characterized by its overt rejection of the establishment of a Palestinian state.

government's push towards peace. After the 1994 massacre, the Oslo Accords were effectively irrelevant.

Both sides failed to meet their end of the bargain. From the perspective of the Israeli government, the Oslo Accords were intended to ensure Israel's internal security. However, Palestinian terrorism against Israeli civilians occurred throughout the 1990s as organizations such as HAMAS attempted to derail the process. April 1994 marked the advent of suicide bombings against Israeli targets. HAMAS claimed the first attack in response to the Goldstein massacre. This new tactic in the Palestinian resistance became more frequent over the late 1990s. Over 100 Israelis died in similar attacks between 1994 and 2000, and a climate of fear permeated the lives of the Israeli public. Suicide bombings served to harden Israeli public opinion and achieved little more than inflicting deep wounds on the psyche of both national communities. Israel's commitment to withdraw from the Occupied Territories under the Accords was constantly stalled by the state's military leadership as the need to protect Israelis from militant groups became of utmost importance. Under the Oslo Accords, the newly created Palestinian Authority was charged with dismantling the terrorist infrastructure of organizations such as HAMAS. The Authority, however, plagued by nepotism and corruption, often used its security forces as an instrument of vendetta and revenge; therefore, its ability to counter HAMAS was seriously questionable. Moreover, the Authority's political capacity to temper HAMAS was limited. HAMAS had built up a significant support base, secured as a result of its leadership in the Intifada, its willingness to take the fight to Israel and its welfare activities. Moving against HAMAS could well have led the Authority into open confrontation. Thus, a game of cat and mouse between the two major power-brokers in Palestinian society continued. Despite these nuances, Israel and the major international actors continued to hold the Fatah-dominated Palestinian Authority responsible for the actions of those opposed to the Oslo Accords (Kurz 2005: 22). The Oslo process was amended in a series of subsequent meetings: in Cairo in 1994; Taba in 1995; and Wye River in 1998.

The deep divisions both within and between the Israeli and Palestinian societies presented serious obstacles for the negotiators at these follow-up meetings. The seething Palestinian discontent with the direction of Israeli politics became more evident at each meeting. Simultaneously, popular Palestinian support for the activities of organizations such as HAMAS continued to grow. It was in this difficult political climate that these meetings were designed to restore hope and add substance to a process that was having little effect on the ground. The optimistic atmosphere that surrounded the announcement of the Oslo Accords declined throughout the 1990s. The Palestinians, embittered by the ongoing military occupation and the expansion of the settlement process, had little faith in Israel's intention to hold to its end of the bargain.

Israelis, on the other hand, were living under a constant threat of terrorism, which reached a peak in February 1996 when several attacks claimed 65 Israeli lives. In an example of the unforeseen consequences of security policy, this radicalization in the Palestinian resistance was strongly influenced by the return of many of the 418 leaders deported in 1992 (*Middle East Report* Editorial Team 1993: 36–7). As the voices of reconciliation were drowned out by extremist action on both sides, many Israelis saw the terrorist campaign against civilian targets as proof that the Palestinian community as a whole had reneged on the peace process.

In 1999 an Israeli Labour government came to power under Ehud Barak. Like most Israeli leaders, Barak had a strong military background. He had commanded the strike force of Israeli commandos that had assassinated PLO members in Beirut in Operation Spring of Youth in 1973. This operation had been launched in reponse to the massacre of Israeli athletes at the Munich Olympics in 1972. However, in contrast to the Likud leadership, Barak had reasonable relations with the Palestinian political elite. Like many before him, Barak attempted to resolve the Israeli–Palestinian conflict. The failings of Oslo had drawn the effectiveness of phased reciprocal negotiations into question. Moreover, the bloodshed of the 1990s created a climate in which neither side could afford another long drawn-out political process while the situation on the ground worsened. Internationally, the Clinton administration was in trouble. The Monica Lewinsky affair had compromised the Clinton legacy, and the administration was casting around for a dramatic political victory. A peace agreement in the Middle East was deemed a perfect fit.

The ensuing Camp David 2000 summit was arguably doomed from the outset. Clinton's team pushed both camps into the summit and brought them to the negotiating table on the basis of a one-time, 'all or nothing' approach. This approach had its own drawbacks. Clinton was correct in surmising that both communities would reject another prolonged process. However, the level of distrust built up over the 1990s was a significant obstacle. A common criticism of Camp David is Clinton's assumption that he could create a lasting agreement by force of his own positions and indeed personality. For both the Israeli and Palestinian teams there were other considerations. The Palestinian team that entered the 2000 summit lacked the cohesiveness that had marked the Oslo Accords. A decade of broken promises had created severe discontent within the Palestinian community, HAMAS had gained strength and Arafat's own position was not secure. Indeed, Arafat had resisted the idea of a summit in 2000 completely. As the negotiations developed Arafat's position was revealed as increasingly precarious. The 'all or nothing' approach meant that Barak made the Palestinian team an offer. The exact nature of this offer is not on the public record: Barak insisted against it being written down. However, it is widely understood that Barak's offer was substantial. It is commonly accepted that it included Israeli redeployment from 95 per cent of the West Bank and 100 per cent of the Gaza Strip; the creation of a Palestinian state in the areas of Israeli withdrawal; and Palestinian control over East Jerusalem, including most of the Old City, and 'religious sovereignty' over the Temple Mount, replacing Israeli sovereignty that had been in effect since 1967. These terms constituted a stunning transgression of traditional Israeli 'red lines', and as word of them filtered out there was shock and surprise in Israel. Barak's ability to implement such expansive terms in practice remains one of the open questions of Camp David. However, as it turned out, the Israeli prime minister was not put to the test.

Arafat rejected the proposal and failed to issue a counter-offer, a situation that reinforced the dominant American and Israeli perception of Palestinian intransigence and Arafat's personal commitment to conflict. In the following years, the Israeli perspective held that Arafat 'critically failed', as he was not committed to the securing of a lasting peace, and furthermore that he negotiated with the view that any political agreement was to be 'a temporary tactical tool' (Sher 2005: 60–1). This interpretation of Arafat, which fails to engage with the reality that the Palestinian leader simply did not have the power to commit to the agreement, remained dominant throughout the remainder of his life. A more nuanced reading of Arafat's actions would take into account the Palestinian leader's initial unwillingness to attend the summit as a result of his clear understanding of the fractious and volatile nature of his own community at that time. As Barak himself pointed out, a peace negotiation takes two, and at Camp David 'the other side was not a willing partner *capable* of making the necessary decisions' (Barak 2005: 117; emphasis added). Indeed, the ability of both Arafat and Barak to convince the more extreme elements in their communities to abide by these terms is open to serious question. In the Palestinian community, many factions already viewed the situation as one of outright conflict and thus viewed a peace agreement as 'surrender'. After the decade of compromise under Oslo, the feeling in the Occupied Territories was that enough concessions had already been made. Indeed, Naseer Hasan argues that 'Oslo had become a symbol of diplomatic paralysis and economic impoverishment for the Palestinian people' (2003: 15). The summit ended in a stalemate, and the situation in the Occupied Territories was ripe for another explosion of discontent.

The spark for the 2000 Intifada came on 28 September, when the Likud Party's Ariel Sharon visited the al-Aqsa Mosque in Jerusalem. Some sources are quick to point out the visit was cleared with Palestinian security forces and thus suggest that the consequent eruption of violence was planned (Levy 2003: 130). However, it is self-evident that Sharon's visit was likely to place further pressure on a situation already at breaking point. Sharon had played a central and controversial role in Israeli politics for several decades before his accession to the position of leader of the Likud Party (then in opposition) in 2000. He had a tense history with the Palestinian people, largely due to his role in the siege of Beirut in the early 1980s. Consequently, when he visited the al-Aqsa Mosque in September 2000 Sharon was accompanied by a significant armed security cohort. Israeli Arabs rioted in response to his presence, and the unrest spread quickly throughout Gaza and the West Bank.

The mutilation of two Israeli reservists in Ramallah on 12 October and the subsequent IDF strike against the Palestinian Authority signalled the move into open conflict. The new Intifada was different from the grassroots activism of 1987, and Israel and the Palestinians were quickly dragged into bloodshed. Palestinian militia groups, including the armed wing of the ruling Fatah Party, commenced a campaign of suicide attacks against Israeli civilian targets. The Israelis responded with targeted killings and helicopter gunships. This horrific cycle of violence seemed self-perpetuating as collective punishment, house demolitions and detentions were matched by firearm attacks against settlements and mass terrorist attacks against cafés, buses and shopping precincts.

The election of Likud with Sharon as its leader in 6 February 2001 was another major development. Israelis elected Sharon, who campaigned under the slogan 'Sharon alone can bring peace', largely as a result of the same attributes that so disturbed the Palestinian community. Sharon, as part of the 1948 generation, was seen as a man of action who would take whatever steps were necessary to protect Israeli lives. As Itamar Rabinovich points out, the fact that Sharon had sparked the 2000 Intifada and was consequently elected with a mandate to resolve it is highly ironic (2003: 182). However, the Israeli need to counter terrorism drove the electoral

BOX 7.6

The **2002 Saudi Peace Plan** was a structural mirror of the Camp David approach. Members of the Saudi royal family produced a one-time offer of complete normalization of all Arab relations with Israel in return for Israel's immediate and unconditional withdrawal to its pre-1967 borders. In accordance with the leadership role assumed by the Saudi royals, this proposal carried some weight in the Arab world and became Arab League policy. The Saudi Peace Plan was met with scepticism in Tel Aviv and Washington. In Israel, concerns over the Saudis' ability to implement the agreement, the lack of a US role and a general determination not to withdraw from the established Jewish settlements in the West Bank prevailed. This proposal did, however, seem to push the United States into a more active engagement with the conflict.

BOX 7.7

President George W. Bush announced his **Roadmap to Peace** in June 2002. This proposal was backed by the Quartet (Russia, the United Kingdom, France and the United States). After a consultation process, the final draft of the plan was submitted to Israel and the Palestinians in 2003. Even during these consultations, it appeared that neither side saw the Roadmap as a likely path to resolution. The Roadmap inherited Oslo's structure: it was a phased process, with an ill-defined final settlement. Unlike its predecessor, the Roadmap explicitly intended a two-state solution. Under this plan, a Palestinian state was to be created by 2005. The failure of the Roadmap led to further stagnation in the peace process between Israel and the Palestinians.

process. The second Intifada led to an Islamization of Palestinian politics, which in turn led to a blurring of the line between secular and religious organizations. At the height of the Intifada, coordination between HAMAS and secular militias became common. In this way, the conflict against Israel generated a sense of unity in the divided Palestinian political scene.

The events of September 11, 2001 had a profound impact on the Israeli–Palestinian conflict. The launching of a 'war on terror' allowed Sharon's government to position the conflict within the broader paradigm of fighting terrorism. The blending of Israeli and American suffering at the hands of suicide bombers served only to obscure the very real differences between the need for political resolution of the legitimate Palestinian grievances, and the agenda of transnational terrorist groups such as al-Qaeda.

The Intifada dragged on and was punctuated by various attempts at peace, including the ill-fated Saudi Peace Plan of 2002 and the Bush administration's Roadmap to Peace. As the Intifada continued, Arafat began a steady fall from grace within the international community. In contrast to the warm welcome he received from the Clinton administration on the lawn of the White House in 1993, Arafat was marginalized by the Bush administration, which tightened ties with Tel Aviv. Traditionally, the Palestinians had been careful to walk a comparatively moderate line on all things related to the United States. Policy in the Occupied Territories was dictated by a long-standing awareness of the pivotal role Washington played in forcing concessions from Tel Aviv.

But Arafat's international standing suffered a serious blow in 2002, from which he never recovered. In Operation Defensive Wall in 2002, the IDF seized documents that indicated Arafat had personally approved salary payments to the families of terrorists (Karsh 2000: 7). This led the IDF to physically confine Arafat in his Muqata headquarters in Ramallah, where Israelis claimed he was hiding several wanted terrorists. In 2004, media reports canvassed the possibility that Arafat could be the next target of an Israeli targeted assassination. This debate regarding the potential killing of an elected national official revealed a whole new side to the 'war on terror' in which, it appeared to many Arabs, all traditional norms of political behaviour were being rendered obsolete. Israeli targeting of Arafat only helped restore his popularity among Palestinians. There had been widespread dissatisfaction with his authoritarian style and the corruption that plagued the Palestinian Authority. However, since the 1970s Arafat had played the central role in Palestinian politics. Perhaps more than any individual, Arafat was the personification of a national cause. The massive public outpouring of grief over his death in 2005, despite his highly controversial status, underscored the sense of solidarity the Palestinian people felt with him.

ISRAEL'S SECURITY WALL

As the Intifada dragged on and policing and military operations, including extra-judicial killings and house demolitions, failed to halt the terrorist tactics of the Palestinian militias, Israel changed its own tactics. Tel Aviv decided to literally wall off the Occupied Territories. This decision was condemned by the Vatican and the European Union (European Union 2003) and even cautioned against by Washington. The Israeli official line remains that the barrier is a required security measure and may be removed should the security situation allow.[2] This unilateral step was decried by the Palestinian political leadership as it was a clear move away from the (largely unsuccessful) bilateral negotiations that had characterized the conflict. From an Israeli perspective, the ethical considerations raised by the walling off of the Palestinians were balanced against the requirement of national security. This decision was validated for many in Israel by the results; during its first year in existence a significant drop was noted in terrorist attacks against Israel. As Tami Jacoby points out, this led to a 'widespread belief in Israel that the separation barrier is an effective counterterrorist strategy' (2005: 35). This outcome may also have been affected by other security measures, such as leadership changes after the targeted killings of a proportion of the HAMAS leadership, including the organization's spiritual leader and founder, Sheikh Yassin.

The erection of the security barrier was seen by many in the Arab world as definitive proof of Israel's tendency to engage with the peace process on a rhetorical level, while displaying a determination to alter the reality on the ground. The wall that now divides Israel from the Occupied Territories roughly follows the pre-1967 borders, the so-called 'Green Line', which is the de facto border accepted by the international community. However, in some areas the wall deviates from this boundary significantly to include on the Israeli side a number of major Jewish settlements in the West Bank. Palestinians view these settlements as illegal and a direct challenge to the peace process. Removing these settlements from the Occupied Territories has been a constant Palestinian demand. The apparent expropriation of Palestinian land by construction of the security wall brought the matter into the international arena.

On 9 July 2004, the International Court of Justice delivered its advisory opinion on the legality of Israel's separation barrier. Israel refused to cooperate in the proceeding, contending that the Court did not have jurisdiction to hear the matter. In a document submitted to the Court, Israel argued that the barrier was a political, as opposed to legal, matter. Thus, the issue should have been dealt with bilaterally between Israel and the Palestinians. This stance was highly ironic, given that the erection of the security wall was a unilateral undertaking. In a majority decision, the Court denied Israel's argument. The main issues discussed in the Court's findings related to the effects of the barrier on the right of the Palestinian people to self-determination, and Israel's contravention of international humanitarian law as such. Israel argued that the violation of Palestinian rights to self-determination was outweighed by the security function of the wall for the safety of both Palestinians and Israelis. The Court stated that, although Israel had the right to protect its citizens against violence, any defensive actions in this respect were required to comply with international law. The Court stipulated that Israel should cease construction of the wall, dismantle the parts of the wall that deviated from the Green Line and compensate Palestinians who had already suffered losses. Israel did not comply with this instruction.[3]

THE GAZA WITHDRAWAL

The inability of the international community to compel Israel to reverse its construction of the barrier lent credence to Arab perceptions that Israel acts outside international law, and is not held fully accountable when it does so. This view was reinforced in early 2005, when Sharon announced Israel's unilateral withdrawal from the Gaza Strip. This tiny area of land had been occupied by Israel since 1967. It is one of the most densely populated tracts of land in the world, being home to approximately 1.3 million Palestinians – 33 per cent of whom live in United Nations-funded refugee camps. In mid-2005, approximately 8,000 Jewish settlers also lived in the Gaza Strip, accompanied by the IDF contingent necessary to provide them protection.

In the context of Israeli politics, Sharon's decision to unilaterally withdraw Israeli settlers from the Gaza Strip was a brave step: in 1995 Yitzhak Rabin was assassinated by a Jewish extremist for his role in the

Oslo Accords. Washington, for its part, welcomed Sharon's move as proof that the Israeli prime minister was committed to advancing the peace process. This was a clear demonstration of the close relationship between the Sharon government and the Bush administration, a relationship fostered in the climate of the 'war on terror'. Bush's earlier endorsement of Sharon as 'a man of peace' (Slevin and Allen 2002) had revealed a lack of familiarity with Sharon's military history. Sharon was seen by many in the Arab world as a figurehead of aggressive Israeli military doctrine. Bush's ill-conceived comment was interpreted as demonstrating a marked willingness to forgive the past transgressions of Israelis, but not those of Arabs. As a result, relations between the Palestinian leadership and the United States grew increasingly complicated. The Bush administration's determination to exclude Arafat from playing a meaningful role in the peace process, while endorsing the ostensible peace-making credentials of Sharon, further entrenched the Arab view of Washington's policy in the region as inequitable.

Moreover, Israel's unilateral withdrawal from Gaza contravened decades of bilateral and multilateral attempts at reconciliation. Amid intense international interest, the planned withdrawal took place in September 2005, and Gaza was 'returned' to the Palestinians. Simultaneously, the Palestinian leadership was at pains to stress to the international community that Israel maintained an ambiguous position on the status of settlements in the West Bank. As a result, the 'natural growth' of Israeli inhabitants of the West Bank continued. In addition, the Israeli government pushed ahead with the E1 Plan, which allows for the literal dissection of Jerusalem from the West Bank.[4] Furthermore, the situation in Gaza – now 'autonomous' Palestinian land – was far from secure. In addition to endemic overcrowding, lack of industry and internal political tension, Israel continued to control maritime, airspace and most land access.

The Gaza pullout also had significant repercussions for Israeli politics. Sharon's decision was not unanimously supported by the Likud Party, and as a result of internal disagreements Sharon left the party that he had helped found. Sharon's spilt with Likud led to the formation of the Kadima Party, essentially a centrist reconstitution of Likud, in November 2005. But in January 2006, the Israeli prime minister suffered an incapacitating stroke that brought his long participation in Israeli politics to a close. The Kadima Party maintained its grasp on power in the March 2006 elections, but failed to secure a parliamentary majority. Sharon's successor, Ehud Olmert, was an anomaly in Israeli politics, having no military background. This lack of experience was quickly tested, as HAMAS and Hezbollah stepped up their military operations against Israel, capturing IDF soldiers in various operations. The July War of 2006, explored in Chapter 3, mired Israel in yet another regional conflict.

The death of Arafat and the incapacitation of Sharon signalled a shift in Israeli–Palestinian politics, as the departure of two men intimately entwined in the crisis left power vacuums in their respective communities. In the territories, the January 2006 elections marked an important turning point in Palestinian politics. HAMAS had played a significant role in Palestinian politics on an unofficial level for nearly two decades. As an Islamist organization committed to the establishment of an Islamic state, HAMAS had a limited relationship with the formal Palestinian political processes then dominated by the secular-nationalist Fatah movement. Despite some internal dissent, in the 1996 elections HAMAS did not field any candidates, as participation in the elections was seen as implicit endorsement of the peace process (Nusse 1999: 161). However, over the subsequent decade, dissatisfaction with Fatah had grown and HAMAS decided to test the election waters. The result was a landslide victory for HAMAS, which won 74 of the 123 parliamentary seats in the election held on 25 January 2006. This electoral victory came as a complete surprise to observers and revealed the extent of dissatisfaction with the Fatah administration. This new development presented a serious challenge to US policy in the Middle East.

A cornerstone of the Bush doctrine has been the call for democratization in the Middle East. The 2006 Palestinian elections were widely acknowledged as free and fair. The expression of popular Palestinian will was the election of an Islamist organization with an explicitly anti-Israel stance. HAMAS had also played a strong social welfare role in Palestinian society, and its lack of corruption in comparison with the Palestinian Authority must have played a significant part in its election victory. HAMAS's rise to power reflected the Palestinian people's frustration with two decades of stagnation and failure in the peace process under the leadership of Fatah-dominated authorities. This was a watershed moment for Washington: either endorse HAMAS in line with the stated policy of supporting the democratization of Arab societies, or reject the results of a democratic process that had delivered victory to a movement listed by the United States as a terrorist organization. Washington followed the latter course. US funding to the Occupied Territories ceased, Arab countries were warned against supporting the new government and Israel withheld customs revenue (Elhadj 2006: 147).

Over the course of 2006, funding was slowly reinstated by the international community, most notably by the European Union. However, Washington maintained a hardline position by refusing to acknowledge HAMAS as a legitimate political player. The major losers in this decision were the Palestinian people. In April 2007, Oxfam reported that, since the election of HAMAS, the Western aid embargo that was intended to influence the Palestinian political process had triggered a humanitarian crisis in the Occupied Territories (2007). In 2007, two-thirds of the Palestinian population was living in poverty, a 30 per cent increase from

2006. The aid embargo greatly affected structures of governance and the provision of public services, most notably from doctors, nurses, teachers and police officers. Salary payments have been sporadic in the public sector since February 2006. In an effort to avoid a humanitarian crisis the European Union set up a Temporary International Mechanism (TIM) to channel aid to the Palestinian Territories while bypassing the HAMAS-led Palestinian Authority. Inadvertently, this served to further undermine Palestinian political structures and entrench divisions within Palestinian society.

Tensions between Palestinian factions continued unabated in this context, and the government began to disintegrate in June 2007. The ensuing split between HAMAS and Fatah further destabilized Palestinian politics, leading to open confrontation in the Gaza Strip. HAMAS supporters carried out attacks on Fatah leaders in Gaza, leading to a division of political authority between Gaza and the West Bank. As Fatah consolidated its hold on the West Bank, the international community moved to resume aid and financial support to the Fatah-controlled West Bank but not the Gaza Strip. This decision belies the international community's commitment to democratization in the Middle East and further underscores the hypocrisy of Washington's approach to Arab politics.

CONCLUSION

The Palestinian–Israeli dispute is one of the most serious causes of instability in the modern Middle East. The ongoing political, social and economic crisis of the Palestinian people has proved a profound challenge to Israel and its Arab neighbours. In the two decades spanning 1987–2007, the relationship between the two national communities was marked by conflict and division. The Oslo Accords stood out as offering the greatest promise for peace. Yet the failure of both communities to achieve peace has placed the Palestinian population in particular in a situation of spiralling misery. The events set in motion by the ascendency of HAMAS to the seat of power were a shock to the Palestinian people. It seemed that the Palestinian democratic desire to elect their own government was not acceptable to the United States and the international community. Under the weight of the international boycott, the Palestinian Authority collapsed and the Territories descended into open hostility, resulting in the separation of the Gaza Strip from the West Bank.

The United States has played a central role in this conflict through its alliance with Israel. Forged in the context of the Cold War, this has proven one of modern history's most enduring state-to-state relationships. However, since the early 1990s, Washington has actively attempted to play a broader role than that of Israel's steadfast ally. The assumption of the 'peace-broker' role was problematic. By claiming the mediation mantle, Washington effectively set itself up for failure. The impossibility of being both loyal ally to Israel and regional peace-broker has been made clear in the last 15 years. Yet, by laying public claim to both titles, Washington brought expectations of fairness and objectivity upon itself. The consistent use of its veto power in the UN Security Council to protect Israel from resolutions that insist that Tel Aviv change its policy towards the Occupied Territories, the continued and increased funding of Israel's already formidable military capacity, and the unstinting political support for Israel's regional policy have all greatly affected Arab views of the United States. Although Washington presents itself as the 'honest broker' in the long search for resolution of this conflict, its actions suggest a nearly myopic endorsement of Israeli policy.

This situation has been further complicated since the launching of the 'war on terror' and the development of regional US policy. As Washington moved to confront transnational terrorism, the Palestinian question became increasingly reframed within the broader conflict. This is highly problematic, as for the Arab world the Palestinian question is one of national liberation. The fundamental differences in political understandings of this conflict feed into the problems of interpretation that the United States currently faces in the Middle East. In the United States, Israel's struggle with the Palestinians is understood as one of confronting terrorism and assuring national security. In the Arab world, the Palestinian struggle against Israel is understood as one of self-defence against occupation. The underlying assumptions of these two narratives are so different that more often than not, each side is entirely unable to comprehend the other's point of view. The reality of Israel's position of absolute power vis-à-vis the Palestinian community reinforces this disparity as well as the sense of powerlessness and inequity felt by many in the Arab world.

The Israeli–Palestinian dispute is a complex equation of nationalism, religion and politics ingrained by selective readings of history and deeply connected to the sense of injustice felt by both communities. The resolution of this conflict is vital to the stability of both Israel and the Middle East. Washington's enduring support for Israel has complicated the search for peace and, subsequently, damaged its standing in the broader Middle East.

NOTES

1 This incident was narrated by President Clinton to Dan Rather of CBS on the news programme '60 Minutes', on 20 June 2004; available at www.cbsnews.com/stories/2004/06/18/60minutes/main624848.shtml.
2 For Israel's perspective, see http://securityfence.mfa.gov.il.
3 The full text of the ICJ ruling is available at www.zionism-israel.com/hdoc/

ICJ_fence.htm. Israel's written submission to the ICJ can be found at http://securityfence.mfa.gov.il/mfm/web/main/document.asp?DocumentID=49708&MissionID=45187.
4 For a detailed overview of the E1 plan by the Applied Research Institute–Jerusalem, refer to www.poica.org/editor/case_studies/view.php?recordID=570.

REFERENCES

Abu-Amr, Ziad (1994) *Islamic Fundamentalism in the Gaza and the West Bank: Muslim Brotherhood and Islamic Jihad* (Indianapolis: Indiana University Press).

Barak, Ehud (2005) 'The Myths Spread about Camp David Are Baseless', in Shimon Shamir and Bruce Maddy-Weitzman (eds), *The Camp David Summit – What Went Wrong?* (Brighton: Sussex Academic Press).

Bizhara, Azmay (1999) 'The Uprising's Impact on Israel', in Joel Beinin and Zachary Lockman (eds), *Intifada: The Palestinian Uprising Against Israeli Occupation* (London: South End Press).

Elhadj, Elie (2006) *The Islamic Shield: Arab Resistance to Democratic and Religious Reforms* (Boca Raton, FL: BrownWalker Press).

European Union (2003) 'Statement to the Tenth Emergency Special Session of the General Assembly of the United Nations by H.E. Ambassador Marcello Spatafora, Permanent Representative of Italy to the UN on behalf of the European Union', 20 October, available at www.eu-un.europa.eu/articles/articleslist_s7_en.htm.

Farsoun, Sami and Landis, Jean (1999) 'The Sociology of an Uprising: The Roots of the Intifada', in Jamal Raji Nassar and Roger Heacock (eds), *Intifada: Palestine at the Crossroads* (New York: Praeger).

HAMAS (1988) 'The Covenant of the Islamic Resistance Movement (Hamas)', 18 August, available at www.mideastweb.org/HAMAS.htm.

Hasan, Naseer (2003) *Dishonest Broker: The U.S. Role in Israel and Palestine* (London: South End Books).

Hass, Amira (2004) 'Israeli Colonialism under the Guise of the Peace Process, 1993–2000', in Dan Leon (ed.), *Who's Left in Israel?: Radical Political Alternatives for the Future of Israel* (Brighton: Sussex Academic Press).

Hassassian, Manuel (2004) 'Why Did Oslo Fail? Lessons for the Future', in Robert Rothstein, Moshe Ma'oz and Khalil Shikaki (eds), *The Israeli–Palestinian Peace Process: Oslo and the Lessons of Failure* (Brighton: Sussex Academic Press).

Hroub, Khaled (2000) *HAMAS: Political Thought and Practice* (Washington DC: Institute for Palestinian Studies).

Jacoby, Tami Amanda (2005) *Bridging the Barrier: Israeli Unilateral Engagement* (London: Ashgate).

Karsh, Efraim (2000) *Arafat's War: The Man and his Battle for Israeli Conquest* (New York: Grove).

Kurz, Anat (2005) *Fatah and the Politics of Violence: The Institutionalization of a Popular Struggle* (Brighton: Sussex Academic Press).

Levy, Joshua (2003) *The Agony of the Promised Land* (New York: iUniverse).

Meir, Hatina (2001) *Islam and Salvation in Palestine: The Islamic Jihad Movement* (Tel Aviv: Tel Aviv University).

Middle East Report Editorial Team (1993) 'From the Editors: Clinton, Israel and the Hamas Expulsion', *Middle East Report* Vol. 181, March–April, pp. 36–7.

Milton-Edwards, Beverly (1999) *Islamic Politics in Palestine* (London: IB Tauris).

Morris, Benny (2001) *Righteous Victims – A History of the Zionist–Arab Conflict 1881–2001* (New York: Vintage Books).

Nusse, Andrea (1999) *Muslim Palestine: The Ideology of HAMAS* (London: Routledge).

Oxfam (2007) 'Poverty in Palestine: The Human Cost of the Financial Boycott', April, available at www.oxfam.org/en/files/bn070413_palestinian_aid_boycott.pdf/download.

Rabinovich, Itamar (2003) *Waging Peace: Israel and the Arabs 1948–2003* (Princeton, NJ: Princeton University Press).

Ruthven, Malise (2005) *Fundamentalism: The Search For Meaning* (Oxford: Oxford University Press).

Sher, Gilead (2005) 'Lesson from the Camp David Experience', in Shimon Shamir and Bruce Maddy-Weitzman (eds), *The Camp David Summit – What Went Wrong?* (Brighton: Sussex Academic Press).

Slevin, P. and Allen, M. (2002) 'Bush: Sharon a "Man of Peace"', *Washington Post*, 19 April.

SUGGESTED FURTHER READING

Beitler, Ruth Margolies (2004) *The Path to Mass Rebellion: An Analysis of Two Intifadas* (Lanham, MD: Lexington Books).

Bisharah, Marwan (2002) *Palestine/Israel: Peace or Apartheid? Occupation, Terrorism, and the Future*, updated edition (London: Zed Books).

Chomsky, Noam (2003) *Middle East Illusions: Including Peace in the Middle East? Reflections on Justice and Nationhood* (Lanham, MD: Rowman & Littlefield).

Dan, Uri (2006) *Ariel Sharon: An Intimate Portrait* (New York: Palgrave Macmillan).

Hart, Alan (1984) *Arafat, a Political Biography*, revised edition (London: Sidgwick & Jackson).

Karsh, Efraim (2003) *Arafat's War: The Man and His Battle for Israeli Conquest* (New York: Grove Press).

Khalid, Harub (2000) *HAMAS: Political Thought and Practice* (Washington DC: Institute for Peace Studies).

Kurz, Anat N. (2005) *Fatah and the Politics of Violence: The Institutionalisation of a Popular Struggle* (Portland, OR: Sussex Academic Press).

The Jerusalem Media and Communications Centre, www.jmcc.org/publicpoll/pop/01/jun/pop4.htm#one.

Leon, Dan (ed.) (2004) *Who's Left in Israel?: Radical Political Alternatives for the Future of Israel* (Brighton: Sussex Academic Press).

Makovsky, David (1996) *Making Peace with the PLO: The Rabin Government's Road to the Oslo Accord* (Boulder, CO: Westview Press).

Mishal, Shaul (1986) *The PLO under Arafat: Between Gun and Olive Branch* (New Haven, CT: Yale University Press).

Mishal, Shaul and Sela, Avraham (2000) *The Palestinian HAMAS: Visions, Violence, and Coexistence* (New York: Columbia University Press).

Nassar, Jamal Raji and Heacock, Roger (1990) *Intifada: Palestine at the Crossroads* (New York: Praeger).

Parsons, Nigel Craig (2005) *The Politics of the Palestinian Authority: From Oslo to al-Aqsa* (New York: Routledge).

Peretz, John (1990) *Intifada: The Palestinian Uprising* (Boulder, CO: Westview Press).

Rashid, Khalidi (2006) *The Iron Cage: The Story of the Palestinian Struggle for Statehood* (Boston: Beacon Press).

Rothstein, Robert, Ma'oz, Moshe and Shikaki, Khalil (eds) (2004) *The Israeli–Palestinian Peace Process: Oslo and the Lessons of Failure* (Brighton: Sussex Academic Press).

Rubenberg, Cheryl (2003) *The Palestinians: In Search of a Just Peace* (Boulder, CO: Lynne Rienner Publishers).

Rubin, Barry M. (1999) *The Transformation of Palestinian Politics: From Revolution to State-Building* (Cambridge, MA: Harvard University Press).

Rubin, Barry and Colp Rubin, Judith (2003) *Yasir Arafat: A Political Biography* (New York: Oxford University Press).

Said, Edward (2002) *The End of the Peace Process: Oslo and After*, revised and updated edition (London: Granta Books).

Said, Edward, with David Barsamian (2003) *Culture and Resistance: Conversations with Edward W. Said* (Cambridge, MA: South End Press).

Shamir, Shimon and Maddy-Weitzman, Bruce (eds) (2005) *The Camp David Summit – What Went Wrong?: Americans, Israelis and Palestinians Analyze the Failure of the Boldest Attempt Ever to Resolve the Palestinian-Israeli Conflict* (Brighton: Sussex Academic Press).

Watson, Geoffrey R. (2000) *The Oslo Accords: International Law and the Israeli–Palestinian Peace Agreements* (Oxford: Oxford University Press).

SUGGESTED STUDY QUESTIONS

1 What were the major obstacles to attaining peace via the Oslo Accords?

2 What was the nature and impact of international involvement in the Oslo Accords?

3 What were the major obstacles to securing a lasting peace agreement at Camp David?

4 What was the nature and impact of international involvement at Camp David?

5 How have Middle Eastern states responded to the increasing role of the United States in the post-Cold War era?

CHAPTER 8

The Iraq 'Adventure' and Arab Perceptions of the United States

The events of September 11, 2001, had a profound and ongoing effect on the Middle East. The initial conflict of the 'war on terror' – the invasion of Afghanistan to oust the Taliban and eradicate al-Qaeda's operational capacity – received reasonable levels of international support. The Taliban was a broadly unpopular organization and its position in Afghanistan was widely condemned. Moreover, UN Security Council Resolution 1267 of 1999, which called for the Taliban to hand over Osama bin Laden, had clearly demonstrated the international community's desire to see the al-Qaeda leader tried on terrorism charges. The terrorist attacks of 2001 imbued this agenda with a new sense of urgency. The US-led invasion of Afghanistan was broadly understood as a legitimate response, and, although many in the international system articulated concerns about its effect on the war-torn country, a military campaign seemed inevitable.

However, the Bush administration increasingly expressed a much more expansive foreign policy agenda. The National Security Strategy of 2002 emphasized unilateralism, Washington's right to undertake pre-emptive military action and the need to promote US values (National Security Council 2002). In many ways, this is consistent with generations of US foreign policy that pivoted on a perception of America's special and unique place in the international system. Washington's focus on pre-emption led military and political planners to consider expanding the horizons of the 'war on terror'. Consequently, the relationship between the Arab world and the United States was dealt another devastating blow as it became clear that Washington was determined to lead a 'coalition of the willing' to invade Iraq and topple Saddam Hussein. The Bush administration's case for war included, at various times, the alleged presence of weapons of mass destruction, Iraqi failure to comply with UN Security Council resolutions, allegations of links between Iraq and international terrorist organizations such as al-Qaeda, Saddam Hussein's dictatorship and its human rights abuses, and finally the perceived responsibility of the United States to 'liberate' the Iraqi people and democratize the state. In early 2008, the state of Iraq appears close to disintegration as the 'post-war' insurgency continues to rage and American troops and civilian Iraqis are indiscriminately killed in ever-increasing numbers. Prisoner abuse scandals, military occupation and the fracturing of Iraq's civil society have all fed popular Arab anger against Washington.

The post-war carnage in Iraq is perpetrated by Iraqi factions determined to gain control of the country and by local and foreign Arab organizations intent on preventing a US 'victory', either military or ideological. In the West, the media focuses on the factional character of the violence. However, in the Middle East, the focus is different: the destabilization caused by the military occupation is widely seen as the catalyst for the growth and entrenchment of these organizations. The organizations tearing the state of Iraq apart appear committed to securing their own positions in a fragile political system and to inflicting as much damage as is possible upon the coalition forces. Despite the reality of intra-Iraqi conflict and the presence of international militants, popular Arab anger and despair have focused largely on Washington's role in creating the conditions that have placed the state of Iraq in a spiral of sectarian violence. Moreover, Washington's failure to comprehend the delicate sectarian situation in Iraq, and to have foreseen the likelihood of communal violence in the aftermath of 'regime change', is singled out for criticism. This chapter explores how the Middle East has responded to the US-led invasion of Iraq. This conflict, widely seen as a neo-colonialist adventure to secure American interests, is an important factor in the pervasiveness of contemporary Middle Eastern anti-Americanism.

IRAQ: THE ROAD TO WAR

In 2007, US authorities estimated the population of Iraq at over 27 million people.[1] Like most Arab states, Iraq has an extremely young population, with nearly 40 per cent of all citizens under the age of 14. The population is predominantly Arab with a 15–20 per cent Kurdish minority. An overwhelmingly Muslim country, Iraq has a Shia majority of 60–65 per cent. Despite this, the Sunni minority, of which Saddam Hussein was a part, ruled the country with repressive force until the government's overthrow in the 2003 US-led invasion. As has been explored, the history of Iraq in the twentieth century was marked by conflict, with Saddam Hussein's regime leading the country into two devastating wars.

Saddam's rule of Iraq was autocratic and characterized by the persecution of the Shia majority and the Kurds and by the suppression of all political opposition. As examined in earlier chapters, Saddam's Iraq experienced costly conflicts with Iran (1980–88) and the US-led coalition (1991) over its occupation of Kuwait. The years between 1991 and 2003 saw Iraq marked by its status as a 'rogue state' on the fringes of the international community. In 1990, the United States imposed a stringent sanctions regime on Iraq through UN Security Council Resolution 661. This resolution was implemented in order to force Iraq's withdrawal from Kuwait, and was later used to strengthen the cease-fire agreements pertaining to the destruction of all Iraq's weapons in the aftermath of the 1991 war. Considering this, as we turn our attention to the lead-up to the 2003 conflict in Iraq, it is important to contextualize this conflict within a decade of political brinksmanship between Baghdad and the international community, or more specifically, Washington.

The 2003 invasion of Iraq was not a sudden knee-jerk reaction by the Bush administration. The 'war on terror' may well have provided the domestic political climate in which this conflict could occur, but the 2003 war resulted from a decision-making process that can be traced to the 1980s. The neo-conservative movement was at the heart of the move to topple Saddam Hussein. This generation of policy-makers, products of the Cold War mindset and now presiding over an unrivalled military apparatus, had long agitated for the removal of the Iraqi regime. In the political 'spin' that marked the lead-up to war, attempts were made to situate Iraq within the broader paradigm of the 'war on terror'. For example, President Bush's 2002 State of Union address, the infamous 'axis of evil' speech, explicitly drew the link.

> States like these, and their terrorist allies, constitute an axis of evil, arming to threaten the peace of the world. By seeking weapons of mass destruction, these regimes pose a grave and growing danger. They could provide these arms to terrorists, giving them the means to match their hatred.
>
> (Bush 2002a)

However, any ideological linkage between al-Qaeda and secular-nationalist Iraq was unlikely. In relation to supporting terrorism, even the White House acknowledged that the focus of the Baghdad regime was on the provision of financial support to Palestinian organizations committed to militant action against Israel, including providing payments to the families of suicide bombers (White House, Office of the Press Secretary 2002). This was a problematic basis upon which to enact a military campaign under the auspices of the global 'war on terror', especially as many of the Palestinian organizations were also supported by US allies such as Saudi Arabia.

The neo-conservative preoccupation with Baghdad pre-dated the events of September 11, 2001. This stream in the Republican Party had faded into the shadows as a result of the disastrous Iran–Contra affair of the 1980s. The latter years of the Clinton administration saw its return to the public eye as the issue of Iraq moved ever more firmly into the spotlight. In 1998, the Project for the New American Century, a Republican-influenced think-tank, petitioned Clinton 'to undertake military action as diplomacy is clearly failing. In the long term, it means removing Saddam Hussein and his regime from power' (1998). Many future heavyweights of the Bush administration – individuals such as Richard Perle, Paul Wolfowitz and Richard Armitage – signed this document. Considering this, the mindset that engendered the invasion of Iraq should be seen as a long-standing trend in US politics. In relation to foreign policy formulation, the neo-conservative impulse can be understood as highly interventionist. More specifically, it has come to designate a willingness to use military force, unilaterally if necessary, to intervene in the affairs of other sovereign states. This mindset was given new force by the relationship between Iraq and the United States in the Clinton years.

In the 1990s, Iraq's relationship with the international community remained difficult. The UN Security Council passed numerous resolutions aimed at the complete disarming of Iraq and the destruction of its weapons capability. In the aftermath of the 1991 conflict, the Security Council, having already passed Resolution 661, moved to strengthen its stance on Iraq. Resolution 687 called for the destruction of Iraq's weapons of mass destruction and established a weapons inspection team to monitor compliance with the directive. But the Iraqi regime angered Washington by continually stymying this process, and the inspection process failed completely in 1998. In 1999, the United Nations attempted to resolve the impasse with Iraq through the establishment of the United Nations Monitoring, Verification and Inspection Commission (UNMOVIC). This commission was established under the mandate established by Security Council Resolution 1284, which explicitly linked the lifting of sanctions on Iraq with Iraqi compliance with the UN inspection regime. However, Baghdad again sought to stall and obstruct the inspections team on numerous occasions and was thus deemed in breach of the resolutions pertaining to its weapons programme. Baghdad's decision to reject Resolution 1284 in December 1999 paved the way for US efforts to build a legal case for invasion.

This game of diplomatic and political brinksmanship was played out in the assembly halls of the United Nations, yet the central role of the United States was evident to the Arab world. As a result, Arab suspicion of American hypocrisy gained strength throughout the 1990s. Washington's eagerness to use military force to resolve the Iraqi question was seen as a transparent contradiction of its willingness to employ different means in other crisis zones, such as North Korea. Moreover, the increasing political bluster against Iraq, ostensibly in response to Baghdad's failure to comply with the will of the United Nations, was seen as a blatant case of double standards when seen in the light of the repeated violations of Security Council resolutions by other states in the region, notably the US allies Turkey (in relation to Cyprus and the Kurds) and Israel (in relation to the occupation of Palestinian territory) (Zunes 2002). Arab discontent focused on Israeli actions, as Israel remained in violation of Security Council Resolutions 1322 (2000), 1403, 1405 and 1435 (2002).[2] Moreover, as Washington sought to coerce Baghdad's compliance, Israel continued to enjoy the protection of the US veto power in relation to the international community's concerns over the Israeli military response to the 2000 Intifada. This diplomatic assault on Iraq in the corridors of the United Nations was matched by an uncompromising public position. Clinton's Secretary of State, Madeline Albright, under media questioning regarding the Iraqi deaths caused by the sanctions, replied with an ill-conceived response that the administration believed that scores of civilian deaths were 'worth it' (Cortright 2001). This fed popular regional perceptions that Arab life was accorded a lower value by Washington.

The neo-conservatives gained a position of prominence with the electoral victory of George W. Bush in 2001. One of the first acts of the new Bush administration in relation to Iraq was to tighten the no-fly zone, which had been established in the aftermath of the 1991 Gulf War. On 16 February 2001, a group of 24 American and British warplanes undertook sorties into Iraq to dismantle anti-aircraft defences in no-fly zone areas (Hallenberg and Karlsson 2005: 83). The neo-conservative agenda for the removal of Saddam Hussein was raised again in the corridors of the White House. The terrorist attacks of September 11 gave the neo-conservative agenda the boost it needed to push it from the periphery of American foreign policy thinking to centre stage. In the new era of heightened security concerns and the emergent military doctrine adopted under Donald Rumsfeld, the United States could not allow 'rogue' or 'failed' states to offer a launching pad for global terror. Drawing from the lessons of Afghanistan, the United States could not ignore the far-reaching implications of local and regional issues for its global interests.

The new policy towards the Middle East was fully supported by the United Kingdom and Australia. Tony Blair, the UK Prime Minister, articulated a similar British agenda in relation to Iraq, although he phrased this policy in terms of preserving the international system:

At stake in Iraq is not just peace or war. It is the authority of the UN. Resolution 1441 is clear. All we are asking is that it now be upheld. If it

BOX 8.1

The **Bush doctrine** refers to the guiding principles of Bush administration (2001–08) foreign policy and its 'war on terror'. After September 11, 2001, President George W. Bush brought about significant change in America's foreign policy. The 2002 National Security Strategy clearly outlines this new direction. Heavily influenced by neo-conservative thinking, the key elements of this new strategy include emphasizing the promotion of democracy and freedom as an antidote to tyranny and terrorism, the pre-emptive use of force against a threat before it has clearly emerged, America's right to act unilaterally in the face of a perceived threat or in the pursuit of American national interests, and the right to utilize the full power of the American military in the pursuit of these goals. The wars in Afghanistan and Iraq are both clear examples of the implementation of the Bush doctrine.

is not, the consequences will stretch far beyond Iraq. If the UN cannot be the way of resolving this issue, that is a dangerous moment for our world.

(Blair 2003)

As the leaders of the United States and the United Kingdom moved to present their case, American and British interests were increasingly equated with the interests of the international community. In this way, Iraqi intransigence was presented as a dangerous snub to the global community.

The doctrine of pre-emption was the product of this new thinking. President Bush's rhetoric left little doubt of the American position, which, for the domestic arena at least, amalgamated the actions of a handful of al-Qaeda operatives and the state policy of Iraq.

[Iraq] possesses and produces chemical and biological weapons. It is seeking nuclear weapons. It has given shelter and support to terrorism, and practices terror against its own people. The entire world has witnessed Iraq's eleven-year history of defiance, deception and bad faith. Some citizens wonder, after 11 years of living with this problem, why do we need to confront it now? And there's a reason. We've experienced the horror of September the 11th. We have seen that those who hate America are willing to crash airplanes into buildings full of innocent people. Our enemies would be no less willing, in fact, they would be eager, to use biological or chemical, or a nuclear weapon. Knowing these realities, America must not ignore the threat gathering against us.

> Facing clear evidence of peril, we cannot wait for the final proof – the smoking gun – that could come in the form of a mushroom cloud.
>
> (Bush 2002b)

London and Washington were conscious of the role that the United Nations could play in legitimizing action against Iraq and were keen to spur it into action. On 8 November 2002 the UN Security Council passed Resolution 1441, which demanded Iraq's immediate cooperation with the inspections process and called for full disarmament. This resolution was understood as a compromise between the strong wording that the United States wanted – wording that would authorize invasion automatically upon non-compliance – and the softer French and Russian versions.

Resolution 1441 signalled the intensification of Washington's journey towards war, as it aimed to provide a multilateral framework for an eventual attack on Iraq. Although sections of the resolution were vague, two major themes emerged. First, the Iraqi regime was required to accomplish a sequence of tasks over the following few months or almost certainly face serious consequences, most likely a US-led attack. Second, in the event of non-compliance, the United States *was not automatically authorized to take unilateral military action*, and certainly not before another meeting of the Security Council. This resolution was very different to UN Security Council Resolution 678 of 29 December 1990, which had provided the legitimate legal framework for Operation Desert Storm. However, the international body's desire to check the US agenda was not internalized in Washington. As the march to war intensified, President Bush outlined his position, which contained significant differences from the British line.

> Intelligence gathered by this and other governments leaves no doubt that the Iraq regime continues to possess and conceal some of the most lethal weapons ever devised . . . The United States of America has the sovereign authority to use force in assuring its own national security. America tried to work with the United Nations to address this threat because we wanted to resolve the issue peacefully. We believe in the mission of the United Nations . . . On November 8, the Security Council unanimously passed Resolution 1441, finding Iraq in material breach of its obligations, and vowing serious consequences if Iraq did not fully and immediately disarm. Yet, some permanent members of the Security Council have publicly announced they will veto any resolution that compels the disarmament of Iraq. These governments share our assessment of the danger, but not our resolve to meet it. Many nations, however, do have the resolve and fortitude to act against this threat to peace, and a broad coalition is now gathering to enforce the just demands of the world. The United Nations Security Council has not lived up to its responsibilities, so we will rise to ours.
>
> (Bush 2003)

With this style of rhetoric President Bush was drawing on a history of American exceptionalism in foreign policy formulation. Moreover, he implicitly identifies the United States as the alternative global force of governance to the United Nations. As Mohammed Ayoob suggests, the US administration made it very clear that 'unless the premier international organization agreed to act as an instrument of American policy it would be consigned to the dustbin of history' (2003: 29). Unlike the broad-based consensus achieved in 1991, the 'coalition of the willing' of 2003 was a haphazard group of states closely aligned to the United States. On 20 March, the United States commenced the invasion of Iraq against the vocal opposition of many of the world's other major powers and against the expressed wishes of the bulk of the Arab states. The Iraqi army folded quickly in the face of the American 'shock and awe' campaign of aerial bombing. President Bush declared victory on 1 May 2003. The US policy of de-Ba'thization and the decommissioning of the national army proved seriously misguided as, stripped of its political and security infrastructure, the Iraqi community lurched towards chaos. Saddam loyalists, various sectarian militias and an unknown number of foreign fighters mounted a costly and horrific resistance to foreign occupation. This violence has set Iraq's sectarian communities against each other and mired the state in a virtual civil war that, in late 2007, shows little sign of abating.

The rationale that the Bush administration employed to legitimize the invasion of Iraq is worthy of investigation here. Essentially, the decision to invade can be understood on three broad lines of argument: the legal, moral and geo-strategic. The legal argument, although limited, was the first line of justification used in the prelude to war and was endorsed on both sides of the Atlantic. This line of reasoning was based on Iraq's failure to comply with Security Council resolutions and on the flawed intelligence regarding Iraq's weapons of mass destruction capability. Across much of the Middle East, the prevailing view was that Iraq's weapons capability was so degraded it posed little threat to the region. However, a US National Intelligence Estimate issued in October 2002 found that, 'since inspections ended in 1998, Iraq has maintained its chemical weapons effort, energized its missile program, and invested more heavily in biological weapons; in the view of most agencies, Baghdad is reconstituting its nuclear weapons program' (Director of National Intelligence 2002). The Bush administration used these conclusions as part of its argument for the March 2003 invasion. However, there was no universal agreement on this point. The Iraq Survey Group, set up to look for weapons of mass destruction or evidence of them in the country, issued a final report stating that it saw no weapons and no evidence that Iraq was trying to reconstitute them (2004).

By April 2005, an internal US commission into weapons of mass destruction suggested that the principal cause of the policy failures was the intelligence community's 'inability to collect good information about

Iraq's WMD programs, serious errors in analyzing what information it could gather and a failure to make clear just how much of its analysis was based on assumptions rather than good evidence'. The letter accompanying the report stated that 'what the intelligence professionals told you about Saddam Hussein's programs was what they believed. They were simply wrong'.[3] This was cold comfort to the state of Iraq, which was in open turmoil by March 2005. These retrospective findings simply revealed the problems with the 'evidence' utilized by the Bush administration in its attempt to make the claim that Iraq had failed to meet the requirements of the UN Security Council and thus to take military action. Leaving the veracity of the evidence provided by the US intelligence agencies aside, the apparent selectivity with which Washington agitated for compliance with Security Council resolutions, especially in relation to Israel's weapons programme, only fanned the flames of Arab discontent.

As the applicability of the legal argument faded, the moral imperative rose to prominence in Washington's assessments of the Saddam regime. This line of reasoning reflected the ideological nature of the Bush administration and its neo-conservative power-brokers, and it was based on the 'need to confront evil' in the international system. This was presented as a 'duty of the civilized world' and often legitimized by recourse to the events of September 11. Saddam's brutal tactics in suppressing political opposition and his persecution of minority ethnic groups were focused upon by a compliant American media. In particular, the Anfal campaigns against the Kurds in 1986–88 and the use of chemical weapons against the Kurdish civilian community were publicized as examples of the oppressive nature of the Iraqi regime. The Anfal campaigns, a systematic programme of destruction and murder against the Kurds, had been ordered by Saddam and led to the razing of 3,000 villages and the deaths of between 50,000 and 100,000 Kurds (Human Rights Watch 1993). The horrific nature of these crimes is without question. It is worthy of note, however, that these atrocities occurred during the Iran–Iraq War, in which Iraq was given logistical, financial and intelligence assistance by the West, in particular by the United Kingdom and the United States (Ayoob 2003: 30). This point has been repeatedly raised in the Arab world as further vindication of Arab perspectives that, in the context of justifying a military invasion, the moral outrage of Washington was simply convenient.

The cracks in both the legal and the moral cases for war led many observers to grant increasing credence to the geo-strategic angle of the Bush administration's plan. This line of reasoning draws strongly on realist conceptions of international relations. Saddam was increasingly seen in Washington as an unpredictable actor in the Middle East. Despite the challenges to his regime and the external pressure applied through the sanctions programme, he had maintained a vice-like grip on power inside Iraq. In neo-conservative circles the removal of Saddam, a step made politically palatable by the post-September 11 political environment, may have been seen as a way to disrupt the status quo and provide new opportunities and benefits to US regional allies. In this way, the decision to invade Iraq reflects existing patterns of US interference in the regional politics of the Gulf region. However, it also reflects a reorientation of US policy aims, which have traditionally held to maintaining the status quo and shoring up friendly regimes. In this, the invasion of Iraq keeps within the US tradition of moving between supporting the status quo, as was the case in 1991, and looking to subvert it, as is demonstrated in the 'regime change' notion of 2003. Such alterations in US policy focus are dependent on prevailing perceptions of American national interest and on the ability of Washington to present its regional agenda to the American public. The establishment of a democratic and pro-US Iraq would have provided Washington with more options in a region where its alliances had often proved tenuous, especially after the events of September 11, which had drawn the status of Saudi Arabia as a lynchpin ally into question. In a linked point, the ideologically motivated Bush administration had propagated the perception that democratization in the Middle East was the key to countering the appeal of militant Islamism.

Even if there was a limited acceptance of the moral and legal arguments, it quickly became clear that other factors were at play in this conflict and that the invasion of Iraq signalled a long-term shift of focus in US regional strategy. The 'war for oil' argument has been raised by a number of observers. To commentators such as the left-leaning intellectual Tariq Ali, oil was the 'principal reason for war against Iraq' (2003: xvi). Economic self-interest in securing the creation of friendly regional regimes to ensure the smooth flow of oil most likely played a part in Washington's agenda. Moreover, the links between major US oil companies and individuals in the Bush administration have received much publicity. However, decades of US foreign policy had pivoted on the approach of drawing oil-rich states into the US sphere of influence through a programme of assistance, support and friendship. Regime change through direct US intervention was an obvious break from earlier tactics and harks back to the 1950s and the coup in Iran that ousted the nationalist government of Mohammed Mossedeq.

In the neo-conservative mindset that dominated the White House at this point, the war against Iraq may well have been seen as the first step toward revamping the entire Middle East. This correlates with the policy statements by the administration that the 'war on terror' is a long-term, even transgenerational, conflict. In this worldview, the political systems of the Muslim and Arab world must undergo a structural change in order to deliver the economic and social prosperity that are the necessary precondition to a definitive victory against terrorism. This argument is an interesting one, as the relationship between democracy and pro-US sentiment is proving difficult to justify. It appears unclear whether policy planners assumed that a democratic Iraq would be pro-American by the virtue of democracy, or out of gratitude for the US role, or as a result of the intended US ability to steer the democratic process. The ferocity of the anti-occupation insurgency has clearly rendered this argument null and void at the current time.

Overall, at differing times, supporters of the war in Iraq have argued that it will yield such future flow-on benefits as the downfall of tyrannical regimes; the curtailment of Islamism, terrorism and the proliferation of weapons of mass destruction; the stabilization of oil prices; and the enhancement of regional security and stability. However, once the overthrow of the Iraqi regime was achieved, the US-backed authorities dissolved the Ba'thist state structure and replaced it with a confessional approach to governance like that used in Lebanon, aimed at giving voice to all of Iraq's sectarian groups. Rather than fostering an inclusive sense of national identity, this approach appears to have only accentuated ethnic and sectarian differences inside Iraq, and rendered any potential flow-on benefits a distant prospect.

ARAB DISCONTENT

The US invasion of Iraq could not but aggravate tensions in the Middle East and give Arabs further reason to view Washington as a global bully. At a political level, Washington and the Arab capitals disagreed about the merits of the invasion, but disagreement was not absolute. Baghdad had proven itself a significant menace, particularly to the Gulf, and the fall of Saddam was not entirely unwelcome. Foreign military occupation and the destabilization of an entire state did not, however, serve the interests of regional leaderships, especially those with a traditional tilt towards Washington. Public anger over the role and actions of the US military stirred popular discontent. More powerfully, there is a major gap between Arab and US public perceptions of the US motivation for the war. In 2004, public opinion in the United States, although revealing concerns regarding the prosecution of the 'war on terror' and the lead-up to conflict in Iraq, consistently showed that the bulk of the American public accepted the sincerity of the US effort as a response to a global threat (Pew Research Center 2004). By 2007, Americans were unsure. By contrast, in Jordan, for example, polling demonstrated that over half the population did not believe the current US strategy was sincere and listed the desire to control Middle Eastern oil, world domination, a vendetta against Muslim states and an attempt to protect Israel as more likely motivating factors for the invasion (Kohut 2007). Such statistics reveal major differences in how Americans and Middle Easterners perceive global affairs and the motivations of the world's only superpower. Moreover, such dramatic differences in perception foster a discourse in which the Middle East and the 'West' are, at least on the level of public opinion, barely engaged in the same debate. A common accusation – that Washington simply did not understand the complexities of Middle Eastern politics and thus the context of the conflict upon which they had embarked – is borne out by public opinion polling. Statistics published in 2004 demonstrated that, although 84 per cent of Americans believed the Iraqi people would be 'better off' in post-Saddam Iraq, 70 per cent of Jordanians felt Iraqis would be worse off in a post-Saddam context (Pew Research Center 2004).

Washington presented the invasion and subsequent occupation as a critical stage in the liberation of the Iraqi people, but to the Arab world it played out as a costly example of America's neo-colonialist tendencies. This interpretation is only strengthened by the power differential between Washington and the region that has so often served as the target of US foreign policy. This perception was hardened by the fact that the 2003 conflict was the first major inter-state regional war that was covered by major non-Western media. The sheer power of the US military might, and the impact of that power on civilians is – in contrast to US media coverage – continually and viscerally covered by regional media. The role of Arab television, especially the Qatar-based satellite network al-Jazeera, was vital to the public interpretation of Washington's actions. Images of US military domination of a once-proud Arab state were beamed throughout the region. As Mohammed Ayoob, among others, points out, unlike the 1991 conflict, the 2003 war was seen and interpreted by Arabs for an Arab audience (2003: 33). This perception of Arab humiliation at the hands of

BOX 8.2

Al-Jazeera, which means 'the peninsula' in Arabic, is a television network based in Doha, Qatar. It began broadcasting in 1996 and since then has expanded beyond the Middle East to reach over 40 million households around the world, rivalling the BBC in number of viewers. In July 2005 al-Jazeera officially launched its English-language channel, which broadcasts news 24 hours a day from its broadcast centres in Doha, London, Kuala Lumpur and Washington DC. Outside the Arabic-speaking world, al-Jazeera only came to prominence in the West after September 11, when it gained notoriety by airing footage of Osama bin Laden. Al-Jazeera has continued to attract controversy, incurring criticism from the US and British governments for its graphic reporting of the war in Iraq and from numerous regional governments for its willingness to critique Arab regimes.

a Western military force was further intensified by the occasional public relations lapse. As Philip Taylor notes, the rhetoric of liberation was often belied by the reality of the conflict, and 'like the Stars and Stripes draped over Saddam's toppled statue, these images will come back to haunt the American occupation of Iraq again and again' (2004).

For many in the Arab world, the Abu Ghraib scandal will stand out as the representative and enduring memory of the US-led 'liberation' of Iraq. Inside one of Saddam's most notorious prisons, the degradation and torture of Iraqi prisoners by US servicemen and women was captured on film. The photographs, which were released on 28 April 2004, shocked audiences throughout the international community and called further into question the morality of the war and the occupation. The photographs were viewed as reflective of a US tendency to disregard human security and dignity in the Arab world. This further substantiated long-standing assumptions regarding the disparate value that Washington places on American and Middle Eastern lives. The role played by the media in the construction of the US image in the Middle East is of vital importance. Attempts by the US administration to 'spin' events in Iraq were extensive. However, Washington's ability to meaningfully alleviate the impact of the Abu Ghraib photographs was limited. The rise of indigenous Middle Eastern media has provided increased access to alternative information in what was heretofore a climate of information control by the state.

CONCLUSION

The question of whether this conflict has advanced America's national interest is, and will for the foreseeable future remain, open to debate. The display of American power in the Middle East has led many to redefine the United States within the paradigm of empire (Vidal 2004; Colás and Saull 2006). Washington's unsurpassed military power is indisputable. The ability of the United States to pursue its political will in far-flung destinations was not in question at the close of the twentieth century. The war in Iraq merely reinforced that reality. As Mary Ann Tetreault points out, the administration paid great attention to 'managing the war as spectacle', with the 'shock and awe' campaign directed at the Iraqi regime, the Arab region and the watching world (2006: 36). Although the initial military conflict was a demonstration of absolute American power, the failure to maintain peace and security in Iraq has encouraged many to raise the possibility of imperial overstretch.

However, for Washington's regional allies the effects of this conflict may well yet prove positive. Should Iraq stabilize, the removal of Saddam Hussein is beneficial for US allies in the Gulf and for the state of Israel. However, the apparent slide of Iraq into civil war and the consequent establishment of the state as a breeding ground for terrorism is a devastating outcome for the Iraqi people, the Arab Middle East, Israel and Washington. Sectarian differences between Sunni and Shia have been amplified in the struggle for power, while many Iraqis view the Kurds as collaborators for their support of US forces during the initial stages of the war (Gunter and Yavuz 2005: 122). Despite the rhetoric of territorial integrity, the de facto separation of Iraq into ethnic cantons appears a serious danger. Indeed the primary outcome of the toppling of Saddam Hussein has been the empowerment of Iran, an eventuality that US policy has explicitly striven to prevent since the Islamic Revolution of 1979. In many ways, the war in Iraq seems to have reversed the aims of decades of US regional policy. 'Dual containment' of Iran and Iraq was the cornerstone of previous US administrations. The toppling of Saddam, the traditional bulwark against Iran, has dramatically altered the Sunni–Shia balance of power in the region. The increased influence of Iran, the dire need for Tehran to be brought into regional diplomatic forums and the increased prominence of Shia organizations throughout the region suggest growing possibilities for Iran. The potential for Iran to claim a prominent role in the region is the unintended, yet, at this stage, primary, outcome of the Iraq adventure.

As the casualties mounted and the internal violence showed little sign of abating, the domestic mood in the United States swung against the continued presence of US troops in Iraq. This shift in public mood and the consequent fall from grace of the Bush administration near the end of its second term reflected the American public's distaste for a conflict in which American soldiers were dying for little tangible gain. Domestically, the political focus in 2007 was squarely upon the need for an 'exit strategy'. For the United States, the disaster that the 'liberation of Iraq' has become will resonate for decades. In relation to national security, the dubious foundations of the 'war on terror' have been highlighted by the conflict in Iraq. Far from achieving its goal of 'securing the homeland', the State Department found that three years into the 'war on terror' the number of 'significant' international terrorist attacks in 2004 reached 655, three times the previous record of 175 in 2003 (Institute for Policy Studies 2005). Moreover, the Pew Research Center's 2006 poll showed that majorities in Jordan, Turkey, Egypt, Indonesia and Pakistan believe the war in Iraq has served to make the world a more dangerous place (Kohut 2007). Globally, the ramifications of this latest Middle Eastern war are also significant. In 2002 world military spending was US$795 billion. With the skyrocketing costs of the war in Iraq, worldwide military spending soared to an estimated US$956 billion. In 2003 and in 2004, the figure spiked again to US$1.035 trillion (Institute for Policy Studies 2005). The increased militarization of international relations, the added potency of Islamist organizations and the devastation, and potential fragmentation, of Iraq appear to be the likely legacy of the Bush administration's foreign policy in the Middle East.

NOTES

1 All population statistics are drawn from the 'CIA World Factbook' (2007), available at www.cia.gov/library/publications/the-world-factbook/geos/iz.html.
2 UNSC Resolutions 1322 (Israel to abide by the Geneva Convention as an occupying power); 1403 (Israel to withdraw from Palestinian cities); 1405 (investigation of the Jenin incident) and 1435 (Israeli to withdraw to the pre-2000 lines).
3 Commission on the Intelligence Capabilities of the United States Regarding Weapons of Mass Destruction, 'Letter to President George W Bush', 31 March 2005, available at www.wmd.gov/report/transmittal_letter.html. The full report is available at www.wmd.gov/report/.

REFERENCES

Ali, Tariq (2003) *The Clash of Fundamentalisms: Crusades, Jihad and Modernity* (London: Verso).
Ayoob, Mohammed (2003) 'The War against Iraq: Normative and Strategic Implications', *Middle East Policy*, Vol. 5, No. 2, pp. 27–40.
Blair, Tony (2003) 'Statement on Iraq', 25 February, available at www.pm.gov.uk/output/Page3088.asp.
Bush, George W. (2002a) 'State of the Union Address 2002', 29 January, available at www.whitehouse.gov/news/releases/2002/01/20020129–11.html.
Bush, George W. (2002b) 'President Bush Outlines Iraqi Threat', 7 October, available at www.whitehouse.gov/news/releases/2002/10/20021007–8.html.
Bush, George W. (2003) 'President Says Saddam Hussein Must Leave Iraq Within 48 Hours', 17 March, available at www.whitehouse.gov/news/releases/2003/03/20030317–7.html.
Colás, Alejandro and Saull, Richard (eds) (2006) *The War on Terror and the American Empire after the Cold War* (London: Routledge).
Cortright, David (2001) 'A Hard Look at Iraq Sanctions', *The Nation*, 3 December.
Director of National Intelligence (2002) 'Key Judgments [from October 2002 NIE]; Iraq's Continuing Programs for Weapons of Mass Destruction', released 18 July 2003, available at www.fas.org/irp/cia/product/iraq-wmd.html.
Gunter, Michael and Yavuz, M. Hakan (2005) 'The Continuing Crisis in Iraqi Kurdistan', *Middle East Policy*, Vol. 12, No. 1.
Hallenberg, Jan and Karlsson, Håkan (2005) *The Iraq War: European Perspectives On Politics, Strategy and Operations* (London: Routledge).
Human Rights Watch (1993) 'Genocide in Iraq: The Anfal Campaigns against the Kurds' (New York: Human Rights Watch).
Institute for Policy Studies (2005) 'The Iraq Quagmire', August, available at www.ips-dc.org/iraq/quagmire/.
Iraq Survey Group (2004) 'Iraq Survey Group Final Report', 30 September, available at www.globalsecurity.org/wmd/library/report/2004/isg-final-report/.
Kohut, Andrew (2007) 'America's Image in the World: Findings from the Pew Global Attitudes Project', 14 March, available at http://pewglobal.org/commentary/display.php?AnalysisID=1019.

National Security Council (2002) 'National Security Strategy of 2002', available at
www.whitehouse.gov/nsc/nss.html.

Pew Research Center (2004) 'A Year after Iraq War', Pew Global Attitudes Project,
16 March, http://pewglobal.org/reports/display.php?ReportID=206.

Project for the New American Century (1998) 'Letter to President Clinton', 26
January, available at www.newamericancentury.org/iraqclintonletter.htm.

Taylor, Philip (2004) 'Image and Reality', *Al-Ahram Weekly Online*, 20–26 May,
No. 691, available at http://weekly.ahram.org.eg/2004/691/re9.htm and http://
ics.leeds.ac.uk/papers/vp01.cfm?outfit=pmt&folder=40&paper=1609.

Tetreault, Mary Ann (2006) 'The Sexual Politics of Abu Ghraib: Hegemony,
Spectacle, and the Global War on Terror', *NWSA Journal*, Vol. 18, No. 3.

Vidal, Gore (2004) *Imperial America: Reflections on the United States of Amnesia*
(London: Clairview).

White House, Office of the Press Secretary (2002) 'Saddam Hussein's Support
for International Terrorism', 12 September, available at www.whitehouse.gov/
infocus/iraq/decade/sect5.html.

Zunes, Stephen (2002) 'United Nations Security Council Resolutions Currently
Being Violated by Countries Other than Iraq', 2 October, available at www.
globalpolicy.org/security/issues/1002resolutions.pdf.

SUGGESTED FURTHER READING

Al-Arian, Laila (2004) 'Perceptions of the US in the Arab World', *The Washington
Report on Middle Eastern Affairs*, Vol. 23, No. 7.

Brigham, Robert K. (2006) *Is Iraq Another Vietnam?*, first edition (New York:
Public Affairs).

Clarke, Richard A. (2004) *Against All Enemies: Inside America's War on Terror*
(New York: Free Press).

Cleveland, William L. (2000) *A History of the Modern Middle East* (Boulder, CO:
Westview Press).

Crockatt, Richard (2003) *America Embattled: September 11, Anti-Americanism,
and the Global Order* (London: Routledge).

Ehrenreich, Barbara (2004) 'Prison Abuse: Feminism's Assumptions Upended', *Los
Angeles Times*, 16 May, available at www.barbaraehrenreich.com/prisonabuse.
htm.

Esposito, John L. (2002) *Unholy War: Terror in the Name of Islam* (New York:
Oxford University Press).

Fadlallah al-Adab, Sayyid Muhammad Husayn (2002) 'Palestinian Armed
Resistance: Questions relating to Its Moral Dimension', *Beirut*, Vol. 50, No.
1–2.

Farber, David (ed.) (2007) *What They Think of Us: International Perceptions of the
United States since 9/11* (Princeton, NJ: Princeton University Press).

Fawn, Rick and Hinnebusch, Raymond (eds) (2006) *The Iraq War: Causes and
Consequences* (Boulder, CO: Lynne Rienner Publishers).

Griffin, David Ray and Scott, Peter Dale (eds) (2007) *9/11 and the American
Empire: Intellectuals Speak Out* (Northampton, MA: Olive Branch Press).

Hersh, Seymour M. (2004) *Chain of Command: The Road from 9/11 to Abu Ghraib*
(Camberwell, Vic.: Allen Lane).

Holbein, James R (ed.) (2005) *The 9/11 Commission: Proceedings and Analysis* (Dobbs Ferry, NY: Oceana).

Katzenstein, Peter J. and Keohane, Robert O. (2007) *Anti-Americanisms in World Politics* (Ithaca, NY: Cornell University Press).

Makdissi, Ussama (2002) 'Anti-Americanism in the Arab World: An Interpretation of a Brief History', *Journal of American History*, Vol. 89, No. 2, pp. 538–58.

Moore, James (2004) *Bush's War for Re-election: Iraq, the White House, and the People* (Hoboken, NJ: John Wiley & Sons).

Omar, Saleh (1996) 'Philosophical Origins of the Arab Ba'th Party: The Work of Zaki Al-Arsuzi', *Arab Studies Quarterly,* Vol. 18, No. 2.

Schostak, Arthur B. (ed.) (2004) *Trade Towers/War Clouds* (Philadelphia: Chelsea House).

SUGGESTED STUDY QUESTIONS

1 What do you understand to be the basis of Arab anti-Americanism?

2 How influential is anti-Americanism in the Middle East?

3 Has US policy in the Middle East advanced the US national interest?

4 Has the US-led invasion of Iraq in 2003 promoted the cause of democracy in the Middle East?

5 What have been the key themes of US foreign policy in the Middle East in the second half of the twentieth century?

Conclusion

The United States emerged as a player in Middle Eastern politics in 1919 when the King–Crane Commission travelled to the region of Greater Syria. From this humble beginning, Washington grew to dominate the political landscape of the region. In the early twentieth century, the anti-colonial history of the United States inclined local leaders to view Washington as a potential friend of the Arab nationalist endeavour. International relations are not, however, based on friendships. Realist understandings of state behaviour in the international system point to the primacy of the principle of self-interest. All states act with the intention of furthering their own position and that of their allies: the United States is no different. In the Middle East, the same principles apply. It is against this backdrop and the broader dynamics of international relations in the twentieth century that the role of the United States in the Middle East must be assessed.

At the close of the First World War, the fall of the Ottoman Empire led to the reconfiguration of the entire Middle East. The colonial powers of France and Britain vied for influence and concessions on the international stage. At the regional level, traditional power-brokers competed with emergent nationalist movements for political authority. The interplay of international politics and regional aspirations triggered a process that redrew the geo-political map of the region. While local actors struggled for self-determination, the international community placed the Middle East under the League of Nations Mandates in the 1920s. These Mandates were clearly products of their time, an uneasy mixture of Wilsonian idealism and imperial impulse. In the inter-war period, the traditional European powers executed their Mandatory duties with an eye to the likelihood of further conflict on a global scale and the role that the various factions and communities of the Middle East could play in influencing events. The states that emerged from this process also acted with their self-interest in mind as they attempted to consolidate their national identities and carve a place for themselves on a changing global stage. As the Second World War loomed, the tenuous nature of the sovereignty achieved by the new Middle Eastern states was tested and once again the needs of the colonial powers emerged as predominant, dictating policy in relationship to Palestine, the Zionist community and Iraq.

The devastation of the Second World War and the subsequent decline of the United Kingdom as a leading colonial power marked the most serious turning point of the first half of the twentieth century. Concurrently, the discovery of oil further entrenched the region in the forefront of Western policy decision-making. The geo-politically and physically vulnerable Gulf sheikhdoms offered both responsibility and opportunity to the West, while the larger states in the region struggled to emerge from the yoke of colonial domination. In the second half of the twentieth century, the Cold War between the Soviet Union and the United States dominated politics internationally, including in the Middle East. The dynamics of the bipolar system and Washington's need to contain Soviet expansion dominated US policy planners. This was reinforced by the direction of ideological trends in the region. In the more populous states, the doctrines of Arab nationalism had come to incorporate socialist undertones and the interplay of geo-political security, economic interests and ideological tension ensured the Middle East would remain a central battleground in the bipolar decades to follow.

The early regional perception of an affinity between American and Arab political worldviews had been slowly eroded as the struggle for the Middle East intensified. The Arab states, symbolically led by Egypt's President Nasser, at times attempted to influence the emergent global system in the attempt to secure their own interests. In this period, Nasser's Aswan Dam project was a clear example of the Middle Eastern determination to extract advantage from the superpower rivalry. Indeed, the Middle East stands out as a region where local leaders were determined to be more than mere pawns for superpowers. Egypt and Israel especially attempted to play the Cold War system to their own best advantage. However, the power differential between Middle Eastern states and the superpowers of the Soviet Union and the United States proved immense. In the Middle East of the 1970s, the Cold War had acquired its own internal logic and the Arab–Soviet relationship sporadically squared off against a regional alliance born out of religious and political links and solidified through geo-strategic calculations.

THE UNITED STATES AND ISRAEL

The establishment of Israel in 1948 marked the culmination of one phase of struggle and the commencement of another between two national communities in one land. The declaration of Israeli independence was a turning point that reconfigured the Middle East, Arab politics and the foreign policies of external players. The Zionist movement had advanced a vigorous programme of local land development, political agitation and, in the final years of the Mandate, military force to secure a Jewish state in the Arab Middle East. This endeavour placed them in direct conflict with the people of Palestine, Arabs who were unwilling to cede their land in order to facilitate the national reconstitution of the Jewish people. As a result of this fractious political scene, Israel became a nation in a near perpetual state of conflict, and security policy dominated national politics.

The Israeli victory of 1967 resulted in an untenable situation. Tel Aviv's conquest of the bulk of Mandate Palestine was not acceptable to Arab actors or to the Palestinian people who found themselves under direct military occupation. As the Intifadas of 1987 and 2000, and the war of July 2006, demonstrated, Israel's authority has been repeatedly tested. But the grievances that underpin these conflict scenarios are often obscured in the rush to defuse political tensions through military means. Security issues dominate every aspect of the Israeli political process and are clearly represented in the Israeli leadership. From Menachem Begin's role in the pre-state militia of the Irgun, to Ehud Barak's role in the commando raids in Lebanon in 1974, to Ariel Sharon's chequered history, the interplay of military might and politics has been instrumental in the formation of the Israeli consciousness.

As has been explored in this book, the United States was not a major player in the political process that led to the establishment of the state of Israel. The King–Crane Commission of 1919, which set the stage for an Arab interpretation of American support, revealed much about the US perspective: awash with Wilsonian idealism, Washington had much to learn about foreign policy formulation. The Biltmore conference of 1942 marks the intensification of US Jewry's support for the Zionist movement, yet the need to balance regional alliances retained significant sway in Truman's White House. The establishment of Israel changed these equations significantly and the United States became a primary backer of the new state. As Israel plunged into consecutive wars, the dynamics of the Cold War drew the United States more closely into local politics in the Middle East. For every step Damascus or Cairo took towards Moscow, a further link in the US–Israeli relationship was secured. Israel's near-miraculous military prowess, mixed with the Arab willingness to apply economic pressure against the United States, further secured Washington's embrace of Tel Aviv. By the end of the 1973 oil embargo, the US policy inclination was clear. This tilt did not balance out as the Cold War came to an end, and by the mid-1990s the sole superpower was seen as wholly situated in Tel Aviv's camp.

The US–Israeli relationship lies at the core of Middle Eastern interpretations of the United States. However, a transformation in the relationship between Washington and Tel Aviv would not automatically resolve the issue of anti-Americanism. Middle Eastern concerns with the use of US power and influence encompass more than a single alliance. In order to contextualize Middle Eastern interpretations of the United States, a more holistic view of the region's political history in the twentieth century is required. The 1950s marked the commencement of a process of US intervention that led Washington down a path that has been marked by double standards. This decision-making process has been, as it is for any state, dictated by self-interest. In Iran in 1953, self-interest dictated that Washington play a part in overthrowing a democratically elected government in order to shore up its influence in that country and to contain the appeal of socialism. Conversely, in 1991 in Kuwait, the status quo was deemed integral to US interests and an undemocratic, oil-rich, US-friendly regime was restored to power. These situations are not related to the conflict between Israel and the Palestinians, but they also inform regional perceptions of the United States as a meddlesome player in regional politics. How then can the claim be made that the US–Israeli relationship lies at the core of Middle Eastern interpretations of the United States? Simply put, the Palestinians. The establishment of Israel and the dynamics of regional politics, especially after 1967, led to the exclusion, marginalization, occupation and demoralization of a society. This is a situation that continues without remedy. The US–Israeli alliance is a mutually beneficial relationship between two states akin in normative political values. As such, the alliance is *in itself* not the point of contention. As the Pew Research Center found in recent global surveys, among Muslim majority countries, 'first and foremost is thinking that American policy is too supportive of Israel at the expense of Palestine' (Kohut 2007). In this way, it is the exclusivity of this relationship in a political context characterized by a complex interplay of grievances, rights and responsibilities that is the point from which the tension emanates. The US–Palestinian relationship, an inverse mirroring of the US–Israeli relationship, is the cause of much popular anger and discontent with the United States.

THE UNITED STATES AND THE PALESTINIANS

The US–Palestinian relationship is marked by contradictions and complexity. The United States, as the self-declared 'honest broker' of the peace process, has played the central role in the conflict resolution attempts that punctuate the Israeli–Palestinian conflict. In this way, Washington's goodwill is vital to the Palestinians, a reality further entrenched by Israel's often isolated international position. Put simply, Washington is the only player in the international system capable of extracting concessions from Tel Aviv. Consequently, Washington's role in relation to this conflict is assessed in terms of outcomes. The stagnation of the peace process and the continued suffering of the Palestinians are perceived as an example of Washington's unwillingness to use its leverage to move Israel towards resolution. In this way, Washington's approach to the Palestinian situation is often understood as representative of the problematic equivocations and double standards that plague broader US policy in the Middle East.

The Palestinian issue permeates the political culture of the Middle East. However, it is an issue internalized and responded to in different ways by the Arab states and the Arab publics. As seen in the wars of 1948, 1967 and 1973, the ideological drivers of conflict between the Arab states and Israel have historically been security, territories and borders. Repeated defeats on the battlefields have been demoralizing for the Arab states, a sense most keenly felt among the Palestinians who continue to live under Israeli occupation or in refugee camps. The growth of the Palestinian nationalist movement has been in part based on the realization that the Arab states could bargain with what does not belong to them. The failure of Arab states to free the Palestinian people underlined for the latter the urgency of self-reliance, a source of dignity and national pride. In this way, the Arab defeat in the Six-Day War of 1967 set in motion the indigenization of the liberation struggle among the Palestinians.

The impact of Palestinian nationalism on regional stability was significant. Since the 1970s, the presence of the armed wing of the Palestinian resistance has contributed to internal destabilization and crises, as was most clearly seen in Jordan in 1970 and Lebanon in the last three decades. Therefore, from a state-level perspective, the provision of meaningful support for the Palestinian cause by Arab states is fraught with dangerous implications. Consequently, Palestinians remain in refugee camps, hamstrung by both political stagnation in the peace process with Israel and an Arab League position that holds that they should not receive citizenship of the states in which they have resided for decades.

This official stance is mirrored by an often conflicted Arab political and public view of the Palestinian community, a tension that is most clearly seen in the state of Lebanon. The violence in the Nar el-Bared camp in northern Lebanon in mid-2007 demonstrated that Palestinian grievances and the failure to alleviate the suffering inherent in a national history played out in refugee camps continues to carry significant risks. These camps, predominantly funded by the international community and relief agencies, are breeding grounds for despair and desperation. This climate proves a tempting opportunity for those committed to destabilization, as the emergence of Fatah al-Islam has shown. This externally led faction capitalized on the depressed situation of the Palestinian refugee community in southern Lebanon to mount a challenge to the Lebanese authorities. In some ways, these issues are part of the political dynamics of the Arab world itself. As the Lebanese response demonstrates (and as the Jordanian response demonstrated previously), a tendency to use military means to resolve political impasses permeates the political culture of the entire region. However, the political systems of Lebanon, Jordan, Egypt or Syria are not the *cause* of the Palestinian situation. Considering this, it is at the headspring of this conflict that resolution must be attained. As the contemporary situation in Lebanon demonstrates, the failure to resolve the Palestinian issue has consequences far beyond the Occupied Territories.

In this protracted conflict, the role of the United States is of vital importance. The events of the 1970s and the consecration of the US–Israeli alliance during the following two decades was an important phase in this relationship. The emergence of a unipolar system in which the United States carries unparalleled military might and political influence has been another. Since the articulation of President Wilson's Fourteen Points, the United States has charged itself with the role of standard bearer for self-determination. It is by this self-articulated criterion that the superpower is judged. In the Middle East, Washington's policy repeatedly fails on the basic criteria of fairness and justice.

The US approach to the Israeli–Palestinian conflict embodies these issues. Essentially, Washington supports Tel Aviv out of a mixture of self-interest, ideological imperatives and domestic pressure. Alliance-building is the right of any state in the international system. But Washington's relationship with Tel Aviv is potentially of less significance than its concurrent assumption of the role of mediator between Israel and the Palestinians. Put simply, it is impossible to be both loyal ally and objective mediator. Arab anti-Americanism has grown exponentially since the 1990s, the years in which the mantle of peace-maker was assumed. As Washington floundered in its approach to the conflict, the lack of parity was repeatedly – and to an Arab audience, painfully – reinforced as Israeli leaders were fêted as peace-makers, while the Palestinian leadership was sidelined.

The 'war on terror' only exacerbated this situation, and Israeli leaders scrambled to situate the Palestinian resistance within the paradigm established by the Bush administration. The use of terrorism by Palestinian organizations is irrefutable and abhorrent. But al-Qaeda and HAMAS are disparate organizations, with widely differing objectives and socio-political contexts. The shared outrage and fear inspired by terrorist acts against civilians, however, served to further unite Tel Aviv and Washington. The state reprisals against terrorism, which exacted a much greater human toll, were thus recast as combating the scourge of militancy, and the reality of Palestinian suffering under Israeli occupation and incursion was downplayed.

Washington's dismissive approach to Arab, and not just Palestinian, suffering was reinforced in July 2006 when the Bush administration stood by as Tel Aviv ordered the partial destruction of a neighbouring state's infrastructure. Israel charts a difficult course in the Middle East, and issues of national security are vital and legitimate in the formulation of any state's policy. But the continued suffering of the Palestinian people works as a potent catalyst for popular anger against Tel Aviv and its major ally. This serves to underscore the central part that the Israeli–Palestinian conflict and the US–Israeli alliance, which is a feature of this conflict, play in accounting for the rise of anti-Americanism in the Middle East. However, this situation is not the sole source of discontent. Since the launching of the 'war on terror', the anger and resentment generated by the Palestinian cause has been eclipsed as US foreign policy has created a new and festering source of discontent.

THE UNITED STATES AND IRAQ

The events of September 11, 2001, set in motion a chain of events that have fundamentally destabilized the Middle East. The fall of the Taliban was a blessing to the people of Afghanistan. However, a sustained US commitment to national reconstruction of the troubled Central Asian state that has proven vital to the stability of the international system was not forthcoming. Washington's planners were encouraged by the apparently 'easy victory' of Operation Enduring Freedom against the Taliban and its al-Qaeda affiliates, and more cautious assessments that pointed to the melting away – as opposed to defeat – of the enemy forces after the battle of Tora Bora in December 2001 were largely discounted. The neo-conservative elite in the United States, committed to expanding the horizons of the 'war on terror', thus construed Afghanistan as a success story for the Bush doctrine. As a result, Washington's power-brokers were able to pass policy that drew only the most tenuous of links between the 'war on terror' and need for regime change in Iraq.

In 2007, the military campaign against Iraq stood out as a US foreign policy disaster of unprecedented proportions. As a result, the broader 'war on terror' has been profoundly compromised from both a military and ideological standpoint. Six years after its liberation from the Taliban, Afghanistan stands on the brink of a resurgent conflict between reinvigorated militants and international forces, and Iraq is devastated by civil conflict. The view is even bleaker from an ideological standpoint. The

United States has deeply damaged its international standing. In the Middle East, a historical tendency to view Washington's actions through the lens of self-interested intervention entered a new phase. Negative Middle Eastern perceptions of the United States, born of the policies of the Cold War, have become entrenched as images of 'collateral damage' have been blended with images of brutal oppression so powerfully displayed in moments such as the human rights abuses in Abu Ghraib. Washington's determination to apply the might of its military power to alter the political structures of the Middle East has badly backfired, and its moral authority lies in tatters. The impact this conflict has had on anti-Americanism cannot be overstated. As the Pew Research Center has chronicled, the fall in support for the United States is steep; in Turkey, for example, favourable attitudes dropped from 52 per cent in 2000 to 12 per cent in 2006. And the damage caused by the Bush administration's foreign policy is not confined to the Middle East, with levels of support for the United States in Indonesia falling from 75 per cent to 30 per cent between 2000 and 2006, and in Germany dropping from 78 per cent to 37 per cent over the same time frame (Kohut 2007).

As a result of the invasion of Iraq, the potential for the regional destabilization of the political system that has been in place since the colonial period is greater than at any other point in modern history. The human cost of the military campaigns in Afghanistan and Iraq is staggering. The intended political outcome of these conflicts – the confrontation and containment of militant Islamism – has not been achieved. In Iraq in particular, the spawning of a newly embittered and empowered militant mindset will have regional ramifications, potentially serving to destabilize and challenge US allies such as the Gulf sheikhdoms and Israel. Although the human suffering created by current US policy in the Middle East cannot be discounted, it is the political impacts of the Bush administration's Iraq war that are most difficult to rationalize. After decades of foreign policy aimed at containing Iran, the central irony of the Bush administration's approach to the Middle East is Tehran's growing assertiveness. Iraq has historically functioned as a check on the Islamic Republic's influence. As the situation spirals in Iraq and Afghanistan, Iran emerges as the sole beneficiary, and Tehran is moving quickly to assert its regional influence and gaining in confidence as a result. A self-assured (and simultaneously defensive) Iran holds serious implications for the Arab political structures of the Gulf and the broader Middle East. As Washington casts around for an exit strategy from the conflict in Iraq, it appears increasingly likely that the only outcomes of the 'war on terror' will be a lasting change to the regional balance of power and the entrenched alienation and embitterment of a new generation in the Middle East.

THE UNITED STATES AND THE MIDDLE EAST: WHERE TO FROM HERE?

A survey of US policy in the Middle East reveals common themes: intervention, the use of influence, alliance-building, questions regarding the parity value ascribed to human suffering, geo-political strategy and the power of economic imperatives. Foreign policy needs to be exacting and calculating as it is the means by which states secure their position in the international system. However, as the most powerful state in that system, the United States is held to different standards. More importantly, the United States has *assumed* the mantle of the global leadership. In the Middle East, this explicitly included the role of peace-broker. However, in the Middle Eastern view, the application of US political and military power is marked by the absence of a central component of leadership: the principle of justice.

The interplay of history and politics explains Washington's interest in the Middle East. The dynamics of the Cold War, the establishment of Israel and the need for energy security ensured that this region would retain a central role in Washington's global calculations. The inevitability of US influence in the Middle East is not under question. It is the application of that influence that is central to understanding Middle Eastern perceptions of the United States. The roots of anti-Americanism lie in the impact of Washington's foreign policy in this troubled region. As has been explored, the modern Middle East is the creation of an often unsteady process of internal intentions and external interference. As demonstrated here, US policy since the 1950s has often served to exacerbate and inflame these tensions.

The US–Israeli alliance, presented here as a byproduct of the Cold War, lies at the heart of these tensions. However, as argued, it is not the sole cause of popular discontent with the United States. Rather it serves as the starkest example of the inconsistency and hypocrisy that permeate US policy towards the Middle East. Be it in Palestine or Iraq, the suffering of Middle Easterners does not appear to figure in US policy in the same way that the suffering of Americans, or Israelis, does. In an era marked by the rise of Arab media and enhanced communications, these inequities are powerfully displayed in a way not experienced in previous generations. The political ramifications of this reality are significant.

The Bush administration's foreign policy leaves the Middle East in a precarious position, and a new American government will face the daunting task of rehabilitating the superpower's role in the region. In addition, the international community, sidelined in the march to war in Iraq, is faced with the challenges of re-engagement with the region. As this process unfolds, greater awareness and understanding of the basis of Middle Eastern discontent with a US-dominated global system is essential.

REFERENCES

Kohut, Andrew (2007) 'America's Image in the World: Findings from the Pew Global Attitudes Project', 14 March, available at http://pewglobal.org/commentary/display.php?AnalysisID=1019.

INDEX

Abbasid dynasty (750–1258) 10
Abdullah (ibn Husayn), King of Jordan 21, 22
Abir, Mordechi 117
Abraham 27
Abrahamanian, Ervand 77, 79
Abu-Amr, Ziad 141
Abu Ghraib scandal 172, 184
active deterrence, military doctrine of 56
Afary, J. and Anderson, K. B. 83
Afghanistan 2, 3; blood-letting of 4; Cold
    War context 89, 90, 91, 92–3, 95, 98, 100,
    105; complexity of history 90; conflict in,
    Gorbachev and resolution of 101–3; Geneva
    Accords (1988) 101; geographical position
    90–1; historical perspective 90–3; human
    cost of conflict in 102; *jihadi* mindset,
    propagation of 104, 105; Mujahideen in
    89, 93, 95–7, 98–9, 100, 101, 103; Pakistan,
    importance in conflict in 92, 96–7; PDPA
    (People's Democratic Party of Afghanistan)
    91–2; Pushtun people 104; Soviet invasion,
    reasons for 93–6; Soviet invasion, regional
    reactions 96–7; Stinger high-tech anti-
    aircraft missiles, transfer to 99–101; Taliban
    in 2, 3, 103, 104, 105, 160, 183; Tora Bora
    183; United States, role in 89–90, 92, 96,
    97–100, 101, 102–3, 104–5
Ajami, Fouad 113
Akbarzadeh, S. and Saeed, A. 72
Al-Aqsa Intifada (2000 onwards) 6, 139, 145,
    146, 148–51, 164, 179
Al-Arian, Laila 3
Al-Jazeera TV 171
al-Qaeda 2, 6, 103, 160, 161, 162, 165, 182, 183

Al-Nakba 37–42; Arab–Israeli force
    differentials 39–40; Palestinian exodus 40–1
Albright, Madeleine 164
Algiers Agreement (1975) 114–15
Ali, Tariq 169
Amal Shia organization 63
American-Arab Anti-Discrimination Board 3
Amin, Hafizullah 94
Amir, Yigal 144
Amnesty International 64
Anfal campaigns against Kurds 168
Anglo-Iraqi War (1941) 110
anti-Americanism: Arab anti-Americanism 3,
    47, 136, 182; complex social and political
    mindset 1–2; essentialist interpretations of
    2; Iraq War and 184; of Islamic Republic
    of Iran 70–1; Middle Eastern 1, 2, 5, 6–7,
    25, 161, 183; modern anti-Americanism 4;
    roots of 185
anticipatory self-defence 51
Arab Higher Committee in Palestine 32, 36, 38
Arab–Israeli Peace Initiative (1982) 62
Arab–Israeli War (1948) 6, 37–42; Arab
    aggression, Israeli perspective on 42;
    controversial nature of 42; Deir Yassin,
    massacre at 38; force differentials 39–40;
    guerrilla war in Palestine 37–8; Hadassah
    Hospital, killings at 38; Israel's 'David and
    Goliath' perspective 39; military capabilities
    of Palestinian fighters 38–9; victory for
    Israel over Arab armies 40–2
Arab–Israeli War (1967) 6, 49–56, 70;
    aftermath of 54–6, 57–8; anticipatory self-
    defence, war of 51; costs of Arab defeat

52, 53; disaster for Palestinians 53; Golan
Heights 51; Israel, siege of 51; post-war
structure of Israel 52–3; provocative actions
by Egypt 49–51; swift victory of Israel in
51–2; territorial advances of Israel in 51–2
Arab–Israeli War (1973) 6, 46, 56–9;
active deterrence, military doctrine of
56; aftermath of 57–9, 138; oil trade,
politicization of 57–8
Arab–Israeli War (2006) 6, 63–5
Arab League 36, 41, 181
Arab nationalism 11, 12, 52, 74, 113, 178
Arab Revolt (1916) 12, 17
Arab Revolt (1936–9) in Palestine 32
Arafat, Yasser: biographical sketch 138; Camp
David negotiations 148; chairman of PLO
60; founder of Fatah 53, 54; handshake
with Yitzhak Rabin 144; imprisonment and
death in Ramallah 150–1, 153–4; insecurity
of position 147; international standing 150;
reputation, requirement for polishing of
143; Saddam Hussein, congratulations for
129
Armitage, Richard 163
Aswan Dam 47, 178
Ataturk, Mustafa Kemal 9
Auto-Emancipation 27
Ayoob, Mohammad 75, 167, 168, 171

Baghdad Pact (1955) 110
Bahrain 84
Baker, James 127
Balfour, Arthur James 15
Balfour Declaration (1917) 8, 15–17, 19, 21,
22, 28, 30
Bali, blood-letting of 4
al-Banna, Hasan 73
Bar-Siman-Tov, Yaaov 48, 52, 57
Barak, Ehud 147–8, 179
Baram, Amatzia 113
Ba'th Party in Iraq 113–14
Bazoft, Farzad 125
Bedouin nomads 31
Begin, Menachim 179
Bekka Valley 60
Ben Gurion, David 35, 36
Biltmore Program (1942) 34, 35
bin Laden, Osama 3, 103, 104, 105, 128, 160,
171

Bizhara, Azmay 141
Black September 60, 139
Blair, Tony 164–5
Boland Amendment (1984) 121
Bolshevik Revolution (1917) 13
Bonney, Richard 71
Bowden, Mark 86n4
Bradsher, Henry 102–3
Bregman, Ahron 51, 56, 61
Brezhnev, President Leonid I. 93, 94, 105n1;
doctrine of 93, 94, 95, 105n1
Britain 77, 164–5, 178; attitudes to King–Crane
Report 19–20; Baghdad Pact (1955) 110;
dominant position in Palestine 21; global
politics and British Mandate in Palestine
29–30; Mandate for Palestine 21, 22–3,
29–30, 32, 33, 34, 37, 42, 46, 67n5; Middle
East, regional alliances in 8, 9, 10–11,
11–12, 13–17; patron of Zionism 46; Suez
War (1956) 47–8; tension with France over
spoils of war 21; White Paper (1922) on
Palestine 30, 31; White Paper (1939) on
Palestine 33
Brown, Leon Carl 21
Brzezinski, Zbigniew 98, 105n2
Bund (Jewish Labor Federation) 28
Bush, President George H. W. 123, 128, 130,
131, 133n3; administration of 120, 123, 124,
126, 150
Bush, President George W. 2, 113, 120, 138,
150, 162, 164, 174n3; administration of
138, 150, 153, 160–1, 162, 163, 173, 184,
185; doctrine of 154, 165, 183; logic of
administration of 3; rationale for invasion
of Iraq 167–70; rhetoric of 165–7; Roadmap
to Peace (G. W. Bush, 2002) 150; 'war on
terror' of administration of 2, 3, 6, 65, 120,
150–1, 153, 156, 160, 162, 165, 169–70, 173,
182–3, 184

Caliphate 10
Camp David Accords (1978) 59, 141, 147, 148
capitalism 76, 85
Carter, President Jimmy 79, 81, 97–8, 99,
105n2; administration of 118; doctrine of
98, 115
Castells, Manuel 76
Central Asia 91, 96, 97, 183
China 95; Chinese–Pakistani relationship 94

Choueiri, Youssef M. 48
Churchill, Winston S. 30
CIA (Central Intelligence Agency) 77, 97, 98, 100, 103; 'CIA World Factbook' 174n1
Clinton, President William J. 147, 156n1; administration of 144, 147, 150, 163, 164; legacy of 147; presidency of, defining moment 144
Cockburn, A. and Cockburn, P. 126
Colás, A. and Saull, R. 172
Cold War 4, 6, 77, 81, 85; Afghanistan in context of 89, 90, 91, 92–3, 95, 98, 100, 105; Arab–Israeli Wars and dimension of 40; development of 37; political domination of 178; US–Israeli alliance and logic of 66
Collins, Joseph 95
Colombia 2
colonialism: Middle East, colonial powers' influence in 9, 25, 177; role of colonial powers in Middle East 8–9, 13–17, 46; traumatic effect in Middle East of 72
confessionalism in Lebanon 20–1
Constantinople 10
Conte, Alex 127
Cordesman, Anthony 122, 128
Cortright, David 164
Crusades 27, 28
Czechoslovakia 40

Davis, Eric 110
Deir Yassin, massacre at 38
Denoeux, Guilain 72
Dershowitz, Alan 16
Donaldson, Gary 129
Donnelly, Thomas 2
Dorronsoro, Gilles 93–4
Dreyfus affair 26
Dupree, Louis 95

Eban, Abba 52, 65
Eden, Prime Minister Anthony 48
Egypt 39, 66, 75, 83, 85, 182; arms assistance from Soviets 56; Aswan Dam 47, 178; Egyptian–Israeli Peace Treaty (1979) 59; Muslim Brotherhood in 73–4, 75; provocative actions against Israel 49–51; Ramadan War (1973) 57; refusal of refuge for PLO 61; Soviet influences in 49–50, 56; Suez War (1956) 47–9; United Arab Republic (1958–61) 48; US formal ties, cutting of 52; 'war of attrition' with Israel 56
Eickelman, Dale 80
El Badri, Hassan et al. 67n2
El-Gemayal, Bachir 61
Elam, Yigal 39, 40
Elhadj, Elie 154
Emunim, Gush 58
Esposito, John 73, 86n1, 104
European Union (EU) 151, 154–5; TIM (Temporary International Mechanism) 155

Faisal (ibn Husayn) 19, 21
Falk, Richard 101
Farouk-Sluglett, M. and Sluglett, P. 131
Farouki, Suha Taji 75
Farsoun, S. and Landis, J. 140
Farsoun, Sami 140
Fatah movement in Palestine 40, 54, 146, 182
Finlan, Alastair 124, 126
First World War 9, 12, 17
Flapan, Simha 36, 38, 39, 40, 42, 43n2, 67n5
France: attitudes to King–Crane Report 19–20; Middle East influence in 8, 9, 13–17, 18; Suez War (1956) 47–8; Syria, Mandate for 20; tension with Britain over spoils of war 21
Freedman, L. and Karsh, E. 118

Galeotti, Mark 94
Galnoor, Itzhak 36
Ganin, Zvi 37
Garthwaite, Gene 3
Gause, F. Gregory 116
Gaza Strip 40, 64, 140, 144, 148, 149, 152–5
Geneva Accords (1988) 101
Germany 184; Ottoman Empire, alliance with 10
Ghareeb, E. and Khadduri, M. 125
Glaspie, Ambassador April 125–6
Golan Heights 51
Goldstein, Baruch 145, 146
Gorbachev, President Mikhail 100, 101
'Green Line' of Israel 151–2
Gulf War (1991) 6, 129–32, 133, 138, 143, 164; post-war confusion 130–1; see also Persian Gulf
Gunter, M. and Yavuz, M. H. 173

Gunter, Michael 131
Gush Emunim 58

Hadassah Hospital, killings at 38
Haddad, Yvonne 73
Haganah 33, 34, 38
Hallenberg, J. and Karlsson, H. 164
HAMAS (Islamic Resistance Movement) 40,
    54, 64, 75, 146, 147, 150, 151, 153–5, 182;
    emergence of 141–2
Hasan, Naseer 148
Hashemite dynasty 14, 19, 21, 22, 110; and fall
    of Ottoman Empire 10–13
Hass, Amira 145
Hassassian, Manuel 144
Hebrew, calls for revival of 28
Hebron, massacre at 145, 146
Heller, Joseph 34
Helmreich, Paul C. 20
Herzl, Theodor 26
Hezbollah 63, 64, 121
Hijaz Rebellion 12
Hilali, A. Z. 99
Hill, Enid 128
Hitler, Adolf 33
Hizb al-Tahrir 75
Hogan, Matthew 38
Holocaust 41, 42; devastation of 34; systematic
    campaign of 35
Holy Land 27–8
Hroub, Khaled 142
Hughes, Matthew 12
Human Rights Watch 168
Huneidi, Sahar 16
ibn Husayn, Ali 11–12, 17, 21
Husayn–McMahon Correspondence 8, 11, 12,
    13, 14, 15
Hussein, Saddam 110, 120, 123, 127, 130;
    aftermath of Operation Desert Storm
    131–2; ambition of 113; biographical
    sketch 113; congratulations from Yasser
    Arafat for 129, 138; decision to invade
    Kuwait 129; dictatorial rule in Iraq 3, 124;
    financial backer of PLO 129; humbling of,
    Israeli national interest 129; international
    confrontation for 128; invasion of Iraq
    and toppling of 160–1, 161–2, 163, 164,
    167, 168–9, 172, 173; media and 125;
    Operation Desert Storm (1991) 128–31;
    outrage focused on Israel 126; perception
    of domestic position 116; perception of
    US 'green light' on invasion of Kuwait 126;
    political beginnings 114; regional intentions
    117; rise to power 114, 115; Sunni tribal
    alliances 116; Tikrit 114; violent resistance
    to 115; Washington's distrust of 123–4

Indonesia 184
Intelligence Capabilities of US Regarding
    WMD, Commission on 174n3
International Court of Justice 152
internationalism 94
Intifada (1987) 64, 140–1, 142, 143, 145, 179;
    see also Al-Aqsa Intifada
Iran 5, 75, 91, 141; Algiers Agreement (1975)
    114–15; Baghdad Pact (1955) 110; Iran Air
    Flight 655, shooting down of 123; Islamic
    Revolution in 6, 70–1, 76–83, 85, 90, 91,
    115, 141, 173; jurisprudence, supremacy
    of (vilayat-i faqih) 79–80, 84; Lebanon and
    121; nationalism in 70, 76, 80, 117; Pahlavi
    regime 77–8, 80, 82; political relationship
    with Iraq 110; revolutionary change,
    clamor for 80; Revolutionary Guards 83;
    Rushdie affair 82; SAVAK (Shah's secret
    police force) 77, 83; sea tensions with US
    122; secularism forced upon 72, 73; Shia
    dimension in Islamic Revolution 83–4;
    White Revolution in 79
Iran–Contra scandal 120–2
Iran–Iraq War (1980–88): aftermath of 123–4;
    costs of conflict 117–18; external influences
    on 117, 118; martyrdom in 117; Soviet
    involvement 119, 120; United States'
    involvement 118–19, 119–23
Iraq 3, 85; aftermath of invasion 172–3;
    Algiers Agreement (1975) 114–15; Anfal
    campaigns against Kurds in 168; Anglo-
    Iraqi War (1941) 110; Arab discontent at
    invasion of 170–2; Baghdad Pact (1955)
    110; Ba'th Party 113–14; blood-letting in 4;
    geo-political structure 111, 161; invasion of,
    events leading to 161–70; Iran, assessment
    of military weakness of 116–17; Iran–Iraq
    War (1980–88) 6, 83; Kurdish community
    in 111; Kuwait, invasion of 126–8; political

relationship with Iran 110; Soviet influence in 113; state of, establishment of 110; United States and 52, 183–4; *see also* Hussein, Saddam

Irgun Zvai Leumi 33, 34

Irish Republican Army (IRA) 2

ISI (Inter-Services Intelligence), Pakistan 92, 97, 100, 102–3

Islam: 'fundamentalism' in 72; Jerusalem, holy site 31; *jihad,* duty of 71–2, 103, 104; political Islam 6; Qur'an 71; Sharia 71, 75; Shia Islam 63, 65, 83–4; Sunnah 71; universality of 74–5

Islamic Jihad 59, 75, 141, 142–3

'Islamism' 2, 6, 85, 90; historical perspective 71–6, 85; identity, communal response and roots of 76; middle-class, educated support for 75–6; national contexts of 75; political movement 72, 73–4; revival in modern times 73

Israel 5–6; active deterrence, military doctrine of 56; Arab aggression, perspective on 42; besiegement of 51; challenge of 1987 Intifada 140–1; conflict engendered by establishment of 25–6, 47; 'David and Goliath' perspective on 1948 War 39; declaration of statehood 37, 39; divisiveness of Israel–Palestine conflict 136, 155–6; Egyptian–Israeli Peace Treaty (1979) 59; 'Green Line' 151–2; Gush Emunim 58; history characterized by war 65–6; Jewish refugees, resettlement of 41; Jewish sovereignty in 55–6; July War (2006) 6, 63–5; Lebanese Maronite Christians, arming of 60; Lebanon War (1982) 59–63, 139; Likud Party 58, 145, 149; as occupying power 65–6; Operation Peace for Galilee (1982) 63; Oslo Peace Accords (1993) 6, 53, 142–4, 155; Oslo Peace Accords (1993), failure of 144–8; refusal to sign NPT 56; Roadmap to Peace (G. W. Bush, 2002) 150; Saudi Peace Plan (2002) 149, 150; security wall 151–2; settler defiance 59, 60; Six-Day War (1967) 6, 49–56, 70; Suez War (1956) 47–9; suicide bombings in 63, 139, 146, 149, 150, 162; territorial advances (1967) 51–2; US relationship with 25–6, 42, 46, 52–3, 66, 136, 138, 155–6, 179–80, 185; victory (1949) over Arab armies 40–2; 'war of attrition' of Egypt with 56; War of Independence 37–42; withdrawal from Gaza Strip 152–5; Yamit settlement, settler defiance and 59, 60; Yom Kippur War (1973) 56–9

Israeli–Egyptian Peace Treaty (1979) 59

Jabotinsky, Ze'ev 31–2

Jacoby, Tami 151

Jawad, Sa'ad 111

Jerusalem 27, 31, 148; King David Hotel, bomb attack on 34; UN-administered trusteeship for 36; West Bank and 41

Jewish community, threats to 26, 29

Jewish Diaspora 27, 29

Jewish identity, tradition and 27

Jewish Labor Federation (Bund) 29

Jewish refugees, resettlement of 41

Jewish sovereignty in Israel 55–6

The Jewish State (Herzl, T.) 26

jihad: Islamic duty of 71–2, 103, 104; *jihadi* mindset, propagation in Afghanistan of 104, 105

Johnson, President Lyndon B. 55

Jordan 11, 83, 85, 124, 181, 182; PLO activism 60–2; US relationship with 52

Jordan River 31–2

July War (2006) 6, 63–5

Junt, Tony 77

jurisprudence, supremacy in Iran of (*vilayat-i faqih*) 79–80, 84

Kahane Commission 62, 139

Karsh, E. and Ratusi, I. 12, 14, 114

Karsh, Ephraim 114–15, 130, 150

Keddie, Nikki 77

Khairallah, David 3

Khalidi, Rashid 39

al-Khalil, Samir 117

Khatab, Sayed 74

Khomeini, Ayatollah Ruhollah 70, 73, 79–80, 80–1, 82–3, 84, 86n2, 115

King–Crane Commission (1919) 18–19, 42, 136, 177, 179

King David Hotel, bomb attack on 34

Kissinger, Henry 57

Kohut, Andrew 170, 173, 180, 184

Kostiner, Joseph 21

Krasno, Jean E. 49
Kuniholm, B. R. 127
Kuperman, Alan 100, 106n3
Kurds in Iraq 111, 168
Kurz, Anat 53, 146
Kurzman, Charles 86n2
Kushner, Harvey W. 103
Kuwait 84, 124–5, 129, 162; Iraqi invasion of 126–8; Iraqi occupation of, response as turning point of politics of Middle East 127–8; US–Kuwait alliance 122

Lacorne, Denis 77
Landis, Jean 140
Lapidus, Ira 86n1
League of Nations 9, 11, 21, 29, 177; Article 22 of Covenant of 17–18
Lebanon 5, 85, 181, 182; Amal Shia organization 63; Bekka Valley 60; confessionalism in 20–1; creation of state of 20; Hezbollah 63, 64, 121; Iran and 121; Maronite Christians in 13, 19, 20, 60, 61; Nar el-Bared 181; Phalange Christian militia 62; PLO activism 60–2; Sabra and Shatila refugee camps 62; Taif Accords (1990) 21
Lebanon War (1982): aftermath 62–3; domestic politics of Israel, effects on 62–3; international reaction to conflict 64; Israeli air and sea blockade 64, 65
Levy, Joshua 148
Lewinsky, Monica 147
liberalism: democracy promotion, dangers of 4; democratic liberalism 97; rejection by Islamicists of 75
Likud Party in Israel 58, 145, 149
Lithuania 29
Litwak, Robert 2
London, blood-letting of 4

McMahon, Henry 11, 13, 14
McNamara, Robert 48
Madrid, blood-letting of 4
Makdissi, Ussama 5, 49, 77, 79
Maley, William 91–2, 95, 96, 101–2, 106n4
Mandate system in Middle East 9, 18–23, 29–30, 32–4, 37, 42, 46, 67n5, 110, 177, 179
Maronite Christians in Lebanon 13, 19, 20, 60, 61

Matthias, Willard 94
Mecca 12, 31
Medina 12, 31
Meir, Hatina 140
Mesopotamia 18
Middle East: Al-Nakba 37–42; anti-Americanism in 1, 2, 5, 6–7, 25, 161, 183; Arab–Israeli War (1948) 6, 37–42; Arab–Israeli War (1967) 6, 49–56, 70; Arab–Israeli War (1973) 6, 46, 56–9; Arab–Israeli War (2006) 6, 63–5; Arab nationalism 11, 12, 52, 74, 113, 178; Arab self-determination, British endorsement of 12–13; Balfour Declaration (1917) 8, 15–17, 19, 21, 22, 28, 30; British attitudes to King–Crane Report 19–20; British regional alliances 8, 9, 10–11, 11–12, 13–17; Caliphate 10; Cold War, effect on 47; colonial period 9, 25; colonial powers, influence of 177; colonial powers, role in 8–9, 13–17, 46; colonialism, traumatic effect of 72; democracy promotion, dangers of 4; divisiveness of Israel–Palestine conflict 136, 155–6; First World War 9, 12, 17; French attitudes to King–Crane Report 19–20; French influence 8, 9, 13–17, 18; geo-political landscape 9, 22–3; Great Powers, regional interference by 77; Husayn–McMahon Correspondence 8, 11, 12, 13, 14, 15; identity, communal response and roots of 'Islamism' 76; imposition by West of territorial boundaries 8; interplay of politics and history 185; Iraqi occupation of Kuwait, response as turning point of politics of 127–8; Israel, conflict engendered by establishment of 25–6, 47; July War (2006) 6, 63–5; Lebanon War (1982) 59–63, 139; Mandate system 9, 18–23, 29–30, 32–4, 37, 42, 46, 67n5, 110, 177, 179; nation-states, establishment of system of 8, 46; national legitimacy, concept of 16; negative conceptions of US 184; Orientalism, study of 31; Ramadan War (1973) 56–9; Russian interests in 14; San Remo Conference (1920) 18, 20; Second World War 9, 178; Six-Day War (1967) 49–56; socialism in 4; Soviet influence, decline of 123; struggle for, intensification

of 178; Suez War (1956) 47–9; Sykes-Picot Agreement (1916) 8, 13–14, 15, 17; United States and, where from here? 185; United States as key player 177

Middle East Report 147

Milestones (Qutb, S.) 74

Milton-Edwards, Beverly 141

Minter, Richard 128

Morris, Benny 67n5, 144

Mossedeq, Prime Minister Mohammed 76, 77, 169

Mueller, John 130

Mujahideen in Afghanistan 89, 93, 95–7, 98–9, 100, 101, 103

Munich Olympic Games (1972) 147

Munson, Henry 80

Musallam, Adnan A. 86n2, 86n3

Musallam, Musallam Ali 115, 125

Muslim Brotherhood 73–4, 75, 141–2

Mutawi, Samir 50, 51

Nar el-Bared 181

Nasser, Jamal 62, 66

Nasser, President Gamal Abdul 47, 48, 49, 50, 52, 53, 74, 90, 178

National Intelligence Estimate (2002) 167

National Security Council (US) 160

National Security Decision Directive 166 (NSDD-US) 100

National Security Strategy (US, 2002) 160, 165

nationalisms 8, 29, 32, 33, 42, 70, 76, 80, 156; nation-states, establishment of system of 8, 46; national legitimacy, concept of 16; secular nationalism 55, 72, 113, 141; *see also* Arab nationalism; Jewish nationalism; Palestinian nationalism; pan-Arabism

Nazi Germany 30, 33, 35

Nicaragua 121

Nidal, Abu 60

North Korea 164

NPT (Non-Proliferation Treaty of 1968) 55, 56

Nusse, Andrea 154

Occupied Territories 5, 58, 62, 75, 145, 146, 151–2, 154–5, 156

oil trade, politicization of 57–8

Olmert, Ehud 153

Omar, Mullah Muhammad 103, 104

OPEC (Organization of Petroleum Exporting Countries) 57, 66, 124, 125

Operation Cyclone (1979) 92

Operation Defensive Wall (2002) 150

Operation Desert Shield (1990) 128–9

Operation Desert Storm (1991) 129–31, 133; outcomes of 131–2, 133

Operation Enduring Freedom (2001) 183

Operation Litani (1978) 60

Operation Musketeer (1956) 47

Operation Peace for Galilee (1982) 63

Operation Spring of Youth (1973) 147

Operation Surprise (1980) 81

Orientalism, study of 31

Orientalism (Said, E.) 31

Oslo Peace Accords (1993) 6, 53, 142–4, 144–8, 155; failure of 144–8

Ottoman Empire 9, 27, 111; division of Ottoman lands 18, 25; fall of 8, 10–13, 22, 46, 177; fear of imperial Russia 10; German alliance with 10; Hashemite dynasty and fall of 10–13; influence of Ottoman norms 22; San Remo Conference (1920) 18; Zionism and lands of 14–15

Ouimet, Matthew 105n1

Oxfam 154

Pahlavi, Reza Shah 70, 77, 79, 83, 90

Pahlavi regime 77–8, 80, 82

Pakistan 75, 84, 91, 95; Baghdad Pact (1955) 110; Chinese–Pakistani relationship 94; importance in Afghanistan conflict 92, 96–7; ISI (Inter-Services Intelligence) 92, 97, 100, 102–3; Pushtun people 104

Palestine 12, 13, 18; Al-Aqsa Intifada (2000 onwards) 6, 139, 145, 146, 148–51, 164, 179; Arab Higher Committee 32, 36, 38; Arab–Israeli guerrilla war in 37–8; Arab revolt (1936-9) 32; Arabs of 31; Balfour Declaration (1917) 15–17; Britain, dominant position in 21; British Mandate for 21, 22–3, 29–30, 32, 33, 34, 37, 42, 46, 67n5; British White Paper (1922) on 30, 31; British White Paper (1939) on 33; Deir Yassin, massacre at 38; divisiveness of Israel–Palestine conflict 136, 155–6; dual claim on lands of 30; exodus from 40–1;

Fatah movement 40, 54, 146, 182; Gaza Strip 40, 64, 140, 144, 148, 149, 152–5; global politics and British Mandate in 29–30; guerrilla war in 37–8; Hadassah Hospital, killings at 38; HAMAS (Islamic Resistance Movement) 40, 54, 64, 75, 146, 147, 150, 151, 153–5, 182; HAMAS, emergence of 141–2; Hebron, massacre at 145, 146; historical perspective 27; Intifada (1987) 6, 64, 140–1, 142, 143, 145, 179; King–Crane Report, attitude to Jewish immigration 19; legitimization of viable Jewish community in 28–9; military capabilities (1948) of Palestinian fighters 38–9; Occupied Territories 5, 58, 62, 75, 145, 146, 151–2, 154–5, 156; Oslo Peace Accords (1993) 6, 53, 142–4, 155; Oslo Peace Accords, failure of 144–8; Palestinian Authority 53, 54, 138, 143, 144, 146, 149, 151, 154–5, 159; Palestinian nationalism 31–2, 61, 141, 181; partition of 35–6, 37; partition of, Arab opposition to 33; Peel Commission (1937) 32, 36; PLO (Palestine Liberation Organization) 53, 54, 60–2, 66, 129–30, 140–1, 142, 143, 144; political identity in 30–1; post-war (1945) chaos in 34–5; Ramallah, Arafat's imprisonment and death in 150–1; referral of matter to United Nations 35; resistance, intractable nature of 65–6; Roadmap to Peace (G. W. Bush, 2002) 150; Saudi Peace Plan (2002) 149, 150; self-determination, desire for 66; 'self-governing institutions', British charged to create 22; United States and Palestinians 180–3; West Bank 41, 140, 144, 148, 149, 152; Zionist General Council in 35; Zionist program of national reconstruction in 28; *see also* Arafat, Yasser
Palestinian nationalism 31–2, 61, 141, 181
pan-Arabism 39, 41, 48, 49, 54, 61, 74, 90, 138
Pappe, Ilan 67n5
Pauly, Robert J. 119
PDPA (People's Democratic Party of Afghanistan) 91–2
Peel Commission (1937) 32, 36
Perle, Richard 163
Persian Gulf 6, 54, 58, 61, 66, 82–3, 84, 90, 97, 98; aftermath of Iran–Iraq War 123–4; battlefield of 109; geo-political vulnerability of 178; Gulf War (1991) 6, 129–32, 133; historical context 110–14; Iran and political structures of 184; Iran–Iraq War (1980–88) 109–10; oil, regional tension over 124–8; Operation Desert Shield (1990) 128–9; Operation Desert Storm (1991) 129–31, 133; outcomes of Operation Desert Storm 131–2, 133; refusal of refuge for PLO 61; Soviet involvement in 118–23; strategic and economic importance 132; tension between Iraq and Iran 114–18; US involvement in 118–23, 132–3, 169, 172–3; water, regional tension over 124–8
Pew Research Center 1, 170, 171, 173, 180, 184
Phalange Christian militia 62
Pinsker, Leo 26, 27
Piscatori, James 80
PLO (Palestine Liberation Organization) 53, 54, 60–2, 66, 129–30, 140–1, 142, 143, 144; activism, Jordan and 60–2; Lebanon, activism and 60–2
Poland 29
Policy Studies, Institute for 173
Prophet Muhammad 10, 11, 12, 65, 71, 83–4
Pushtun people 104

Qasim, Brigadier General Abd al-Karim 111, 114, 125
Qassem, Naim 67n6
Quandt, William B. 67n3
Qur'an 71
Qutb, Sayyid 73–4, 80, 86n2, 86n3

Rabat Conference (1974) 62
Rabin, Yitzhak 138, 144, 152
Rabinovich, Itamar 149
Ramadan War (1973) 56–9
Ramallah, Arafat's imprisonment and death in 150–1
Raphel, Gideon 52
Rather, Dan 156n1
Ratusi, Inari 114
Reagan, President Ronald W. 62, 81, 99, 100, 121; administration of 119, 120, 121, 122, 123, 124; Arab–Israeli Peace Initiative (1982) 62; doctrine of 132
Revisionist Zionism 31–2, 34

Rezun, Miron 113, 114, 117, 120, 129
Ricker, Laurent 47
Roadmap to Peace (G. W. Bush, 2002) 150
Rodman, P. W. 102
Rogan, Eugene L. 22
Rogerson, Barnaby 86n4
Rostow, Eugene V. 55
Rothschild, Lionel, Lord 15
Roy, Arundhati 92, 94
Roy, Olivier 103
Rubenstein, Amnon 55
Rumsfeld, Donald 120, 164
Rushdie, Salman 82
Russia: anti-Jewish agitation in 29; Bolshevik
    Revolution (1917) 13; Middle East interests
    of 14; see also Soviet Union
Ruthven, Malise 145

al-Sabah family of Kuwait 124
Sabra refugee camp 62
Sachar, Howard 15, 16, 27, 42
Sadat, President Anwar 56, 59, 141
Sadiki, Larbi 72
al-Sadr, Muhammad 115, 116
Sahliyeh, Emile F. 67n4
Said, Edward 31
Saikal, A. and Maley, W. 101, 102
Saikal, Amin 93, 94, 97, 102, 106n5
Salibi, Kamal 21
Samoza dynasty in Nicaragua 121
San Remo Conference (1920) 18, 20
Sandanistas in Nicaragua 121
Sardar, Z. and Davies, M.W. 1
The Satanic Verses (Rushdie, S.) 82
ibn Saud, Abdul Aziz 21
al-Saud royalty of Saudi Arabia 127, 149
Saudi Arabia 9, 11, 83, 84, 89, 125, 126, 129;
    Iraqi invasion of Kuwait, response to
    127–8; Mujahideen in Afghanistan, financial
    support for 97; politicization of oil trade
    57–8, 66; refusal of refuge for PLO 61;
    Saudi Peace Plan (2002) 149, 150
SAVAK (Shah's secret police force) 77, 83
Second World War 9, 33–6, 42, 46, 178
September 11 terrorism 1, 105, 113; global
    community, perspective on 3–4; Middle
    Eastern contextualization of 3, 150, 160,
    163, 164, 165, 168, 169, 183

Sharia 71, 75
Sharon, Ariel 61, 139, 148–9, 150, 152–3, 179
Shatila refugee camp 62
Shatt al-Arab 114, 124
al-Shawwa, Mayor Rashad 142
Sher, Gilead 148
Shia Islam 63, 65, 83–4
Shlaim, Avi 15, 16, 39, 41, 54, 57, 67n5
Sick, Gary 81
Sinora, Hanna 54
Six-Day War (1967) 6, 49–56, 70
Slevin, P. and Allen, M. 153
Smith, Charles D. 62
socialism 4, 49, 76, 85, 93, 95, 113, 180; power
    of ideology 28, 31; rejection by Islamicists
    of 75
Soviet Union 4, 40, 66, 84, 91–2, 178;
    Afghanistan invasion 6, 89, 90, 93–7;
    Afghanistan invasion, reasons for 93–6;
    Afghanistan invasion, regional reactions
    96–7; arms assistance for Egypt from 56;
    Egypt, influences in 49–51, 56; emergent
    superpower (1948) 37, 46; Iran–Iraq War
    (1980–88), involvement 119, 120; Iraq,
    influence in 113; Israel, recognition of
    independence of 39; KGB 97; Middle East,
    decline of influence in 123; misjudgment
    of Afghan conflict 101–2; Persian Gulf,
    involvement in 118–23; Suez War (1956)
    47–9
Spiegel, Steven 52
Sprinzak, Ehud 67n1
Stern Gang (Lehi) 34
Stinger high-tech anti-aircraft missiles 99–101
Suez War (1956) 47–9
suicide bombings in Israel 63, 139, 146, 149,
    150, 162
Sykes–Picot Agreement (1916) 8, 13–14, 15,
    17
Syria 11, 13, 18, 84, 141, 177; deployment to
    Lebanon 59–60; French Mandate for 20;
    Lebanon War (1982) 61; Ramadan War
    (1973) 57; United Arab Republic (1958–61)
    48; US formal ties, cutting of 52

Taif Accords (1990) 21
Tal, David 37, 38
Taliban in Afghanistan 2, 3, 103, 104, 105, 160,
    183

Tanner, Stephen 100
Taylor, Philip 172
Tetreault, Mary Ann 172
Thomas, Baylis 39
Tora Bora 183
Transjordan 39, 41
Tripp, Charles 115
Truman, President Harry S. 37, 179; doctrine of 77
Tunisia 61
Turkey 10, 72, 164; Baghdad Pact (1955) 110

United Arab Emirates 83, 84, 124
United Arab Republic (1958–61) 48
United Kingdom see Britain
United Nations 11, 22, 35, 37, 46, 49, 51, 60, 113, 164; Iran–Iraq conflict 118, 130; Jerusalem, UN-administered trusteeship for 36; Mandates confirmed by (1922) 20; Resolution 37/37 102; UNMOVIC (UN Monitoring, Verification and Inspection Commission) 163
United Nations Security Council 11, 48, 102, 156, 168; Resolution 181 35, 36, 37; Resolution 242 54–5; Resolution 598 118, 122, 123; Resolution 660 127, 128, 130, 131; Resolution 661 127, 162, 163; Resolution 678 128, 166; Resolution 687 131, 163; Resolution 1267 160; Resolution 1284 163; Resolution 1322 164, 174n2; Resolution 1403 164, 174n2; Resolution 1405 164, 174n2; Resolution 1435 164, 174n2; Resolution 1441 164, 166
United States 178; Afghanistan, role in 89–90, 92, 96, 97–100, 101, 102–3, 104–5; American-Arab Anti-Discrimination Board 3; anti-Americanism 1–2, 3, 4, 5, 6–7, 25–6, 47, 70–1, 136, 161, 180, 182–4, 185; 'Arab-Afghan' movement and 6; arms sales to Iran 120–2; Boland Amendment (1984) 121; Camp David Accords (1978) 59, 141, 147, 148; centrality in global politics of 1, 2, 6; CIA (Central Intelligence Agency) 77, 97, 98, 100, 103; emergence into international spotlight 15–16, 17; emergent superpower (1948) 37, 46; hostage crisis in Iran 81; hostility in Iran towards 81–2; Iran–Contra scandal 120–2; Iran–Iraq War (1980–88), involvement in 118–19, 119–23; Iranian Revolution and response of 80–2; Iraq and 183–4; Israel, recognition of independence of 39, 179; Israel, relationship with 25–6, 42, 46, 52–3, 66, 136, 138, 155–6, 179–80, 185; Israeli–US alliance 66, 136, 138, 155–6, 179–80, 185; Jordan, relationship with 52; key player in Middle East 177; major force in Middle East politics 2; Middle East and, where from here? 185; mixed blessing of Israeli statehood for 42, 46; National Intelligence Estimate (2002) 167; National Security Decision Directive 166 (NSDD) 100; National Security Strategy (2002) 160, 165; negative conceptions of 184; neo-conservative preoccupation with Baghdad 163, 164–5, 167–70; Palestinians and 180–3; Persian Gulf, involvement in 118–23, 132–3, 169, 172–3; regional role in Middle East 6; relationship with Middle East, changes and context 4–5; revolutionary history of 5; self-determination, support for 5; Suez War (1956) 47–9; suppression of Soviet allies 85; USS Samuel Roberts, Iranian mine incident 122; USS Stark, Iraqi airstrike on 122; Yom Kippur War (1973) 57
UNMOVIC (UN Monitoring, Verification and Inspection Commission) 163

Vidal, Gore 172
Vital, David 43n1

Wahhabism 2, 22
al-Wahhad, Muhammad Ibn 'Abd 22
Walker, Martin 99
Walsh, Lawrence 133n2
'war on terror' 2, 3, 6, 65, 120, 150–1, 153, 156, 160, 162, 165, 169–70, 173, 182–3, 184
water, regional tension over 124–8
Weizmann, Chaim 35
West Bank 140, 144, 148, 149, 152; Jerusalem and 41
Wilson, Mary C. 12
Wilson, President Woodrow 5, 49; Fourteen Points, articulation of 15, 17, 182; idealism of 9, 179; self-determination, vision of 19
Wolfowitz, Paul 163
World Health Organization (WHO) 102

World Zionist Conference (1897) 16

Yamit settlement, settler defiance and 59, 60
Yassin, Sheikh 142, 151
Yetiv, Steve 130
Yom Kippur War (1973) 56–9

Zionism 5–6; aspirations in Middle East of 14–15; Biltmore Program (1942) 34, 35; Britain as patron of 46; Bund (Jewish Labor Federation) 28; claim to Palestinian lands 27; coining of term 27; declaration of State of Israel 37, 39; dual claim to lands of Palestine, belief in resolution of 30; General Council in Palestine 35; Haganah 33, 34, 38; Irgun Zvai Leumi 33, 34; Israel, origins of 26–33, 42; Jewish nationalism, foundations of 26–7, 28; King–Crane Report, stance on 19; 'national home,' concept of 16, 22, 32; national reconstruction program in Palestine 28; Ottoman Empire and 14–15; Plan Dalet (Plan D) 38, 40; program of national reconstruction in Palestine 28; Revisionist Zionism 31–2, 34; Second World War 33–6, 42; Stern Gang (Lehi) 34; World Zionist Conference (1897) 16; Zionist settlement in Middle East 12
Zunes, Stephen 164